THE FAILURE OF REMAIN

McGill-Queen's Studies in Protest, Power, and Resistance

Series editor: Sarah Marsden

Protest, civil resistance, and political violence have rarely been more visible. Nor have they ever involved such a complex web of identities, geographies, and ideologies. This series expands the theoretical and empirical boundaries of research on political conflict to examine the origins, cultures, and practices of resistance. From grassroots activists and those engaged in everyday forms of resistance to social movements to violent militant networks, it considers the full range of actors and the strategies they use to provoke change. The series provides a forum for interdisciplinary work that engages with politics, sociology, anthropology, history, psychology, religious studies, and philosophy. Its ambition is to deepen understanding of the systems of power people encounter and the creative, violent, peaceful, extraordinary, and everyday ways they try to resist, subvert, and overthrow them.

1 New Media and Revolution
 Resistance and Dissent in Pre-uprising Syria
 Billie Jeanne Brownlee

2 Games of Discontent
 Protests, Boycotts, and Politics at the 1968 Mexico Olympics
 Harry Blutstein

3 Organizing Equality
 Dispatches from a Global Struggle
 Edited by Alison Hearn, James Compton, Nick Dyer-Witheford, and Amanda F. Grzyb

4 The Failure of Remain
 Anti-Brexit Activism in the United Kingdom
 Adam Fagan and Stijn van Kessel

The Failure of Remain

Anti-Brexit Activism in the United Kingdom

ADAM FAGAN AND
STIJN VAN KESSEL

McGill-Queen's University Press
Montreal & Kingston • London • Chicago

© McGill-Queen's University Press 2023

ISBN 978-0-2280-1412-6 (cloth)
ISBN 978-0-2280-1413-3 (paper)
ISBN 978-0-2280-1510-9 (ePDF)
ISBN 978-0-2280-1511-6 (ePUB)

Legal deposit first quarter 2023
Bibliothèque nationale du Québec

Printed in Canada on acid-free paper that is 100% ancient forest free (100% post-consumer recycled), processed chlorine free

Library and Archives Canada Cataloguing in Publication

Title: The failure of remain : anti-Brexit activism in the United Kingdom / Adam Fagan and Stijn van Kessel.
Names: Fagan, Adam, 1969– author. | Van Kessel, Stijn, author.
Series: McGill-Queen's studies in protest, power, and resistance ; 4.
Description: Series statement: McGill-Queen's studies in protest, power, and resistance ; 4 | Includes bibliographical references and index.
Identifiers: Canadiana (print) 20220439044 | Canadiana (ebook) 20220439133 | ISBN 9780228014126 (cloth) | ISBN 9780228014133 (paper) | ISBN 9780228015109 (ePDF) | ISBN 9780228015116 (ePUB)
Subjects: LCSH: Referendum—Great Britain. | LCSH: European Union—Great Britain. | LCSH: Protest movements—Great Britain.
Classification: LCC JF497.G7 F34 2023 | DDC 328.241—dc23

This book was typeset in 10.5/13 New Baskerville ITC Pro.
Copy-editing and composition by T&T Productions Ltd, London.

Contents

Tables and Figures vii

Acknowledgements ix

Abbreviations xi

1 Introduction 3

2 Theorising and Analysing Pro-European Activism in the United Kingdom 16

3 The Politics of Europe in the United Kingdom 42

4 Mapping Anti-Brexit Activism in the United Kingdom 67

5 Framing Leave and Remain 107

6 Conclusion 140

Appendix A: List of Interviews 155

Appendix B: Survey Questionnaire 156

Notes 163

References 167

Index 187

Tables and Figures

TABLES

1.1 Selected key events in the Brexit process. 6

1.2 Anti-Brexit mass demonstrations in London. 7

4.1 Typology of mobilising agents. 69

FIGURES

2.1 Analytical framework. 31

4.1 Timeline of anti-Brexit mobilisation in the United Kingdom. 76

4.2 Personal reasons for becoming involved in the anti-Brexit movement. 93

4.3 Activists' perspectives on the Brexit process. 103

5.1 Personal views on the European Union. 109

5.2 Pre-selected terms associated with membership of the EU. 110

5.3 Personal views on the referendum and the Brexit process. 111

5.4 Prevalence of frame categories in the campaign materials of the anti-Brexit movement. 114

Acknowledgements

The usual gnawing pressure to complete a book is even greater when writing about an issue, Brexit, that is contemporary and on which the dust has certainly not settled. Thankfully, we were fortunate to receive support from a host of academic friends and colleagues. In particular, we owe gratitude to Sarah Childs, Tim Bale, and Daniel Gover for their extensive comments on early drafts of the manuscript, and for helping us to improve the quality of our analysis and argument.

Besides offering a case study of the UK's anti-Brexit movement, this is primarily a book about the politicisation of Europe through social movements. The support and guidance in this area that were offered by Catherine de Vries, John Fitzgibbon, Maria Grasso, and Swen Hutter were very much appreciated. We owe particular thanks to Donatella della Porta and her colleagues at the Scuola Normale Superiore in Florence. A very early draft of the research and preliminary findings was presented at a Cosmos research seminar, at which John D. McCarthy acted as discussant. The study was also presented at the Global Governance Colloquium, chaired by Michael Zürn, at the WZB Berlin Social Science Center. On both occasions, and at various other conferences, we were offered fantastic scholarly insights and commentary on our work by all who participated, for which we are most grateful.

We owe our greatest thanks to our numerous interviewees. Whether in Liverpool, Newcastle, London, or elsewhere, in person or on Zoom, it was always fascinating and a pleasure for us to learn of your activism and dedication to the anti-Brexit cause. Without a single exception, you were extremely generous with your time and patience. We are particularly grateful to those who spoke to us more than once and/or commented extensively on our written drafts – Brenda Ashton, Andrew Atter, Audrey Gaffney, Mike Galsworthy, Simon Gardner, Nick Hopkinson, and Zoë Genevieve Perry – particularly when we seemed overwhelmed by the various configurations of the anti-Brexit movement.

Our fieldwork was supported by the Economic and Social Research Council, which funded the project '28+ Perspectives on Brexit: A Guide to the Multi-stakeholder Negotiations', led by principal investigator Helen Drake (grant number ES/R001847/1).

We were fortunate throughout the research and writing period to have the support of Kristina Tokic, our research assistant, who ingeniously created timelines, tables, and graphs, and sifted through our recorded interviews and transcripts for minuscule details and quotes. None of this would have been possible without the institutional support offered by our universities: the School of Politics and International Relations at Queen Mary University of London, and the Department of Political Economy at King's College London. We would also like to thank Richard Baggaley at McGill-Queen's University Press, who immediately grasped the merit in our project and was able to steer us towards writing a book that would resonate with as wide an audience as possible. We hope we have succeeded. Finally, we would like to express our gratitude to Sam Clark of T&T Productions for his meticulous work during the copyediting process.

Abbreviations

BAME	Black, Asian and minority ethnic
BfE	Britain for Europe
DiEM25	Democracy in Europe Movement 2025
EEC	European Economic Community
EM	European Movement
FFS	For our Future's Sake
LGBT+	lesbian, gay, bisexual, transgender +
MP	Member of Parliament
NHS	National Health Service
OFOC	Our Future Our Choice
POE	Pulse of Europe
POS	political opportunity structure
PV	People's Vote
RMT	resource mobilisation theory
SMO	Social Movement Organisation
SNP	Scottish National Party
SODEM	Stand of Defiance European Movement
UKIP	UK Independence Party

THE FAILURE OF REMAIN

1

Introduction

On the eve of the UK's departure from the European Union (EU) – something that is commonly referred to as Brexit – activists adorned in blue and gold flags, and holding homemade banners, could be found protesting in most cities and towns across the country. After months of street stalls, online petitions, and demonstrations, the myriad small local organisations and networks revealed their hastily built capacity to mobilise a diverse array of citizens to challenge Brexit. Who were the activists, what were their claims, and who were they addressing? To what extent did they challenge the narrative of the Eurosceptics? Had they managed to politicise 'Europe', and if so, how? And, crucially, how can we explain the movement's emergence and its ultimate failure to prevent a 'hard Brexit' from happening?

While a great deal has been written about Brexit – why and how it happened; who and what were its main drivers – the focus has largely been on the role of politicians and political parties on the one hand, and the characteristics of 'Leave' and 'Remain' voters on the other. This book adopts a different perspective and offers the first comprehensive study of the UK's grassroots anti-Brexit[1] movement that emerged and developed after the June 2016 referendum. Our extensive study is based on original interview data, complemented with results from our survey of anti-Brexit activists and analysis of their campaign materials. It provides an in-depth assessment of the discourse, ideology, and strategies of the UK's anti-Brexit movement. We trace the movement's internal political and ideological divisions, analyse the interaction between movement actors and their relation to political elites, and generate new knowledge about the referendum and its impact on UK politics.

But the book also makes a significant contribution to the wider comparative literature on the politicisation of European integration (Hutter et al. 2016). Most recent accounts and commentaries concentrate on what is presented as a populist or anti-liberal and xenophobic political maelstrom (e.g. Mudde 2019); the incipient counter-reaction and resurgence of pro-EU politics has received much less attention. While it is hard to deny that the rise of populist Euroscepticism denotes a serious challenge to established politics, pushing defenders of 'liberal-cosmopolitanism'[2] onto the defensive, the extent to which it is being actively challenged has yet to be comprehensively studied or fully understood. In an increasingly Eurosceptic era, we examine how and why citizens defend the principle of European integration, for which we will use the broad term 'pro-European' activism. While the UK case is by no means typical, it is nevertheless very revealing of how difficult the formulation of effective pro-European counter-narratives can be.

We conclude that while the anti-Brexit movement did represent the first iteration of a UK-wide pro-European movement that was genuinely 'bottom-up', the capacity of its activists to challenge Eurosceptic discourses was, and continues to be, limited due to the absence of a cogent and clear stance on the United Kingdom's relationship with the EU. The movement was primarily occupied with reversing a domestic political decision (Brexit) instead of formulating clear visions about the future of European integration – it could best be described as 'anti-Brexit' first and 'pro-European' second. The movement's efficacy was also hampered by several other factors. In the period prior to the United Kingdom's formal departure, the movement was riven by profound internal divisions and ideological differences, beset by weak links to political elites and institutions, and wedded to strategies and tactics that were unlikely to have a lasting effect on the politicisation of Europe within UK politics.

The United Kingdom ultimately left the EU with a 'hard' Brexit deal. While the government remains embroiled in what are likely to be long and bitter negotiations with Brussels regarding the Northern Ireland protocol and other key areas of contention, an efficacious social movement asking for the United Kingdom's re-entry into the EU is unlikely to develop any time soon. What does seem probable, however, is that the case for the United Kingdom remaining as closely integrated with the EU as possible is likely to be part of the agenda of a variety of progressive campaigns and mobilisations. With such a scenario in mind, we offer a series of conceptual and theoretical conclusions that may inform future research on pro-European activism and the politicisation of 'Europe'. More broadly, we identify the challenges that are faced by liberal-cosmopolitan movements that emerge not to strive for radical change, but to defend established political institutions.

FLAGS, STREET STALLS, AND BADGES: THE UK'S ANTI-BREXIT MOVEMENT

Had he been alive to witness the spectacle of British citizens assembled in town centres draped in the EU flag, Harold Wilson – the prime minister at the time of the first referendum on UK membership of the European Economic Community (EEC) in 1975 – may well have dismissed the spectacle as a new-fangled 'common market theology'. Winston Churchill might have gone further and concluded that those marching through central London had forgotten that 'we are with Europe, but not of it' (Saunders 2018, 39). De Gaulle, the French president who vetoed Britain's application to join in 1967, may have concluded that despite Brexit, the United Kingdom's 'deep-seated hostility' towards European integration was perhaps less febrile than he had imagined.

Much has been written and said about how the referendum result on 23 June 2016 confounded academics, politicians, and pundits alike (e.g. Hobolt 2016; Clarke et al. 2017; Evans and Menon 2017). The intervening four and a half years between the referendum and the end of the transition period, after which the United Kingdom in effect left the EU's single market and customs union, was perhaps the most tumultuous period in British post-war politics (see table 1.1). The proroguing of Parliament, which was then deemed to be unlawful and was overturned, and the 2017 and 2019 general elections are but examples of a series of tempestuous episodes. Some have contended that the political crisis of Brexit had more to do with issues of sovereignty than membership of the EU as such; that it represented an overwrought eruption of deep-seated domestic divisions, with the vote having enabled an outpouring of frustration at the inequality and dislocation of contemporary Britain (Bickerton 2019).

Table 1.1 Selected key events in the Brexit process.

Date	Event
23 June 2016	UK referendum on membership of the EU; 51.9% voted to leave, 48.1% to remain
13 July 2016	Theresa May succeeds David Cameron to become the new UK prime minister
29 March 2017	Theresa May triggers Article 50, starting the EU's legal process for leaving the bloc; the negotiation period would later be extended three times, in March, April, and October of 2019
8 June 2017	General election results in a 'hung parliament'; Conservative Party remains in power with support from the Northern Irish Democratic Unionist Party
25 November 2018	EU leaders approve a withdrawal deal reached with the United Kingdom after months of difficult negotiations
15 January 2019	The government loses the first 'meaningful vote' in Parliament on the Brexit deal, by 432 votes to 202
18 February 2019	The Independent Group for Change, known as Change UK, is founded as a cross-party initiative of members of parliament opposing Brexit
24 July 2019	Boris Johnson succeeds Theresa May to become the new UK prime minister
28 August 2019	The government initiates the prorogation of Parliament between September and October 2019, with the apparent intent to avoid further opposition to its Brexit plans; the prorogation was later ruled to be unlawful by the Supreme Court
12 December 2019	The general election results in a large Conservative Party majority; Johnson pledges 'to get Brexit done' by 31 January 2020
31 January 2020	At 11 p.m. the United Kingdom leaves the EU and enters the transition period
24 December 2020	Following arduous negotiations, the Brexit deal (the EU–UK Trade and Cooperation Agreement) is sealed
31 December 2020	At 11 p.m. the transition period ends, and the United Kingdom leaves the EU single market and customs union

Yet little has thus far been written about a startling political phenomenon of the era: the grassroots anti-Brexit movement that emerged gradually in the aftermath of the referendum vote (Brändle et al. 2018, 2022). The mobilisation of local people across the United Kingdom, often with no previous experience of activism, forming community-based campaign organisations and establishing social media groups, was unprecedented. Demonstrations were arranged and mass protest marches were attended, with families, friends, and neighbours rapidly mobilised. On Saturday mornings,

Table 1.2 Anti-Brexit mass demonstrations in London.

Date	Name
July 2016	March for Europe
September 2016	March for Europe
March 2017	Unite for Europe
September 2017	People's March for Europe
June 2018	People's Vote March
October 2018	People's Vote March for the Future
March 2019	Put It to the People
July 2019	March for Change
October 2019	Let Us Be Heard

in towns and cities across the country, street stalls festooned in the blue and gold of the EU would be hastily set up; a small band of volunteers, usually middle-aged men and women, predominantly white and middle class, would distribute leaflets and engage in conversation with those members of the public who ventured near. In some cases there were megaphones, placards, and almost ructious behaviour, but mostly the activism was calm, and the activists engaged in persuasion rather than protest.

Street marches were an important component of the activism repertoire of the anti-Brexit movement. The ones in London attracted most public attention (see table 1.2), certainly when the number of participants swelled to hundreds of thousands from the second half of 2018 onwards (e.g. BBC 2018; Townsend 2019). At various points, as the anti-Brexit demonstrations in London grew bigger and louder, it looked as though the movement might stand a chance – either in forcing a second vote or stopping Brexit altogether. On 19 October 2019, as lawmakers huddled inside the House of Commons on a Saturday to debate Prime Minister Boris Johnson's Brexit deal, hundreds of thousands of protesters gathered outside the Palace of Westminster to demand that voters be given the final say on Brexit. However, despite the crowds, the placards, and the mushrooming of local organisations, the movement ultimately failed. Not only did it fail to stop the UK leaving the EU in January 2020, but it also proved incapable of bringing forth a 'People's Vote' or even altering the terms and conditions of the country's departure and subsequent trade deal.

British citizens are certainly not averse to protest, and neither is grassroots activism unusual in the United Kingdom. Indeed, in addition to local chapters of the Campaign for Nuclear Disarmament (CND), Amnesty International, and Greenpeace, genuinely local environmental activism has been part of the political landscape of towns and cities for decades (Griggs and Howarth 2007). Furthermore, from the demonstrations protesting against nuclear weapons in the 1950s, to the anti-Poll Tax protests in the 1980s and the mobilisation against the Iraq war in 2002–3, political rallies have been a leitmotif of the progressive left for decades. With the exception of the 1975 referendum campaign, however, protest politics never centred on the issue of EU politics, certainly not from a pro-European perspective.

As Euroscepticism gained political momentum in the following decades, no counter-movement was in evidence. While the UK branch of the European Movement (EM), established in the late 1940s, hosted speakers and events pertaining to the advantages of continued membership, its support base was small and it was drawn from a narrow demographic. EM members did not flaunt their support publicly, nor could they be described as activists. There had been a mobilisation of citizens in the run-up to the 1975 referendum in favour of continued EEC membership, but this was hardly a grassroots movement: it was orchestrated by trade unions, churches, and other organisations as part of the broader 'Yes' campaign (Saunders 2018). Similarly, the official pro-Remain movement, Britain Stronger In Europe, which emerged after the latest referendum was announced in early 2016, was also not a bottom-up initiative. Rather, it was established by politicians and members of what might be termed a 'Westminster elite', and it was heavily London-centric. Although regional and local chapters were established, the emergence of a genuine grassroots movement, which is the focus of our research, did not occur until after the June vote.

What was so striking about the anti-Brexit movement was, first, that it largely emerged spontaneously, without an initial over-arching structure, and in the absence of any direct linkage to a national campaign organisation or political party. Second, grassroots movements usually emerge either to campaign for progressive reforms or as conservative reactions to such reforms (e.g. the anti-abortion movement). There are no obvious examples of grassroots social movements in the UK that have emerged to defend the liberal cosmopolitan order rather than to campaign for change.[3]

THEORETICAL CONTRIBUTION

Beyond an analysis of the emergence and efficacy of the anti-Brexit movement as such, our study makes a twofold theoretical contribution. First, to the scholarly literature on the 'politicisation of Europe', by shifting the focus from Eurosceptic political parties to grassroots movements that are supportive of European integration. Second, we contribute to the social movement literature by focusing on a particular category of movement organisations: liberal-cosmopolitan movements that emerge not to directly challenge established institutions, but to defend them. As discussed in the next chapter, the extensive existing scholarship has focused almost exclusively either on what might be termed left-liberal 'pro-change' movements or on right-wing conservative organisations that seek to resist permissive and progressive reforms.

Politicisation of Europe

In the decades after World War II, citizens across EU member states were observed to lack genuine interest in the presumed technocratic process of European integration, and to passively trust their political elites to proceed (Lindberg and Scheingold 1970). Mainstream parties, which still enjoyed a dominant electoral position and generally supported further European integration, thus relied on a so-called permissive consensus. In the past few decades, however, the salience of, and political contestation around, the issue of European integration has increased (Brack and Startin 2015), and so have levels of public Euroscepticism, which also found expression in the party-political arena (Taggart 1998; Pirro et al. 2018). Most scholars thus agree that the permissive consensus has significantly weakened, having effectively been replaced with a 'constraining dissensus' (Hooghe and Marks 2009). The financial and migrant crises since the beginning of the twenty-first century have certainly accelerated this politicisation of Europe, heightening contestation on both the political left and right, and moving the EU higher up several countries' political agendas, even if only temporarily (Hutter and Kriesi 2019).

The focus of academic enquiry into the politicisation of Europe has mainly been on Eurosceptic forces in the 'conventional' party-political arena, not least parties on the radical right (see Hutter et al. 2016), or within the context of policy debates (Schmidt 2019). The limited attention to pro-European expressions at the grassroots level is hardly surprising given that, until recently, very few citizens came out to defend either the EU or the broader principle of European integration. There are examples of social movements engaging with aspects of EU politics, but these have typically expressed fundamental criticism of the current form and direction of European integration. Several 'left-progressive' movements, for instance, have supported closer European cooperation from their cosmopolitan and anti-nationalist perspective while lamenting the supposed neoliberal nature of the EU in its present form (della Porta and Caiani 2009; della Porta 2020a). Movements wholeheartedly supporting the EU are still rare, although pro-European citizens have been forming local grassroots organisations as well as cross-national networks, with the predominantly Germany-based Pulse of Europe being one example. By focusing on possibly the most salient expression of pro-European mobilisation – the anti-Brexit movement in the United Kingdom – our research fills a gap in the existing scholarship. Our study not only investigates a novel empirical phenomenon, it also explores the potential of pro-European movements – particularly grassroots mobilisations – to contribute to the politicisation of Europe.

The social movement literature

Given that our empirical study is concerned with political mobilisation around the issue of EU membership in the protest arena – thereby distinguishing it from most of the existing studies on the domestic politics of European integration – the most obvious starting point is the literature on social movements and contentious politics (Tarrow 1996). As discussed in some detail in the next chapter, the early social movement literature focused exclusively on political processes and the mobilisation of resources to explain the emergence of societal activism (McAdam et al. 1996; McAdam and Snow 1997; McCarthy and Zald 1977). By contrast, later scholarship has centred on the concept of 'framing' to describe the 'process of negotiating shared meaning' that movements undertake in order to articulate their grievances and galvanise support (Gamson 1992). This shift is in large part borne out of the need to explain why – given similar resource endowment, and operating in the same political context – some organisations achieve greater success than others.

In our evaluation of the anti-Brexit movement we focus on all three dimensions: the combined impact of the political opportunity structure, resource mobilisation, and framing. In terms of our theoretical contribution, it is the latter dimension that is of particular interest. Given that the main political parties remained divided over the issue of 'Europe', grassroots activists were key players in the months and years following the referendum. Local activist networks were mobilising not only to oppose Brexit and offer solidarity to other pro-Remain citizens, but also to define what it meant to defend EU membership and to support 'Europe'. To use the language of the social movement literature, through their activism they offered 'interpretative schemata that simplifie[d] and condense[d] the "world out there"' (Snow and Benford 1992, 137), and they helped 'to fashion shared understandings of the world and of themselves that legitimate and motivate collective action' (McAdam et al. 1996, 6).

Our starting premise is that movement organisations and networks have the potential, through their activism, not only to raise grievances but also to articulate understanding of the problem and propose alternatives. This tallies with the distinction made throughout the social movement literature between 'diagnostic' and 'prognostic' frames (Benford and Snow 2000). Studies have sought to differentiate between strategic processes involved in frame production (Snow et al. 1986) and observed the inter-connectedness of identifying the problem, apportioning blame, and devising solutions. In the words of Benford and Snow (2000, 616), 'the identification of specific problems and causes tends to constrain the range of possible "reasonable" solutions and strategies advocated'. While further understanding of the interconnectedness between the two framing components is important for all social movement campaigns, we deem it particularly critical for movements such as the anti-Brexit movement that exist primarily to defend established institutions.

For 'pro-change movements' the framing task primarily involves envisioning an alternative future. In the case of conservative (counter-)movements, the primary focus is to critique policies that are seen to undermine the established order and the interests of groups and individuals that are typically in a position of power and privilege (McVeigh 1999). As we illustrate, for pro-European movements that seek to defend *aspects* of the status quo of EU membership while also offering a 'progressive' vision – but one that is not dissimilar from what currently exists – frame construction is far more complex. Our study reveals what specific dilemmas these movements face in constructing ideational frames and formulating their messages. In their attempt to gain public support, how do they formulate a critique of the established order that they ultimately wish to defend, and how do they construct an alternative vision of the future that is not substantively different to the existing reality?

METHODOLOGY

The focus of our study is the various organisations and initiatives that comprised the anti-Brexit movement, and particularly the local groups and networks that were its backbone in the aftermath of the June 2016 referendum. Although local chapters of Britain Stronger In Europe and the European Movement existed during the 2016 referendum campaign itself, there was little evidence of community-level, self-organising activism (Fuchs 2006). Our research centres on the activism of such local organisations from their formation in the immediate aftermath of the referendum through to the United Kingdom's formal departure from the EU in January 2020. Our geographic focus includes all four nations of the United Kingdom.

In terms of methodology, we triangulated several methods and primary and secondary sources. We primarily relied on a series of semi-structured interviews with individuals and groups of activists. We held thirty-one interviews between February 2019 and June 2021, some of which were with multiple interviewees (see appendix A for the list of interviews). The majority of these were held in person, but several of them were organised via Zoom – including the seven conducted from May 2020 onwards, a period that was marked by the Covid-19 pandemic. Interviews were structured around two main themes: the (local) organisation and its activities (mainly generating data for chapter 4 on mobilising structures), and its aims and ideology (providing data for chapter 5 on framing processes).

Although we arranged some of our interviews using a 'snowballing' technique, whereby local activists recommended others with whom they collaborated, we deliberately sought to interview activists in regions of England where there was a high level of support for Leave (e.g. the North-East, Lincolnshire) and in others with strong local support for Remain (e.g. London, Bristol, Liverpool). In addition, we held several interviews in each of the other countries of the United Kingdom: in Scotland and Northern Ireland (where a majority voted Remain) and in Wales (where a majority voted Leave). In addition to local activists, we also interviewed leading figures within a number of prominent anti-Brexit initiatives (Scientists for EU; Another Europe is Possible; Best for Britain; Stand in Defiance European Movement; Our Future Our Choice; For Our Future's Sake; March for Change) and national umbrella organisations (European Movement; Britain for Europe; People's Vote). These organisations typically worked with, or had established connections with, local activists.

Complementing the interview data, we conducted an online survey as well as a content analysis of campaign materials. The aim of the survey was to capture demographic information as well as attitudinal data (see appendix B for the questionnaire). We asked how activists articulated and perceived their support for the EU; about their previous political engagement, party affiliations, and links with other activists; and for details of their activism. The survey was distributed through the networks of anti-Brexit organisations, most notably those affiliated with Britain for Europe and the European Movement – invitations were sent to the email addresses of local branches, which were available on the organisations' websites. Some interviewees also assisted with further distributing the survey. Only individuals who engaged in anti-Brexit activism at least occasionally were asked to complete the survey – responses concerning levels of activism confirm the sample only includes 'genuine' activists and not merely sympathisers. Almost all responses were collected between late July and late October of 2019, with a total of 563 individuals completing the full survey.[4]

A key focus of our research was to capture how organisations and activists framed their critique of Brexit, their support for Remain, and their vision of the EU. In addition to the above methods, we sought to do this via content analysis of online and printed campaign materials, including leaflets, posters, and edited photos/memes on social media. These items were retrieved from the Facebook and Twitter pages of the national organisations previously mentioned, and from local activist groups affiliated with Britain for Europe and/or the European Movement across all of the United Kingdom's regions and countries. In some cases activists provided materials by email. The eventual sample consisted of 547 items, all posted online between the date of the referendum (23 June 2016) and the general election of 12 December 2019.

STRUCTURE AND CONTENT OF THE BOOK

We begin (in chapter 2) by discussing the extant literature on the 'politicisation of Europe', which predominantly focuses on the conventional party-political arena, and outlining our conceptual and analytical framework. With regard to the anti-Brexit movement, we explain how the social movement literature provides a logical starting point for studying this particular iteration of activism, which emerged not from within established organisations or political parties, but from the grassroots and as a reaction to the perceived failure of politicians and the political elite. We discuss the importance of political processes, resources, and frames as key variables to explain the emergence and efficacy of a particular movement. Accordingly, we outline the analytical framework that structures the subsequent three empirical chapters. These respectively focus on political opportunities, mobilisation structures, and framing processes.

Chapter 3 charts the political opportunity structure in which the anti-Brexit movement emerged and operated. We take a long view of how pro-European perspectives evolved in the United Kingdom between the 1975 referendum and the 2016 vote and its aftermath, paying particular attention to the shifting positions of the two main political parties. The intention is to contrast the two periods but also to highlight continuity in terms of the UK public and political perspective on EEC/EU membership.

Chapters 4 and 5 provide an exposition of our original empirical data and analysis. The former sets out the parameters of the movement and its mobilising structures, and it traces the movement's evolution and fragmentation. The latter analyses how the content and nature of the ideational framing evolved, including conceptions of 'Europe' held by activists and the movement's claims and messages used to rally support.

Our final chapter (chapter 6) brings together the findings from the previous chapters and identifies implications for the academic literature. We convey the significance of our findings for understanding Brexit and the domestic political impact, and we relate our data and arguments to the wider academic debate on the contestation and politicisation of Europe.

2

Theorising and Analysing Pro-European Activism in the United Kingdom

> If we are trying to account for mobilization, we have to ask, under what conditions do outraged forms of knowing lead to social mobilizations and movements? So awareness alone does not suffice, and neither does outrage.
>
> Judith Butler (2016)

The unprecedented mobilisation of a pro-European movement in the United Kingdom that took place in the wake of the 2016 referendum is worthy of study in its own right. Yet the movement should be seen and studied in a broader context, as its emergence is indicative of wider trends in contemporary European politics. This chapter thus takes a step back from the British context, based on the assumption that Brexit is but one iteration of the increased visibility of European integration in domestic political debates across the continent. EU-wide discussions about pan-European debt mutualisation – not least in the context of the Covid-19 crisis – and the more general role of the EU in dealing with politically salient global challenges such as Russia's military aggression, migration and climate change are certainly no longer peripheral.

The salience of 'Europe' as an issue in public debates is, however, a relatively recent phenomenon. For a long time most citizens lacked genuine interest in the presumed technocratic process of European integration; they simply passively trusted their political elites to proceed (Lindberg and Scheingold 1970). It was not until the conception of the Maastricht Treaty at the start of the 1990s and the move towards a more multilevel (and increasingly supranational) form of governance that this 'permissive consensus' started to weaken, being replaced by a 'constraining dissensus' (Hooghe and Marks 2009). Since that time, political elites have faced an increasingly Eurosceptic public. According to Brack and Startin (2015, 239), the 'mainstreaming' of Euroscepticism has become 'discernible across Europe at the level of public opinion, among political parties and civil society groups, within the EU institutions themselves and in terms of changing and more challenging media discourses'. Opposition to the EU – including concerns about specific policies, the power of its institutions, the so-called democratic deficit, and national sovereignty – has generated considerable and cross-ideological mobilisation (Pirro et al. 2018; della Porta 2020a). Meanwhile, civil society-based activism in defence of European integration and in support of the EU has been barely visible, sporadic, and confined to certain EU countries (della Porta and Caiani 2009).

In terms of the above trends, the United Kingdom can be seen as somewhat of an outlier in the sense that attitudes towards European integration have always been lukewarm at best, and hostile at worst, among both party elites (the political 'supply side') and the electorate (the political 'demand side') (see, for example, Diez Medrano 2003; Hobolt 2016). According to Eurobarometer survey data collected in spring 2015, the British public was split on the question of whether their country could better face the future outside of the EU: 43 per cent agreed, 43 per cent disagreed, and 14 per cent did not know (European Commission 2015, 99). With these numbers, the United Kingdom ranked at the very bottom of EU member states as far as support for EU membership was concerned – the European average was 58 per cent 'disagreed', 30 per cent 'agreed', and 12 'did not know'. That said, as in other countries, European integration has not always been a very *salient* issue for the British public (Baker et al. 2008). Moreover, while the main political parties have long been internally divided over the issue, successive Labour and Conservative governments have accepted and defended EU membership when in power, up to the June 2016 referendum vote.

As will be further discussed in the next chapter, the referendum result changed the political situation, with leaving the EU becoming the default scenario. Given the lack of sufficient allies among the political elite, it is unsurprising that opposition to the United Kingdom's departure from the EU eventually found expression in the arena of protest politics. In view of the unprecedented grassroots anti-Brexit mobilisation that took place in the United Kingdom, but also the emergence of pro-European organisations such as the Pulse of Europe elsewhere, it is necessary to look beyond party-political mobilisations around European integration. The anti-Brexit movement in the United Kingdom presents us with quite an exceptional case, and also a crucial one, to study the politics of 'Europe' in the protest area.

This chapter presents the theoretical premise and the analytical framework on which our research is based. It starts with an overview of the general literature on political contestation around, and public attitudes towards, European integration. It continues with an overview of the literature on the 'politicisation of Europe' in the party-political and protest arenas. We observe the limited attention given in the extant literature to the phenomenon of pro-European politics and the role of social movements in the politicisation of Europe. Given our empirical focus, the social movement literature nevertheless provides both a conceptual and an analytical framework for studying such mobilisations. In adopting this perspective, our study seeks to make three contributions: first, to the existing literature on anti-Brexit protest (Brändle et al. 2018; Goodwin et al. 2020); second, to the more sizeable literature on the politicisation of Europe; and third, to the very limited scholarship on pro-European activism and, more generally, social movements that essentially seek to defend the status quo or, in the case of the anti-Brexit movement, the status quo ante.

Most of the latter half of the chapter is devoted to presenting the analytical framework for our empirical analysis of the anti-Brexit movement that emerged after the referendum vote. We start from the conceptual framework provided by Doug McAdam, John McCarty, and Mayer Zald (1996), who identify three key dimensions that are relevant to understanding the mobilisation, as well as the efficacy, of social movements: political opportunities, mobilising structures, and framing processes. This dynamic model allows us to explain in the chapters that follow both the emergence of the anti-Brexit movement and its ultimate failure.

'EUROPE' IN THE CONVENTIONAL POLITICAL ARENA

Our empirical study is specifically concerned with political mobilisation around the issue of EU membership in the protest arena, and it thereby distinguishes itself from most of the existing studies on the domestic politics of European integration, which tend to concentrate on public opinion and the way different positions on the EU are expressed by political parties. We start with a brief overview of this literature as it provides us with an important premise for our own study of the United Kingdom's anti-Brexit movement. In particular, the existing literature reveals who is likely to support and oppose European integration, and how the political conflict around Brexit fits into a more general 'cultural' dimension of political competition that is highly salient across Europe. In this respect, much of the scholarly literature has explicitly concentrated on *opposition* to European integration, or 'Euroscepticism'. The traditional mainstream 'default' position of support has received less attention, as have expressions of explicit support for European cooperation among culturally liberal parties with a cosmopolitan ideology (Hooghe and Marks 2018).

It is also worthwhile pointing out that the literature on the domestic political impact of the EU is relatively recent. It was initially assumed that European integration constituted a 'sleeping giant' in terms of the issue's potential for mobilisation (van der Eijk and Franklin 2004): mainstream parties were seen to have few incentives to politicise the issue because doing so risked exposing internal divisions (see, for example, Steenbergen and Scott 2004; Green-Pedersen 2012). In the past few decades, however, the salience of the issue of European integration, as well as political contestation around it, have increased (see, for example, Hooghe and Marks 2009).

Considering the political 'supply side' and the connection between party ideology and positions on European integration, it has been observed that mainstream parties tend to support European integration (Marks and Wilson 2000; Hooghe et al. 2002; Aspinwall 2002; de Vries and Edwards 2009). This is not surprising given that the traditionally dominant mainstream parties have in fact shaped the process of European integration. While they may express certain grievances with the EU in its current form (see, for example, Kriesi 2007; Helbling et al. 2010), few mainstream parties fundamentally question the general merits of European integration. The UK Conservative and Labour parties have been notable exceptions, in that they are mainstream parties that have vocal Eurosceptic factions. In general, however, the loudest Euroscepticism can be found among parties at the fringes of the ideological spectrum. Paul Taggart, who initially defined Euroscepticism as 'the idea of contingent or qualified opposition, as well as incorporating outright and unqualified opposition to the process of European integration' (Taggart 1998, 366), asserted that these parties often take such positions to dissociate themselves from (generally pro-European) mainstream parties.

The Euroscepticism of parties is not only strategic, but is also rooted in ideology. Parties on the (culturally conservative) radical right portray the EU as a project that threatens the sovereignty of their country's 'native' people and, through the opening of borders, the cultural homogeneity of nations (Pirro and van Kessel 2017; Vasilopoulou 2018). Parties of the radical left, which are primarily concerned with socio-economic issues, typically describe European integration as a neoliberal project that encourages a 'race to the bottom' in terms of welfare entitlements and working conditions. Given that radical left and radical right parties are very dissimilar in terms of both their ideology and the key issues they focus on, their interpretation and problematisation (i.e. their 'framing') of European integration is very different (Pirro et al. 2018). What they nevertheless share is a populist critique of the EU, which they portray as an undemocratic and elitist organisation that acts against the interests of 'ordinary people' (van Kessel 2015).

While traditional mainstream parties are still generally supportive of the EU, the end of the permissive consensus has meant that political leaders must now look over their shoulders, so to speak, when they are engaging in EU-level negotiations, and take into consideration the higher levels of Euroscepticism among the public (Hooghe and Marks 2009, 5). What is more, many (radical right) Eurosceptic parties have increased their electoral strength and have also gained representation in government in a number of countries, including Austria, Italy, and Greece (Albertazzi and McDonnell 2015; Pirro et al. 2018). In turn, this electoral pressure has induced some traditional parties to curb their enthusiasm for further European integration (Meijers 2017). In more recent years, the distinction between 'pro-Europeans' and 'Eurosceptics' has thus become more blurred, and some scholars have spoken about the 'mainstreaming' of Euroscepticism (Taggart and Szczerbiak 2013; Brack and Startin 2015). This does not necessarily mean that the EU is in immediate existential danger. Even parties on the radical right – the most vocal critics of the EU – rarely prioritise the issue of European integration, and few advocate following the United Kingdom's example of leaving the bloc (Heinisch et al. 2021; van Kessel et al. 2020).

With regard to the political 'demand side', citizens' attitudes towards the EU vary both within and across EU member states. Once more, the United Kingdom can be seen as an extreme case here, given that 'the British public has consistently been the most Eurosceptic electorate in the EU ever since the UK joined in 1973' (Hobolt 2016, 1,259–60). It is important to recognise that, like parties, citizens are often not simply 'for' or 'against' the EU but have more nuanced ideas about specific EU policies or regime characteristics (Boomgaarden et al. 2011; Garry and Tilley 2015; Hobolt and de Vries 2016; de Vries 2018a). Broadly speaking, public support/opposition maps onto party positions: citizens on the extremes of the ideological spectrum tend to be less supportive of the EU (Steenbergen et al. 2007; Lubbers and Scheepers 2010; van Elsas and van der Brug 2015), but they also vary in terms of their specific grievances according to whether their ideology is 'left' or 'right' (van Elsas et al. 2016). Right-wing Eurosceptics are in agreement with radical right parties in objecting to the EU mainly on cultural grounds, and in being more fiercely opposed to the principle of European integration. On the radical left, parties and their voters are much less opposed to the principle of European cooperation but are nevertheless critical about the current (supposedly neoliberal) direction the EU takes. There is also evidence that parties on the fringes of the political spectrum can attract voters on the basis of their Eurosceptic platform (de Vries 2010; de Vries and Edwards 2009), although more specific issues, such as immigration for radical right voters, tend to be more important in explaining party support (Werts et al. 2013; McDonnell and Werner 2019).

Political contestation around Europe has often been considered from a broader perspective of societal and party system change. In a series of contributions that bring together the political supply and demand sides, Hanspeter Kriesi and colleagues (2006, 2008, 2012) relate political conflict around EU issues to the broader process of globalisation (or 'denationalisation') and its impact on national party systems. According to these scholars, a new structural conflict has materialised in Western European countries, pitting the so-called winners and losers of globalisation against each other. The winners are typically more highly skilled citizens with cosmopolitan attitudes; the losers are individuals who identify strongly with the national community and who lose out, or perceive themselves to lose out, from globalisation. The conflict between these groups – which are heterogeneous in terms of composition and which must be mobilised by political elites – can be defined as one between 'integration' and 'demarcation'. These concepts can be interpreted in an economic sense (free trade versus protectionism) as well as a cultural one (cosmopolitan versus nationalist), and the scholars hypothesise and find that the contemporary Western European political space is structured around two corresponding dimensions.

Crucially, the transformation of party systems is found to be driven primarily by radical right challengers, which managed to mobilise the globalisation 'losers' by appealing to their *cultural* anxieties – around immigration, not least, but also around the process of European integration (see, for example, Hobolt 2016; Hooghe and Marks 2018). The extent to which Eurosceptic individuals objectively are losers from globalisation and European integration can be questioned, certainly where it concerns their material position, yet concerns related to other types of *perceived* loss – namely of national sovereignty and identity – have certainly been key right-wing Eurosceptic themes. The thrust of Kriesi et al.'s argument is illustrated empirically by the recent electoral rise of populist radical right parties in many European countries, as well as their apparent impact on the electoral programmes of centre-right mainstream parties, especially in the areas of immigration and cultural diversity (Bale 2003; Wolinetz and Zaslove 2018; Abou-Chadi and Krause 2020; Bale and Rovira Kaltwasser 2021). Parties with a cosmopolitan agenda, such as green parties, have also had relatively good results in a handful of European countries, but their performance is generally overshadowed by the rise of the radical right. The Brexit vote, too, has often been interpreted as an indication of liberal-cosmopolitanism being pushed onto the defensive in the contemporary European context (de Vries 2018b).

POLITICISATION OF EUROPE

The discussion above showed how a great deal of the literature has approached the politics of European integration from the perspective of broader societal trends and a changing political space, emphasising the recent upsurge of nationalist and culturally conservative politics. Recent academic contributions have also focused on the politicisation of European integration as a topic on its own (see Hutter et al. (2016) for the most comprehensive collection of studies). While the conceptualisations of this phenomenon vary, scholars generally refer to 'the process through which European integration has become the subject of public discussion, debate, and contestation' (Schmidt 2019, 1018). These studies typically consider the politicisation of Europe in the party-political arena and mainly emphasise Eurosceptic actors as being the main drivers. We argue that the anti-Brexit movement constitutes a crucial case of an understudied form of EU politicisation: namely, one driven by pro-European actors in the domain of protest politics.

We follow Hutter and Grande (2014, 1,003), who identify three main conceptual dimensions of politicisation: issue salience (visibility), actor expansion (scope), and actor polarisation (intensity and direction). Only salience can be considered a necessary condition: politicisation can manifest itself as long as increased salience occurs in combination with either actor expansion or polarisation (Grande and Hutter 2016a). Accordingly, politicisation of Europe implies (a) increasing *salience* of the theme in terms of, for example, media coverage, public awareness, and the actions of politicians; in combination with (b) *expansion in terms of the scope of actors and audiences* involved in EU issues; and/or (c) *polarisation* of attitudes in favour of and against different aspects of EU governance (see also de Wilde et al. 2016).

Many scholars have observed an increasing politicisation of European integration along these or similar lines (see, for example, Statham and Trenz 2015; Börzel and Risse 2018; Zürn 2019). This trend has been related to the EU's increasing political authority, in combination with a variety of intermediating variables (such as national narratives, competitive party politics, and crises or external shocks), which together form the political opportunity structure for EU politicisation (de Wilde and Zürn 2012). Some scholars note, however, that there is no clear upward trend of EU politicisation over time, and that there are significant differences between countries and arenas of political contestation (Hutter et al. 2016; Hutter and Kriesi 2019). Grande and Kriesi (2016, 283) speak of 'a patchwork of politicising moments across European countries' and of a general process of '*punctuated politicisation*, in which a significant but limited number of singular events produce high levels of political conflicts for shorter periods of time' (original emphasis).

Critical events such as EU-related referendums and treaty reforms act as important stimulants for such temporary politicisation (Grande and Hutter 2016b). Yet events alone are not sufficient to explain EU politicisation; one also needs to consider the interpretation and strategic deployment of these events by political actors (Grande and Hutter 2016a). The politicisation of Europe, in this regard, has mainly been discussed with reference to actors resisting further European integration, not least political parties of the radical right (see, for example, Hutter and Grande 2014; Kriesi 2016; Dolezal and Hellström 2016). According to de Wilde, Leupold, and Schmidtke (2016, 6), the increasing electoral success of such parties and the more general public criticism of the EU 'indicate that politicisation is driven primarily by those critical of the integration process rather than by those who are supportive' (see also Schmidt 2019). Many scholars therefore perceive politicisation to indirectly act as a brake on the European project, certainly at a time when the EU has been facing a multitude of crises (Zeitlin et al. 2019; but see also Jabko and Luhman 2019). Limited scholarly attention has been given to the mobilisation of political actors that defend the EU or the more general idea of European integration.

As noted above, however, politicisation either requires *polarisation* of attitudes and positions, and thus an expression of pro-European views as well, or an *expansion of actors*, which can come in the form of political mobilisation beyond the conventional party-political arena.

Regarding polarisation, a number of political actors, including France's president Emmanuel Macron and various social-liberal and green parties, have in recent years spoken out in defence of deeper European integration. Some of these parties also performed well during the 2019 European Parliament elections, which were marked primarily by high levels of voter fragmentation rather than by an across-the-board victory for Eurosceptic radical right parties (Hobolt 2019). The politicisation of the EU has, in other words, tended to accentuate the previously introduced cleavage of 'integration versus demarcation' or 'cosmopolitanism versus parochialism' (Zürn 2019; de Vries 2018b).

When it comes to the expansion of actors, there is evidence that citizens supportive of the EU can be mobilised in the protest arena: Börzel and Risse (2018) cite the pro-European Pulse of Europe (PoE) street demonstrations as an example. PoE's foundation was a reaction against what were considered illiberal and nationalist tendencies, exemplified by the Brexit vote in June 2016 and the election of Donald Trump as US president in November that same year (van Kessel and Fagan 2022a). Initially a small network of local acquaintances in Frankfurt am Main, PoE soon grew when citizens across the country as well as a number of individuals outside Germany sought to join. In early 2017, PoE developed a formal organisational structure, and weekly demonstrations commenced across (mainly German) cities and towns. The organisation was able to sustain its levels of mobilisation over the subsequent couple of years, especially around a series of national elections in Europe. Large-scale and regular PoE gatherings practically ended, however, after the European Parliament elections of 2019.

As we discuss in the following section, such protest activities around the various aspects of European integration have remained rare. Assessing whether social movement activism has become more 'Europeanised', Dolezal, Hutter, and Becker (2016, 134) conclude that 'while we observe some politicisation of Europe from below, mass protest mobilisation related to the issue is definitely slow in coming' (see also Hutter 2012). The unprecedented mobilisation of grassroots pro-European activism in the aftermath of the UK Brexit vote can thus be seen as an exception to the rule, but also as a crucial case if we wish to understand the politicisation of Europe in the protest arena.

SOCIAL MOVEMENTS, PROTESTS, AND EUROPE

Various studies have considered the way in which the EU and its institutions are perceived, accessed, and approached by a variety of social movement organisations (SMOs). Such analyses often centre on sector-specific protests against EU policies (such as farmer blockades), transnational social movement mobilisation and coordination, how and to what extent SMOs employ the EU as an arena in which to voice their specific interests, and the related challenges and opportunities of the EU's system of multilevel governance for SMO and interest group activities (see, for example, Reising 1999; Marks and McAdam 1999; Imig and Tarrow 1999, 2001; della Porta and Caiani 2007, 2009; Monforte 2014; della Porta and Parks 2018). Scholars have identified several practical and institutional obstacles that SMOs face in trying to coordinate transnational action targeted at EU institutions. One key observation from these studies is that the national arena still offers greater mobilisation opportunities. Another is that protests about European issues and institutions have tended to be dominated by famers and occupational groups rather than by organisations with more 'postmaterialist' aims, such as environmental and anti-racist movements (Imig 2004).

Literature that concentrates on the general course of European integration as the *subject* of politicisation in the protest arena remains scarce, but Balme and Chabanet (2008), FitzGibbon (2013), Caiani and Weisskircher (2019), and della Porta (2020a) are exceptions. As already noted, this scarcity is in large part due to such protests having remained relatively uncommon: the issue of 'Europe' has been more salient in the electoral arena than in the protest arena (Kriesi 2012, 202; Hutter 2012a,b). In general, protest mobilisations around European integration have remained far less frequent in comparison with other issues, and they have also failed to show any increase over time (Uba and Uggla 2011; Dolezal et al. 2016). The politics of Brexit in the aftermath of the 2016 referendum was therefore somewhat unusual in the sense that the mobilisations that occurred for 'Remain' primarily manifested themselves within the realm of protest politics.

As also noted above, the most tangible expression of the politicisation of European integration has been, and remains, Euroscepticism. In terms of the integration–demarcation cleavage, those opposing European integration from a culturally conservative perspective are more likely to be aligned with parties of the radical right. The support base of radical right parties typically has a greater inclination to participate in elections than in the arena of protest politics (Kriesi et al. 2012). Opposition to deeper integration, further enlargement, or the transfer of additional power from national governments to the EU has therefore been more likely to find political expression within electoral politics than within the realm of protest politics. Dolezal, Hutter, and Becker (2016, 129) indeed find that 'the Eurosceptics from the right … were hardly ever seen on the streets protesting against European integration'. Notwithstanding the recent rise of far-right movements such as PEGIDA and the Identarians, which have often expressed a critical 'Europe of sovereign nations' vision (see, for example, Caiani and Cisar 2019; Caiani and Weisskircher 2019), 'Europeanised' protest behaviour has still predominantly been driven by the 'left'.

Such left-wing activism dates back to the 1990s and the signing of the Maastricht and Amsterdam Treaties. It also played a role in the French and Dutch rejection, by referendum, of the Treaty for the European Constitution in 2005, and in opposition to the so-called Bolkestein Directive, which sought to remove obstacles from the common market in the area of services (see, for example, della Porta and Caiani 2007, 2009). What was fuelling such opposition was a sense that the Maastricht Treaty of 1992 had shifted European integration from being a project of solidarity to being one of austerity and neoliberal economics. Similar mobilisations against the EU from the left were also visible during the signing and ratification of the Lisbon Treaty (2007–9), with large demonstrations and counter-summits accompanying all the major EU summits that took place. In addition, the European Social Forum – a rolling conference organised by the Global Justice Movement between 2002 and 2010 – provided a platform and an opportunity for left-wing mobilisation and critique of the EU.

What has arisen from such activism is the notion of a 'Europe from below': a reimagining of Europeanisation that prioritises economic and social justice, as well as democratisation (Chabanet 2002; della Porta and Mosca 2005; della Porta and Caiani 2009). While this is not an iteration of pro-EU activism as such, it is also not an entirely Eurosceptic position either. Organisations of this kind have typically shunned nationalistic arguments and welcomed European cooperation in principle; they have also perceived protest campaigns to be 'occasions to build a European identity' (della Porta and Caiani 2009, 124). The activists' critique of the EU has been part of a broader mobilisation against neoliberal globalisation and international financial institutions. What was articulated through the various counter-summits and protests was a 'critical Europeanism' and a recognition of the opportunities that EU institutions provided for cross-national grassroots activism against a neoliberal form of globalisation.

A recent 'special issue' of the *European Journal of Cultural and Political Sociology* interrogated the effects of the financial crisis in the late 2000s on the positions of 'progressive' social movements towards the Europeanisation process (della Porta 2020a). Individual contributions focused on the claims, frames, and justifications of youth activists (Milan 2020); secessionist organisations (Portos 2020); environmental movements (Bertuzzi 2020); feminists, and lesbian, gay, bisexual, and transgender (LGBT+) organisations (Chironi 2020); labour movements (Zamponi 2020); and 'Blockupy' (della Porta 2020b). Based on the findings of these studies, della Porta (2020, 228) observes

> the increasing criticism of existing EU institutions at the level of politics (with the democratic deficit perceived as increasing during the financial crisis); policy (seen as less and less driven by considerations of social justice and solidarity); and polity (with proposals to go 'beyond Europe'). While federalist visions are less and less supported, a soft cosmopolitanism aims at combining different territorial levels, regaining control at the national but also local level, within mutualist conceptions. In fact, even within more critical visions of the EU and greater concerns for issues of national sovereignty, the progressive movements we look at still continue to call for another Europe.

While progressive SMOs are thus highly dissatisfied with the current state of the EU, they acknowledge 'Europe' as an inescapable reality. Activists have not necessarily been keen, however, to openly debate visions of Europe, given the risk of internal divisions and the perception that Euroscepticism is the domain of the far right (della Porta 2021). Furthermore, despite occasional periods of intensity, EU-critical activism on the left has ebbed and flowed. For example, in the aftermath of the Great Recession of 2007–9, the EU – as part of the troika of global financial power – was very much a target of political opprobrium from the newly energised left (as well as the radical right). However, this quickly dissipated once national economies appeared to stabilise. As Diani and Kousis (2014, 400–1) conclude in their study of Greece (where anti-EU sentiment on the left had been unsurprisingly strong), by 2012 protest events had taken on more distinct agendas, and domestic political issues had become increasingly salient. The Democracy in Europe Movement 2025 (DiEM25) is a more recent example of a left-wing exponent of 'critical Europeanism', and it launched a transnational alliance for the 2019 European Parliament elections. Spearheaded by former Greek finance minister Yanis Varoufakis, the movement called for a radical democratisation of Europe (de Cleen et al. 2020), but its affiliated parties failed to win seats at the European level.

Explicitly pro-European street protests, whether in the United Kingdom or elsewhere in Europe, are a recent phenomenon. For instance, PoE, one of the most notable pro-European citizens' initiatives, was only established at the end of 2016. While a cornucopia of organisations and movements (such as the European Movement) have existed across the continent since the late 1940s onwards, these were more akin to professional lobbying organisations and interest groups than being protest movements as such. Apart from when citizens came out in favour of the ratification of particular EU treaties, pro-EU activism has been largely conspicuous by its absence, not just in the United Kingdom but across member states.

ANALYSING THE EMERGENCE AND EFFICACY OF THE ANTI-BREXIT MOVEMENT IN THE UNITED KINGDOM

The social movement literature provides a comprehensive intellectual framework for our research on the emergence and efficacy of the United Kingdom's anti-Brexit movement. From a 'bottom-up' perspective, it enables us to both interrogate how local activists can influence political contestation around European integration and to look at the formation of cleavages more generally. In addition, our particular empirical focus enables us to also make a significant theoretical contribution to the existing social movement literature by considering how movements that emerge not to directly challenge established institutions but to defend them construct ideational frames to convince the wider public of their cause.

The classic social movement literature is configured by a combination of structural and agency-related factors offered as determinants of the potential efficacy of movement actors and organisations. Early studies tended to depict collective action as a reaction to crisis or tension, and emphasised political processes and the mobilisation of resources to explain the emergence of societal activism. If the key question asked by scholars is why certain organisations are able to exert influence at a particular time, the answer is explained in the early literature either in terms of structural opportunities afforded by the domestic political system (McAdam et al. 2001) or the availability and deployment of resources (Kitschelt 1986; Tilly 1978). Social movement scholars initially employed one of two broad approaches: the political opportunity structure (POS) approach or resource mobilisation theory (RMT). Later analyses of collective action, protest, and the emergence of conflict adopted the constructivist perspective of framing, whereby the success or failure of actions was understood in terms of the particular discursive and cognitive schema employed by activists (Gamson 1992).

Contemporary studies of contentious politics posit social movements as being critical in cleavage formation and in the emergence of new issue agendas and forms of politics. Indeed, those who now study social movements do not view them as merely reflecting social tensions and crises, but as producers and developers of political responses. This transformation has been assisted by more nuanced methodological approaches that facilitate fine-grained analysis of 'impact' (Tarrow 1996; Amenta and Polletta 2019). Through their activism and campaigns, social movements are seen as being able to redefine both the political space and the ways of 'doing politics'; through their composite organisations and networks and by linking ideas, individuals, organisations, and events, social movements are seen as creators of new norms and solidarities, and therein lie their power and influence (della Porta 2016).

In developing our analytical framework, we start from the notion that existing approaches need to be combined in order to fully capture the emergence and performance of contemporary protest and contentious politics (McAdam et al. 2001). More precisely, we start out from the suggested analytical framework of Doug McAdam, John McCarty, and Mayer Zald (1996), who identify three key dimensions that are relevant to understanding the mobilisation as well as the efficacy of social movements: political opportunities, mobilising structures, and framing processes (see figure 2.1). The scholars stress that the relative importance of these dimensions may fluctuate over time: the model, in other words, is *dynamic*. For instance, while the political opportunity structure may be crucial in explaining the emergence of a given movement, the other two dimensions, which are related to the movement's agency, may become more important in the subsequent stages of that movement's life cycle. We also agree with the McAdam et al. assertion that the three dimensions are *interdependent*. Thus, while we will now introduce the three dimensions separately, and also focus on each of them in turn in the following three chapters of this book, the concluding chapter draws all three together and discusses how the political opportunity structure, mobilising structures, and framing processes potentially interacted in the emergence and development of the anti-Brexit movement.

```
┌─────────────────────────┐
│  Political opportunities │
│    Political system      │
│    Elite alignments      │──→  Stage 1
│    Elite allies          │     Social movement emergence
│    Actor configuration   │
│    Discursive context    │
└─────────────────────────┘
            ↕
┌─────────────────────────┐
│  Mobilising structures   │
│    Organisation          │
│    Activists             │
│    Repertoires           │
└─────────────────────────┘
            ↕                 ──→  Stage 2
┌─────────────────────────┐        Social movement efficacy
│  Framing processes       │
│    Issues and themes     │
│    Diagnostic frames     │
│    Prognostic frames     │
└─────────────────────────┘
```

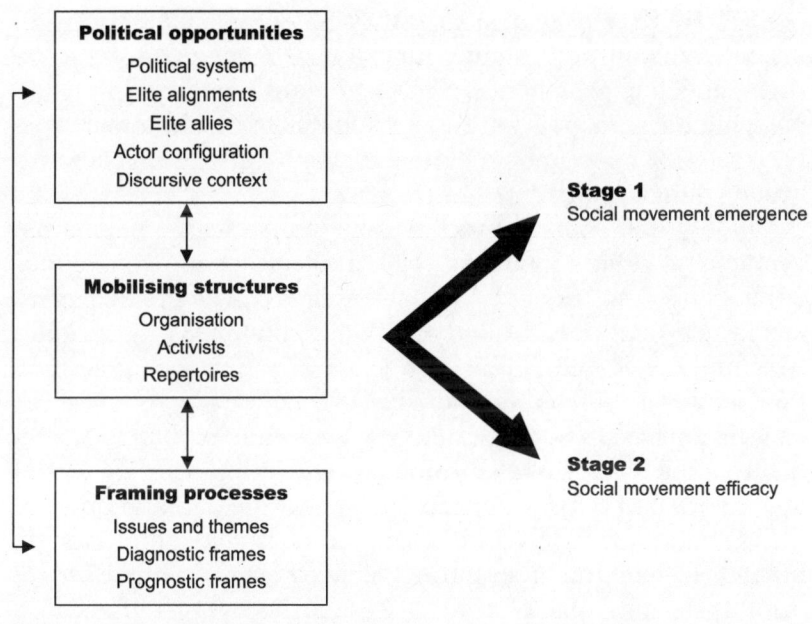

Figure 2.1   Analytical framework.

Political opportunities

As mentioned previously, the POS concept has featured prominently in the social movement literature (Tilly 1995). The classical early literature explained patterns of mobilisation and strategies of collective action in terms of the distribution of power within the state, the extent to which political institutions provided access for social movements to the public sphere and the political decision-making arena, formal and informal networks and institutions, and the cultural setting in which organisations interact with the governing and state institutions (Eisinger 1973; Tilly 1978; Kriesi 1995a; Piven and Cloward 1977; McAdam and Snow 1997). Regarding the formal institutional setting and its impact on movements, Kitschelt (1986, 62) notes that '[the] rules allow for, register, respond to, and even shape the demands of social movements that are not yet accepted political actors'. In his comparative analysis of new social movements across Europe, Koopmans identified the party and electoral systems as critical determinants of social movement access. He concluded that '[systems] which are highly resistant to the penetration of new conflict dimensions ... structurally block the breakthrough of new politics' (Koopmans 1996, 44–5). Variation in policy-making styles, institutional and procedural settings for deliberation, and the capacity and fragmentation of the institutions concerned with the implementation of policy are also acknowledged as important variables that will impact upon the capacity of movements and collective action (Kitschelt 1986, 64).

Although the political process approach became somewhat hegemonic in terms of studying social movements and contentious politics, there are two fundamental and interrelated problems with analysing protest from the perspective of institutional processes and structural opportunities. First, the concept of 'political opportunities' can be interpreted in a very broad manner, which reduces its analytical value. To a large extent this has been rectified in the literature, which has tried to provide greater clarity regarding formal and informal structures. For our analysis, we seek inspiration from McAdam (1996), which distils from the earlier literature four dimensions of political opportunity, including elements of the formal institutional structure of political systems, as well as more informal power relations. Given that the dimension of 'state repression' is not genuinely relevant in the democratic context of the United Kingdom's Brexit debate, we select McAdam's three remaining dimensions for our research: relative openness or closure of the institutionalised political system; the stability or instability of elite alignments; and the presence or absence of elite allies. Drawing on Kriesi's (2008) more recent theorisation, we add a fourth dimension to our understanding of the political opportunity structure: the configuration of actors. This refers not just to the presence of elite allies, but also to the particular dynamic or relational power between 'protagonists, antagonists and bystanders' within a political system. The configuration of political actors will determine the way the campaign or action is formulated, its efficacy, and its ultimate success. While they are shaped by the broader political context, actor configurations are less stable and more volatile, and they are therefore a critical component of the opportunity structure.

The second problem with the original POS approach is more fundamental and relates to the inherent and rationalist assumption that available opportunities, however extensively they are understood and defined, will be both recognised and used by activists. This is essentially a 'cause and effect' issue: one cannot simply assume that the availability of certain opportunities explains patterns of activism and the success or failure of campaigns. While some protests and campaigns will respond instantly to new opportunities, other movement actors will not necessarily be aware of, or be prepared to make use of, such opportunities for a host of reasons. What the more recent literature highlights is that there are filtering processes taking place between structural opportunities and activists. Kriesi (2008) talks about the importance of 'prevailing strategies' within a political system, as well as 'cultural or symbolic opportunities' as determinants of particular forms of action. Rather than viewing a country's opportunity structures as being universally available to all movements, he refers to the emergence of 'opportunity sets' that reflect the particular interaction between cultural models and political–institutional structures. These may differ depending on how and when a social movement emerges. Elster (1989) adds further nuance by identifying two intervening filtering mechanisms that will determine which available actions are utilised. These are broadly the actor's beliefs about and understanding of opportunities, and their desire to use them.

What the more recent literature highlights is how the efficacy and availability of systemic political opportunities are also conditioned by what Koopmans and Statham (1999) refer to as 'discursive opportunity structures': that is, the prevailing discourse and norms that condition the efficacy of particular campaigns and actions. Why some mobilisations make use of certain opportunities and others do not is explained in terms of a more subjective evaluation and understanding of such opportunities. In other words, actions are not governed entirely by the 'rationality principle' but are shaped by both personal and systemic constraints on individual actors, including prevailing discourse and understanding, as well as the agency of individuals to engage available material and non-material resources.

Other more recent research has emphasised the dynamic and interactive nature of protest, breaking down the movement and its environment into component players and arenas (Jasper 2015). This brings the POS approach much closer to the other two strands of the social movement literature: resource mobilisation and framing (discussed below). Understanding the web of intervening variables that determine and shape campaigns is particularly relevant for our study insofar as we set out to understand why a mass mobilisation of anti-Brexit and pro-EU activists across the United Kingdom seemingly had limited efficacy. In chapter 3 we pay particular attention both to the discursive opportunity structure as well as to the role of crucial players in the party-political and media arenas.

Mobilising structures

While the political process literature of the 1970s paid too little heed to the agency of actors in the deployment of strategies and opportunities, the literature in later years does acknowledge the extent to which the agency of individual activists – what systemic and non-systemic resources they mobilise – is critical to understanding particular actions. The concept of mobilising structures can be associated most clearly with resource mobilisation theory (RMT), the other strand of the classical social movement literature.

RMT challenges the notion that the presence of grievances and a conducive POS alone is enough to explain protest, and instead portrays SMO activists as rational actors who consciously decide to organise and mobilise on the basis of the availability of resources (Oberschall 1973; McCarthy and Zald 1977; Tilly 1978; Zald and McCarthy 1987). The capacity for mobilisation is dependent on the existence of various material and non-material resources, such as money, the availability of benefits, and the expertise available to a particular movement organisation: 'the type and nature of the resources available explain the tactical choices made by movements and the consequences of collective action on the social and political system' (della Porta and Diani 1999, 8). Although such a perspective shifts the emphasis from the system towards the activists, and is therefore seen as being closely aligned to rational choice theory, it is usually inferred or at least implicit that structural realities generate resources and that mobilisations are constructed in the context of constitutional, political, and economic situations.

Resource mobilisation theorists make a number of basic but highly significant points that are relevant to our study. Most notably, they claim that the greater the amount of discretionary resources among citizens and the elite, the greater the amount of resources available to SMOs: higher incomes, 'the satiation of other wants', and the extra time that citizens have available to them as a consequence of increased prosperity deliver benefit to organisations (McCarthy and Zald 1977, 1224). According to McCarthy and Zald (1977, 1226), 'it is only when resources can be garnered from conscience adherents that viable SMOs can be fielded to shape and represent the preferences of such collectivities'. As an approach, what the RMT literature confirms is that crisis and the existence of social or economic problems, sympathy for a particular cause among the population, or political opportunities alone will not result in the emergence of efficacious organisations. What also matters is the agency of individuals, their capacity to mobilise various systemic and non-systemic resources, plus their initial endowment of such resources.

POS and RMT approaches dominated social movement studies during the 1970s and 1980s, and they were often deployed in tandem (Kitschelt 1986; Rüdig 1988). Within much of the classical literature it is acknowledged that agency and structure are closely interconnected, with structural realities, both formal and informal, providing particular resources for collective action (della Porta 1988). Most studies are underpinned by the assertion that while the deployment of particular resources will be determined by the systemic opportunities available to movement organisations, it is the political system that essentially provides many of the resources that organisations employ.

In our study, we follow McCarthy's (1996, 141) interpretation of 'mobilising structures' as 'those agreed upon ways of engaging in collective action which include particular "tactical repertoires", particular "social movement organizational" forms, and "modular social movement repertoires"'. To put it more plainly, we are interested, first, in the organisations and activists that constituted the anti-Brexit movement, the relationship between these organisations, and how they employed material and non-material resources. Second, we focus on the types of organised action undertaken by the activists, and the activists' potential to reach out to, and sway, a large audience beyond ardent 'Remainers'. In the words of della Porta (2020c), did their actions ever constitute transformative 'eventful protests' that acted as 'exogenous shocks' altering the course of events? As we have already suggested, it is important to analyse mobilising structures in conjunction with the more general POS, but also with the movement's messages and claims. It is these 'framing processes' we discuss next.

Framing processes

A further strand of the literature analysing collective action, protest, and the emergence of conflict has adopted the constructivist perspective of framing (Gamson 1992). Frame analysis attempts to understand mobilisations in terms of attributed meaning and how the conflict is understood, articulated, and interpreted (della Porta and Diani 1999, 69). One question that has dominated the contemporary social movement literature is why some organisations seem better able to use systemic opportunities and resources than others. The issue strikes at what is arguably the major shortcoming of the POS model in isolation: namely, that it assumes that actors react rationally to the opportunities and constraints of the domestic structural context in which they operate (Eder 2003). As discussed above, a major shortcoming of the original POS approach was the tendency to see the individual actor as being linked to the macro-structures without heed to the complexities of social relations. Scholars who reject such a rationalist direct link identify a host of 'irrational' motives for mobilisation (emotions, identity), or they seek to explain the differential interaction with structural opportunities in terms of the deployment of particular discursive or interpretive frames. Understood as 'schemata of interpretation' that allow individuals 'to locate, perceive, identify and label' (Snow et al. 1986, 465), frames become the mechanism via which SMOs communicate with individuals and with elites. The precision of the discourse can therefore be critical in terms both of mobilising popular support and in gaining traction with elites.

If we accept that it matters how organisations articulate their campaigns and demands, then the congruence and dynamic between particular societal frames is also critical. This is referred to in the literature as 'framing alignment' (della Porta and Diani 2020) and 'resonance' (Snow et al. 2018). The greater the alignment between a movement organisation's framing of an issue and the discursive frames employed by state and civil society actors, the greater the chance of positive impact or 'resonance' with elites and the public. Insofar as frames are understood as 'a general, standardised, predefined structure which allows recognition of the world, and guides perception ... allowing [actors] to build defined expectations about what is to happen' (Donati 1992, 141–2), the obligation rests with movement organisations to 'frame' their campaigns in a way that resonates with dominant or existing interpretive frames. The ability of an organisation to reinterpret an issue so that it resonates with dominant frames but in such a way that the policy debate is altered, or popular opinion is changed, becomes a powerful means by which movement organisations can have an impact. This relates most closely to the notion of 'discursive opportunity structures' – the prevailing discourse and norms that condition the efficacy of particular campaigns and actions. Put simply, a social movement stands the best chance of generating traction if its actors articulate their campaign frames to resonate with extant discursive frames and prevailing meaning and cultural understandings. This does not mean that campaigns must agree or align with dominant understandings but that they must engage critically with their discourse and meaning.

Overall, what the focus on framing tells us is that the availability of resources and the relative openness or closure of the political system are insufficient variables to explain empowerment; the intervening variable is the interpretative frame that is selected and deployed by movement organisations. In this regard, a distinction is made throughout the literature between 'diagnostic' and 'prognostic' frames (Benford and Snow 2000). The former refers to social movements identifying 'a problem that deserves to be changed ... and an assertion of its cause (or causes) that warrants a response' (Smith 2020, 4); the latter is understood as the articulation of solutions and the course of action to be taken to remedy the identified problem. Prognostic framing involves social movement supporters proposing 'a plan of attack, and the strategies for carrying out the plan' (Benford and Snow 2000, 616). Benford and Snow (2000, 617) also identify 'motivational framing' as a core framing task, and this entails a '"call to arms" or rationale for engaging in ameliorative collective action'. This latter type of framing is integrated in chapter 4, which focuses on the evolution of the movement as well as activists' motivations. Chapter 5 engages more explicitly with 'diagnostic' and 'prognostic' framing, as its main focus is on the efforts to convince the wider public by means of messages and claims – *consensus* mobilisation in the words of Klandermans (1988).

In our research, we determine how anti-Brexit SMOs framed the 'event' of Brexit as well as European integration more generally. In particular, we seek to assess how pro-European activists and organisations interpreted and problematised the Brexit process ('diagnostic' framing), but also how they sought to sway Eurosceptic citizens by providing alternative solutions and visions of 'Europe' ('prognostic' framing). Furthermore, in line with McCarthy (1996, 149) and Zald (1996, 269), we note that framing can have an 'internal' dimension as well as an 'external' one. The former type of framing is connected to the mobilisation structures of a movement, as internal 'framing contests' have the potential to cause organisational tensions, which in turn may limit a movement's efficacy and its capacity for concerted action.

While framing processes form an essential part of explaining the emergence and efficacy of the anti-Brexit movement, our analysis of its frame construction and articulation per se also offers specific insights for the social movement literature. Before we conclude this chapter we discuss the specific dilemmas the anti-Brexit movement was likely to face in terms of its strategic messaging, given that it constituted a rare instance of a liberal–cosmopolitan movement that emerged not to directly challenge the EU's institutions but to defend them.

THE STRATEGIC DILEMMAS OF LIBERAL MOVEMENTS DEFENDING ESTABLISHED INSTITUTIONS

While there exists an abundance of comparative and single-case analysis of social movements as 'meaning-makers', the focus of such studies has largely been on progressive left-liberal identity-based movements that challenge the establishment and strive for change. Notably, Gamson and Meyer (1996, 283) defined a social movement as 'a sustained and self-conscious challenge to authorities or cultural codes by a field of actors'. To create a political opportunity for themselves, the authors argue, they typically rely on an 'optimistic rhetoric of change': 'their job is to convince potential challengers that action leading to change is possible and desirable' (Gamson and Meyer 1996, 286).

Some movements, however, exist to defend long-established political institutions against forces that desire radical change. The literature has primarily devoted attention to culturally conservative or reactionary 'counter-movements' (see Vüllers and Hellmeier (2021) for an exception). Studies in this field focus mostly on movements that emerged to oppose the agenda of left-liberal organisations: in the areas of civil rights (Mottl 1980), LGBT rights (Ayoub and Chetaille 2020), abortion law (McCaffrey and Keys 2000), environmental protection (Hess and Brown 2017), and the politics of immigration and race (Blee and Creasap 2010; Blee and Yates 2015; Smith 2020), for example. This literature focuses on the dynamic interaction between movement and counter-movement, whereby the latter is almost invariably a conservative or right-wing response to a 'progressive' liberal reform. The counter-movement's primary focus is to critique policies that are seen to undermine the established order and the interests of groups and individuals that are typically in a position of power and privilege. Following McVeigh (1999, 1,463), conservative movements engage primarily in 'defensive' collective action: they 'emerge in reaction to shrinking, rather than expanding, levels of power and influence'.

In terms of its framing strategies, explicitly pro-European movements face a more challenging task in comparison with left-liberal 'pro-change' movements on the one hand, and conservative 'counter-movements' on the other. For pro-European movements that seek to defend *aspects* of the status quo while also offering a 'progressive' vision – but one that is not dissimilar to that which currently exists – frame construction is far more complex. While conservative movements refer back to a previous era that was ostensibly better, the *raison d'être* of movements with a socially or culturally liberal character is to strive for a fairer future and winning new rights, especially for those who lack privilege and power (Schradie 2019, 157–8). This puts liberal–cosmopolitan pro-European movements in a difficult position. How much criticism of the current situation can be articulated without calling into question the merits of the status quo (or the status quo ante in the case of the anti-Brexit movement: the situation prior to the referendum)? To what extent can a vision of the future be promoted without sowing the seeds of discontent with the current or previous state of affairs?

Our study will thus reveal what specific dilemmas pro-European movements face in constructing ideational frames and formulating their messages. Furthermore, although studies have sought to differentiate between strategic processes involved in frame production (e.g. bridging, amplification, extension, and transformation) (Snow et al. 1986), the interconnectedness of identifying the problem, apportioning blame, and devising solutions has not been fully considered (Gerhards and Rucht 1992; Nepstad 1997). Indeed, Benford and Snow (2000, 616) merely observe that 'some research suggests that there tends to be a correspondence between an SMO's diagnostic and prognostic framings ... [and that] the identification of specific problems and causes tends to constrain the range of possible "reasonable" solutions and strategies advocated'. Put simply, if the diagnostic frame only partially articulates the problem and its culprits, the prognostic frame will not be able to comprehensively map the way ahead. How the two frames are intrinsically linked has recently been discussed and illustrated in the context of anti-racist activism (Smith 2020): if racism is depicted and diagnosed (framed) narrowly in terms of *racist* individuals (rather than institutional or systemic *racism*), or the extent of the problem is denied, then the emergent solutions will likely be ineffective (see also Bacchi and Eveline 2010).

It is our assertion that diagnostic and prognostic frame development are intrinsically connected, with each emerging via a process of constructing and then communicating 'a perceived reality' that informs the notion of 'the problem', 'the culprit', and 'the solution' (Entman 1993). The process of frame construction involves consideration of how a movement 'chang[es] old understandings and generates new meanings' (Benford and Snow 2000, 625). These meanings then determine not just its vision of the future but also how it articulates its critique of the status quo, the apportioning of blame, and how it sets out to mobilise activism.

CONCLUSION

A key objective of this theoretical chapter has been to make the case for studying the anti-Brexit movement that emerged in the United Kingdom after the 2016 referendum from the perspective of protest politics. We began by discussing how the 'politicisation of Europe' has primarily been studied outside of the realm of social movement and protest politics. The literature has mainly focused on rising opposition to European integration, captured by the term Euroscepticism, which was primarily expressed by political parties on the edges of the political spectrum. We then sought to illustrate the relevance of the social movement literature as both a conceptual and an analytical framework for this study and its underpinning research.

While debates about European integration have previously played a relatively minor role in the arena of protest politics, we should not overlook Eurosceptic social movement activism from the left, which associated EU policies and the deepening of integration with globalisation and neoliberal economics. Its reimagining of Europeanisation prioritising economic and social justice was relevant in the emergence of a 'constraining dissensus' and the notion of a

'Europe from below' as the basis of an alternative vision of integration. Some of this activism appeared to dissipate after the Great Recession of 2007–9, yet in more recent years there have been examples of more overtly pro-European actors emerging from within the realms of civil society and protest politics, with the Pulse of Europe and, indeed, the anti-Brexit movement being the most prominent examples. These potentially mark a significant politicisation of Europe 'from below' (see van Kessel and Fagan 2022b).

Drawing on the extensive social movement literature, we provided an analytical framework for studying the anti-Brexit movement in the United Kingdom, and for considering the extent to which networks of citizens, movement organisations, and protest politics manage to impact on the politicisation of Europe. In highlighting (i) political opportunities, (ii) mobilising structures, and (iii) framing processes as determinants of social movement emergence and efficacy, we capture the significance of structures, resources, actors, and the attribution of meaning in assessing the impact of popular movements on cleavage formation and the politicisation of issues. In tune with most contemporary scholars, we assert that the three broad approaches need to be used in tandem to fully capture the rise and performance of social movements. For analytical purposes, however, the following three chapters will consider each of the three dimensions in turn, before drawing together the findings in the concluding chapter.

3

The Politics of Europe in the United Kingdom

We have our own dream and our own task. We are with Europe, but not of it. We are linked but not combined. We are interested and associated but not absorbed. If Britain must choose between Europe and the open sea, she must always choose the open sea.
Winston Churchill, Speech to the House of Commons, 11 May 1953

There is no question of any erosion of essential national sovereignty.
Edward Heath, British prime minister, 1970–74

While subsequent chapters of this book are endogenous in their focus – the campaign tactics of the movement, the deployment of its resources, and the way the anti-Brexit message was framed by activists – this chapter adopts an *exogenous* perspective: the political context in which the anti-Brexit movement emerged and operated. Given that social movement scholars have from the outset pointed to the 'political opportunity structure' to explain and understand the efficacy of any popular movement (Kitschelt 1986; Tilly 1995), this is a good place to start our analysis. The core question here is: to what extent can we explain the emergence and political efficacy of the anti-Brexit movement in terms of the political opportunity structure?

As was highlighted in the previous chapter, the early social movement literature explained patterns of mobilisation and strategies of collective action in terms of the following: the distribution of power within the state; the extent to which political institutions provided access for social movements to the public sphere and to the political decision-making arena; formal and informal networks and institutions; and the cultural setting in which organisations interact with the governing and state institutions (Eisinger 1973; Tilly 1979; Kriesi 1995; Piven and Cloward 1977; McAdam and Snow 1997). Regarding the formal institutional setting and its impact on movements, Kitschelt (1986, 62) notes that '[the] rules allow for, register, respond to and even shape the demands of social movements that are not yet accepted political actors'.

In terms of analysing how the political system and its institutions shaped the UK's anti-Brexit movement, the discussion will consider the following dimensions identified by McAdam (1996): relative openness or closure of the institutionalised political system; the stability or instability of elite alignments; and the presence or absence of elite allies. Again, as already introduced, we add two further dimensions to our analytical framework. Drawing on Kriesi's (2008) theorisation we additionally include the so-called configuration of actors. This refers not just to the presence of elite allies, but also to the particular dynamic or relational power between 'protagonists, antagonists and bystanders' within a political system. The configuration of political actors will co-determine the way the campaign or action is formulated, its efficacy, and its ultimate success. While they are shaped by the broader political context, actor configurations are less stable and more volatile, and they are therefore a critical component of the opportunity structure. Finally, we include a consideration of what Koopmans and Statham (1999) refer to as the 'discursive opportunity structures': the prevailing discourse and norms that condition the efficacy of particular campaigns and actions. Discursive opportunity structures, as we demonstrate, interact with the above dimensions, in particular the openness or closure of the institutionalised political system and the configuration of actors.

We understand political opportunities as entry points to the system and available resources to enable efficacious mobilisation, and we see them as being subjective rather than objective. They are perpetually in flux and repeatedly negotiated and challenged, and, most importantly, they are a product of discursive communication across actors and activists. Insofar as they are the product of the interaction between movements and counter-movements, and the machinations between elites and the masses, access will always be conditioned by the specific campaign or issue on which activism is focused. Social movements exist to challenge and reinterpret prevailing norms, but their efficacy is also determined *by* such norms. In other words, the success or failure of a movement and the degree of access to elites is determined by salient attitudes, beliefs, and values. Any change in attitude – expressed in terms of popular and/or political discourse – will potentially impinge upon the opportunity structure. When assessing how the extant political system has shaped and determined a social movement, it is therefore imperative to consider prevailing narratives and discourses.

What follows below is, first, a consideration of the relative openness or closure of the British political system for social movements and contentious politics in general, and for pro-European activism in particular. The analysis will consider formal political institutions as well as the prevailing discursive opportunity structure. The discussion will focus particularly on continuity and change in the political opportunity structure between the referendum of 1975 and the United Kingdom's departure from the EU at the start of 2020.

In some respects, the movement to campaign for the UK to remain in the EEC in 1975 and the anti-Brexit movement operated in comparable political contexts. In both periods, the two main parties were internally divided (though in 1975 the division was greatest in the Labour Party rather than the Conservatives). Prior to both referendums, the public's stance on EEC/EU membership appeared to be unenthusiastic but, on balance, just about supportive (Miller 2015; Evans and Menon 2018, 47). In May 1975, the European Commission's polling agency Eurobarometer asked the question: 'Generally speaking, do you think that UK membership of the European Community (Common Market) is a good thing, a bad thing, neither good or bad, or don't know?' Forty-seven per cent of UK respondents thought it a good thing, compared with 21 per cent who thought it a bad thing (Miller 2015). When asked the same question in 2015, little had apparently changed: 43 per cent of respondents thought it a good thing and 23 per cent thought it bad. British Social Attitudes data from 2015 revealed that 37 per cent of respondents wanted to remain in a reformed EU, 26 per cent were happy to remain in the EU as it existed, and only 18 per cent favoured leaving (Evans and Menon 2018, 47). In the period after the 2016 referendum, public opinion was notoriously divided and polarisation intensified, but successive opinion polls still mostly indicated a small majority being in favour of remaining in the EU (WhatUKThinks n.d.).

Yet in other respects the political context in which the 2016 referendum took place was profoundly different. In the four decades since the 1975 vote, a climate of rabid Euroscepticism had built up in the media – particularly the print media – and within politics. Furthermore, even if citizens often remained ambivalent about the issue of European integration, attitudes towards the EU have consistently ranked among the least favourable in comparison with other European countries (see, for example, Baker et al. 2008). The existing literature places considerable responsibility on how a 'hostile' British print media pursued a persistent campaign of 'othering' of Europe and the EU (van der Zwet et al. 2020). This matters given that perceptions of the EU and of European identity are shaped by exposure to positive and negative news coverage of European matters (Bruter 2003) – despite the fact that research conducted via focus groups has revealed that a majority of UK participants thought that coverage of the EU by the print media was overly negative and lacking objectivity (Bruter 2004). More significant still is the fact that although in recent years the circulation of national newspapers in the United Kingdom has declined overall, in the period between 1975 and 2016 Eurosceptic national titles were dominant among the traditional working class and those with lower levels of education (Grant 2008; Galpin and Trenz 2017), the demographic that overwhelmingly voted Leave in the June 2016 referendum (Moore 2016).

Our analysis then goes on to focus on elite alignments/allies as well as the configuration of two key actors: the UK Independence Party (UKIP) and the official 'Remain' referendum campaign. The United Kingdom had experienced monumental social, economic, and cultural transformation in the period between the two referendums, and it was a profoundly different country in 2016, with new social cleavages and identitarian politics characterising the political debate (Lord 2018). One key upshot from this was the growth of UKIP as an overtly Eurosceptic political party, syphoning support from both Labour and the Conservatives (also known as the 'Tories'). Furthermore, as Sobolewska and Ford (2020, 121–53) illustrate, the link between voters and (the traditional) political parties had seriously weakened. This was not simply about parties becoming 'catch-all' and attempting to appeal to a wider segment of the electorate, and nor was it just about the decline of deference to elites. Rather, it was about the erosion of trust in politicians and political parties (Pattie and Johnston 2001; Evans and Menon 2017). In terms of anti-Brexit activism this mattered because it meant greater instability of elite alignments and the weakened functioning of political parties in linking citizens with power and elites. This concerned not only political elites, but also the economic and academic elites who dominated the Stronger In 'Remain' campaign in the run-up to the 2016 referendum (Clarke et al. 2017).

What is also important to recognise is that the referendum outcome itself gave a democratic mandate to the decision to leave the EU. This meant that it became even more politically perilous for either the Conservative or Labour leaderships to support EU membership (Hayton 2021). Such reluctance to adopt an unequivocal pro-European position was enabling for the emergence of the grassroots anti-Brexit movement. If, as was the case immediately after the referendum vote, politicians are trusted less and parties are perceived to be disconnected from public demands and opinion, then citizens are likely to turn to social movements. However, the lack of elite allies ultimately weakened the efficacy of the movement. Indeed, what the discussion below highlights is how, in the aftermath of the referendum, the link between local activists, the remnants of the central Remain campaign, and political parties was tenuous at best and non-existent at worst. As will become clear from our analysis, the anti-Brexit movement needed, but did not get, the linkage to power and elites that political parties are able to provide.

THE POLITICAL SYSTEM: OPEN OR CLOSED FOR PRO-EUROPEAN MOBILISATION?

Formal political institutions

How open or closed is the British state? Underpinning this question is a consideration of the extent to which there is devolution of power and authority, where both are located, but also the degree to which formal structures and informal practices or the realities of power are aligned. While much does depend on the issue at stake, there is a style and character of national decision making that will determine and shape the opportunities afforded to any social movement campaign. While some scholars have pointed to the relatively entrenched lobbying system and the proliferation of a plurality of interest groups in the United Kingdom as evidence of openness (Koopmans 1996), others conclude that despite devolution in the early 2000s, the British state remains overly centralised both in nature and in practice, with power concentrated in the national executive based in Westminster, London. Civil society activists in the United Kingdom enjoy few formal guarantees of representation in the political process (Dryzek et al. 2003, 42–8), and it is only in the past twenty years that they have won the right to appeal directly to the judiciary (Cichowski and Stone Sweet 2003). Though social movement organisations, particularly environmental NGOs, have pursued legal means to advance their campaigns, this has met with limited success (Vanhala 2012).

The House of Lords – the country's second legislative chamber – has exerted significant influence over the Commons (Russell 2013), and it is often receptive to debating a wide variety of societal interests. However, neither citizens nor their movements can appeal directly to the Lords, and, given that its members are unelected, its legitimacy is somewhat compromised. When conflicts between the two chambers arise, it is invariably the Commons that prevails (Russell and Gover 2017). Thus, the UK political system affords few points of access to social movements, particularly those that are not well networked into elite social circles. As Kollman and Waites (2011, 183) observed in their study of the LGBT+ movement in the United Kingdom, 'interest groups and social movement organizations … must rely on the good will of either elected politicians or Whitehall [national civil service] officials to be heard and have their concerns fed into decision-making processes'.[1]

Those advocating in favour of EU membership in 2016 faced a political opportunity structure that was not particularly open, either in general or in respect of their particular concern. With reference to the period after the referendum, access for pro-Remain activists was further limited due to the fact that the decision-making process in the post-referendum period was entirely centralised. The first and most obvious reason for this was that, given the enormous trade and security implications of Brexit, it was somewhat inevitable that the negotiations and decision-making process were based in Westminster and Whitehall. Irrespective of devolution and the authority granted to the Scottish and Welsh political institutions over various social and economic issues, the United Kingdom's relationship with the EU, the referendum, the ensuing negotiations, and the political decision-making process were the purview of Her Majesty's Government in London. Both the Scottish National Party (SNP) and the Welsh Labour Party (then in power in Scotland and

Wales, respectively) had been unequivocally pro-Remain. However, the Scottish and Welsh First Ministers were, to a large extent, marginalised in terms of the negotiations with Brussels from the day after the referendum until the day the United Kingdom left the EU (Wincott 2020). The entirely centralised nature of the Brexit process was even more galling for Scottish voters, a majority of whom were pro-Remain and who had an elected government at Holyrood that was steadfastly opposed to Brexit (BBC 2020). Indeed, for those anti-Brexit activists north of the border, the political opportunity structure could not have been more closed and restrictive.

Discursive context

That the political opportunity structure was so closed for pro-EU activists certainly also related to prevailing public and political opinion – what we identify in our conceptual framework as the *discursive opportunity structure*. Political access, however centralised the decision-making process, is conditioned by public opinion and prevailing attitudes. A social movement campaign able to galvanise public support is more likely to exert influence or at least gain an audience with elites. It is fair to say that support in the UK for European integration among both ordinary citizens and political elites has always been temperate at best, lukewarm at worst. Where and when it has existed in the post–World War II period, support for 'Europe' has been couched in pragmatic, transactional, and instrumental terms – framed in the language of national self-interest rather than ideological creed or conviction (Diez Medrano 2003). As the then prime minister Harold Wilson observed during the 1975 referendum, there was little appetite in the United Kingdom for 'common market theology' (Saunders 2018, 115).

Despite a landslide result in favour of staying in the EEC in the 1975 referendum, the public and political enthusiasm for 'Europe' was mostly tepid thereafter. The *Daily Express*, which had campaigned for a 'Yes' vote to stay in in 1975, captured the prevailing mood at the time in its post-referendum editorial: 'We are still a United Kingdom … We are still a sensible kingdom. The most encouraging lesson of the [1975] referendum is that the centre held' (Saunders 2018, 3). In other words, the United Kingdom's membership was to be tolerated as long as it delivered economic benefits and did not fundamentally threaten national sovereignty. This was the underpinning political consensus of the next four decades, and it constituted the parameters of the political debate on Europe within the United Kingdom. What united the political mainstream with a sizeable proportion of the British population was a lack of enthusiasm for the EEC/EU, and a phlegmatic acceptance borne out of a recognition that the economic rationale is broadly in the country's best interests (Saunders 2018). Any attempt to be more enthusiastic or to be more pro-integration would seemingly struggle to gain political traction.

Several critical changes took place between 1975 and 2016 that altered the political climate and the opportunity structure for those wishing to defend the United Kingdom's membership of the EU. This chapter later turns to the creation of UKIP in September 1993 and looks at the pressure the party exerted on the Conservatives (Bale 2018). More fundamentally, the cumulative impact of an unremitting Eurosceptic campaign by the print media meant that the discursive political opportunity structure for pro-EU activists became increasingly inhospitable. Indeed, the significance of the Eurosceptic media should not be overlooked. As well as enjoying a wide national distribution, a large share of the British printed press is owned and controlled by a handful of Eurosceptic proprietors and editors. Throughout the decades between the two referendums the British tabloid press pursued various 'crusades' around different Euro-myths and sustained a long tradition of Eurosceptic and Europhobic editorial stances (Zappettini 2019). Popular titles such as the *Daily Mail*, *The Sun*, and the *Daily Express* were particularly active in portraying the United Kingdom as a victim of a Brussels conspiracy to force the British government to surrender sovereignty in all shapes and forms. Unsubstantiated allegations and provocative reporting were often part and parcel of these outlets' EU reporting, with one well-known example being *The Sun*'s 'Up Yours Delors' headline in 1990, referring to the then European Commission president's plans to introduce a common currency. Perhaps equally notable was the tabloids' trivialisation of European politics. Indeed, the most popular titles have made little attempt over the years to cover European issues in any depth. As Grant (2008) notes, only three national daily newspapers – *The Guardian*, *The Times* and the *Financial Times* – have staff correspondents in Brussels. This perhaps explains why, according to Eurobarometer data from 2015, UK respondents performed worse than citizens from any other member state when asked factual questions about the EU (European Commission 2015).

If the prevailing political discourse was inhospitable for pro-EU activists before and during the referendum campaign, it shifted even further in the Brexit direction in the aftermath of the 2016 vote. Indeed, the day after the 2016 referendum, when the veteran BBC political commentator David Dimbleby announced the result of the referendum with the statement 'the British people have spoken ...and the answer is we're out', he was articulating the mantra that would frame the political debate in the ensuing three and half years. In the view of many politicians – even those supportive of the Remain position – the referendum vote represented a democratic mandate for the United Kingdom to leave the EU: something that could not be ignored nor simply overturned. This undoubtedly altered the political opportunity structure; it changed the calculations that individual politicians were prepared to make and constrained the articulation of an unequivocally pro-Remain position.

ELITE ALIGNMENTS AND ALLIES: A CONTEXT OF DIVISION AND FLUX

In addition to how open or closed the political system is, and the location of power and authority, it is critical to consider the link with parties, and the patronage and support of leading party figures. While this has long been acknowledged in the social movement literature (Koopmans 1996), it has recently received renewed scholarly attention due to the emergence of contemporary movements such as the People's Assembly Against Austerity (Rhodes 2020) and Momentum (Dennis 2019), as well as the broader phenomenon across Europe of so-called movement parties (Kitschelt 2006). For any social movement in the United Kingdom, gaining access to politicians and political elites is, to a large extent, contingent on the position adopted by the two main parties on the issue in question. Consideration should be given to how internally united the parties are, the extent to which there are divisions between the party elite and the rank and file, and how those divisions are managed.

In terms of the anti-Brexit movement's ability to gain political access, or at least a degree of political traction, links with political parties and the positioning of those parties were critical. When David Cameron announced the referendum date in February 2016, the parliamentary arithmetic favoured Remain: out of 329 Conservative MPs, 185 declared their intention to vote for the United Kingdom to stay in the EU; all but 10 of Labour's 232 MPs, all 8 Liberal Democrat MPs, and all 54 SNP MPs also pledged to support Remain. Despite campaigning to leave in 1975, the Welsh nationalist Plaid Cymru also campaigned for a Remain vote in 2016. Of the 138 MPs who declared their intention to vote Leave, the majority were Conservatives, plus the single UKIP MP and 8 Democratic Unionist Party MPs (Clarke 2017, 30).

Despite the fact that most MPs, at least prior to the referendum, supported 'Remain', forging an alignment with either of the two main political parties in 2016 was more difficult for anti-Brexit activists than had been the case forty years earlier. There are two fundamental reasons for this. First, despite the importance of elite linkage and alignment for social movements, in contemporary politics having the support of politicians – even the leaders of large parties – is far less of a guarantee that one's cause will gain traction and salience than it once was. The period between the first EEC/EU referendum and the second witnessed a decline of deference and a growing reluctance among voters to follow the 'cues' (Hooghe and Marks 2004) of their leaders. A process of dealignment between parties and their traditional voter base was taking place during this period. Referring to the 1997–2010 period, Sobolewska and Ford (2020, 8–9) contend that 'voters and parties steadily drifted apart. Both Labour and the Conservatives changed in ways which alienated voters and eroded traditional partisan political identities.' This meant that even if one of the main parties had been steadfastly pro-Remain, this would not necessarily have delivered the same dividend in terms of winning over voters as it would have in the past. In terms of social movement efficacy, elite alignment is therefore still important, but the benefits are mitigated by a decline in deference and trust, and by the dealignment that has taken place between parties and voters. In addition to this, the position of the two main parties had radically shifted vis-à-vis EU membership. It was not simply that by 2016 Labour had become more pro-EU and the Tories less so; it was that the internal divisions *within* the parties had become much more acute, complex, and pronounced, resulting in a stark division between the parties' leaderships, their rank and file members, their parliamentarians, and the voters. This amounted to a further weakening of the cueing function of the two political parties regarding the issue of European integration.

In 1975, the debate about whether the United Kingdom should stay in or leave the EEC mapped much more closely onto the left–right ideological cleavage that underpinned the party system. Although there were certainly internal divisions within both Labour and the Conservatives, anti-Common Market sentiment was much more associated with the left (which saw the EEC as a capitalist club that threatened jobs), whereas the pro-European position was laced in the right-wing rhetoric of security, strengthening the British economy, free trade, and countering the Soviet threat (Saunders 2018). Such a left–right divide is reflected in the percentage of party supporters voting to stay in the EEC by party identification: just under 90 per cent of Conservative supporters said they voted to stay in the Common Market, compared with 58 per cent of Labour supporters (Clements 2017).

By 2016, the situation had changed quite remarkably. Forty years since the first referendum, support for the EU was now much more a phenomenon of liberal-left Labour voters than centre-right Tories (Cole 2020). This largely reflects the fact that EU membership had in the ensuing period become associated with greater social protection and the regulation of labour, and with liberal/progressive social policies. For many Tory voters, the EU was no longer a free-market club but an expensive regulatory leviathan that threatened to strangulate the British economy. In the absence of the Soviet threat and with the UK economy now performing better than, or at least as well as, other EU member states, many Conservative voters had long since abandoned their pragmatic and tepid enthusiasm for European integration (Dorey 2017). If they supported staying in the EU at all, it was because the economic case for doing so was sufficiently compelling (Curtice 2016). Unsurprisingly, therefore, in the weeks prior to the 23 June referendum vote, polling indicated that around 58 per cent of Conservative supporters backed Brexit, whereas more than 75 per cent of Labour voters supported Remain (Clements 2017).

However, changes in party supporters' preferences on Europe amounted to much more than simply a left–right realignment on the issue of Europe. Three fundamental shifts had occurred in the forty years between the two votes. First, the EU had fundamentally changed from being a rather loose economic project to becoming a supranational political system based on a distinct model of multilevel governance (Hooghe and Marks 2009). Through various treaties, integration had touched all policy spheres and thus, being a supporter of the EU in 2016 meant something very different from what it had meant in 1975. Second, as discussed in detail below, the support base of the Labour Party had dramatically altered. Third, the rise of UKIP and the impact of both large-scale EU immigration after 2004 and the Great Recession of 2007–8 had completely reconfigured the political debate concerning EU membership. While both main parties articulated a formal position in favour of the status quo – that is, the United Kingdom remaining in the EU – deep divisions had emerged by 2016 between party members, voters, MPs, and the leaderships of both the Conservatives and Labour.

In terms of attitudes, the most significant shift had occurred within the Conservative Party. In 1975, despite the manifestation of Euroscepticism within the rank and file and among some Tory parliamentarians, most of the shadow cabinet and most backbench MPs backed a pro-membership position. By 2016 the party had become much more internally divided than it had been forty years earlier. The schism was in large part a consequence of, on the one hand, the party having moved in a more liberal and cosmopolitan direction during the 2000s (Ford and Goodwin 2014), and, on the other hand, the influx of Tory MPs that had entered Parliament in 2010 and 2015 being much more Eurosceptic (Heppell et al. 2017). The latter, combined with growing support for UKIP across parts of England, had pushed the party much more towards Euroscepticism than the leadership intended (Bale 2017). Indeed, the disunity and tension are captured in the scenario of a majority Conservative government led by a leader, David Cameron, who was openly pro-Remain calling an in/out referendum against the backdrop of a divided cabinet and frontbench. The party officially remained neutral, but a corps of the parliamentary party and the rank-and-file membership staunchly favoured Leave. In early 2016, months before the referendum, an internal survey within the party revealed that approximately two-thirds of Conservative MPs supported Britain's exit from the EU despite Cameron's clear preference for staying in (Helm and McDonald 2016). Compare that with 1975, when the Conservative Party officially supported the United Kingdom remaining in the EEC: Margaret Thatcher, as party leader, supported the 'yes' campaign, as did most of the shadow front bench, the parliamentary party, and the rank-and-file members (Saunders 2018). If a group of citizens or local campaigners sought to mobilise in favour of Britain remaining in the EEC, it was reasonably clear that the Tory party, and any local Conservative MP or councillor, would have been their ally, or at least a good point of access. In contrast, after the 2016 referendum, and even more so upon Boris Johnson's rise to power in July 2019, the Conservative party became the party of 'getting Brexit done' (Hayton 2021).

What had befallen the Conservatives by 2016 was an almost exact copy of the 1975 divisions within Labour, when senior ministerial figures were campaigning openly for and against the EEC and Labour voters were given conflicting advice on how to vote (Saunders 2018). The Labour Party decided not to adopt an official position in 1975. Harold Wilson and several members of his cabinet unenthusiastically supported the 'yes' campaign, but the government was split: its members actually campaigned on each side of the question. A significant proportion of the parliamentary party, the unions, and the rank-and-file members of the Labour Party were anti-EEC, based largely on a defence of UK workers' rights against migrant workers from Europe, cheap labour, and a loss of jobs. The fact that the leadership gave tacit support for the United Kingdom to remain in the EEC while the party refused to adopt this as an official stance reflected the strong anti-common market sentiment that dominated all echelons of the party.

From having been a broadly Eurosceptic party in 1975, the Labour Party had unceremoniously ditched its anti-EU stance by the late 1980s and early 1990s (Cole 2020). This was indicative of the more fundamental shift that was taking place within the party. No longer solely a party of the industrial working class, Labour became more a party of the white-collar worker, of the professional, university educated, and liberal urban middle class, and of younger women (Campbell 2006; Sobolewska and Ford 2020). While blue-collar and semi-skilled and unskilled workers were still more likely than not to vote Labour, the party's agenda and policies had shifted considerably. This transformation was particularly evident under the leadership of Tony Blair and during the creation of 'New Labour', which promoted a battery of policies that in fact reflected the internationalist, pro-market, socially liberal, and pro-EU values of liberal-minded Tory voters and Liberal Democrat supporters. While the party shifted ideologically, the beliefs and opinions of those voters in its former heartlands did not necessarily follow a similar trajectory.

What had occurred by 2016 was a growing dislocation between the party's former voter base in the north of England and the Labour Party at Westminster and its more affluent and socially mobile supporters (Evans 2017). To employ Sobolewska and Ford's (2020) terminology, the party and many of its voters in London, Manchester, and other large cities were outwardly and ideologically 'identity liberal'. However, many Labour voters in post-industrial towns and parts of northern England, who had suffered most from the Great Recession and the ensuing austerity, were 'identity conservative' and much more wary of immigration – and supportive of Leave.

In the aftermath of the 2016 referendum, although formally committed to supporting Remain, the Labour party's position on future UK–EU relations was cautious at best, ambiguous at worst (Diamond 2018; Hayton 2021). This was due not only to the referendum result making it difficult for politicians to disregard a 'democratic mandate', but also to the election of Jeremy Corbyn as party leader a year earlier. Under Corbyn, ideological divisions between the leadership, the parliamentary party, members, and voters intensified, including over Europe and Brexit. The newly elected left-wing leader was a long-term Eurosceptic and was extremely reticent to parade the pro-EU credentials he claimed to harbour. The parliamentary party, far more centrist than the new leader, were overwhelmingly in favour of Remain, as were most members of Corbyn's first shadow cabinet (Pogrund and Maguire 2020). The Labour Party largely remained a party of the liberal centre left and, unsurprisingly, most members were pro-EU and aghast at the prospect of the United Kingdom leaving. Even those who had joined (or rejoined) the party to support Jeremy Corbyn tended to be pro-Remain (Crines et al. 2017). However, many (erstwhile) Labour voters in post-industrial northern English towns – some of them with relatively high levels of socio-economic deprivation – were Brexit supporters (Sobolewska and Ford 2020). The Labour Party was, in 2016 and the years that followed, pro-Remain at its core but led by a left-wing Eurosceptic and wary of losing Brexit-supporting voters in English northern constituencies (Batrouni 2020).

In the aftermath of the 2016 referendum, it was unclear to pro-Remain and anti-Brexit activists – whether they were in the liberal heartlands of London or in Sunderland or Stoke – where the Labour Party stood on Brexit. This mattered a great deal for the anti-Brexit movement that emerged in the period after the referendum vote. As Koopmans (1996, 44) observed in his comparative analysis of new social movements across Europe, progressive liberal campaigns benefit greatly from the patronage of the established left. Had the Labour Party been led by a staunchly anti-Brexit leadership after the referendum, a grassroots movement across the country may not have emerged in the way that it did. However, those campaigning against Brexit would arguably have fared better.

Thus far the focus of the discussion has been entirely on the two main parties that have dominated the UK party system. Because of the staunchly pro-European stance of the United Kingdom's main 'third party', the Liberal Democrats have also been a potentially important elite ally for any pro-European movement in the country. Support for the party and the number of seats it holds in Parliament have seen considerable fluctuation, but the Liberal Democrats had played a key role in recent years, being part of a coalition government between 2010 and 2015. More importantly, the party has been an unequivocal supporter of remaining in the EU, and in its former guise as the Liberal Party, it had formed the backbone of the European Movement in the United Kingdom. The elections of 2005 and 2010 represented an all-time highpoint for the party in terms of share of the popular vote and number of seats in Parliament. Under the leadership of Charles Kennedy (2005) and then Nick Clegg (2010), the party secured 22 per cent and 23 per cent of the popular vote, translating into 62 out of 646 seats and 57 out of 650 seats, respectively.

In the subsequent years, however, the party's support plummeted. Clegg took the party into coalition with the Conservatives between 2010 and 2015, and for many commentators this explains the haemorrhaging of the party's support in the 2015 election, when they won 7.9 per cent of the popular vote and only eight seats in Parliament. The demise of the Liberal Democrats was such that at the start of 2016 they were polling at 6 per cent – at a time when 17 per cent of respondents had indicated their intention to vote for UKIP (Cutts and Russell 2015). This led many to question whether the party could still in fact be considered the third party in British politics. Had the Liberal Democrats still been a significant force in Parliament and across the country during the referendum and in its aftermath, this may well have enabled the anti-Brexit movement to have gained greater elite-level traction. Yet the Liberal Democrats, the most staunchly pro-EU party in the United Kingdom, were relegated to mere bystanders.

While there were leading politicians in both of the main parties that were staunchly pro-Remain, and with a groundswell of parliamentary support for voting in favour of staying in the EU, the dynamic within the two main parties was complex, with Brexiteers forming a substantial part of the parliamentary party (the

Conservatives) or Remainers afforded, at best, only ambivalent support by their leadership (Labour). The referendum result itself further incentivised politicians from both parties to, reluctantly or otherwise, support some form of Brexit. For grassroots activists seeking to stop the United Kingdom leaving the EU, this meant that their elite allies were essentially marginalised. The situation did not genuinely change when, in February 2019, seven centrist and pro-European MPs resigned from the Labour Party, dissatisfied with the party's leftist course under Corbyn (Marsh 2019). Three frustrated Conservative MPs would later join the group to form Change UK – The Independent Group. Anna Soubry (former Conservative) and Chuka Umunna (former Labour) were among its more prominent faces, and they would also engage with the grassroots anti-Brexit movement, as described in the next chapter. However, the new political party failed to muster popular support and did not win any seats in the May 2019 European Parliament elections or in the December 2019 general election (Adams 2020).

CONFIGURATION OF ACTORS: THE ROLE OF PROTAGONISTS AND ANTAGONISTS

The social movement literature posits that the ability of activists to gain access, mobilise support, and ultimately exert political influence is dependent not just on the presence of elite allies, but also on the particular dynamic or relational power between the 'protagonists, antagonists and bystanders' within a political system (Kriesi 2008). As identified in our conceptual framework, the configuration of actors, their proximity to sources of power, and their interaction with social movement organisations is a key determinant of access and efficacy. We identify two crucial actors outside of the political elite who have impacted on the grassroots anti-Brexit movement's mobilisation potential and efficacy: the UK Independence Party (UKIP) and the official Remain campaign that emerged prior to the referendum.

The impact of the UK Independence Party

It has been claimed that 'the rise of UKIP helped to pave the way for the historic Brexit vote' (Clarke et al. 2017, 111). Irrespective of the number of seats the party won or its share of the popular vote, UKIP's appeal and the attention it received had a significant impact on the grassroots anti-Brexit movement's mobilisation potential and efficacy. The party's main impact was in disrupting the configuration of actors, fracturing the fragile political consensus, and giving political voice to full-throated Euroscepticism within the mainstream. The political presence of UKIP altered both the tone and substantive content of the debate about the United Kingdom's membership of the EU. In particular, UKIP's impact on the Conservative Party's position on Europe and on Cameron's decision to hold the Brexit referendum should not be underestimated (Bale 2018).

UKIP's growing popularity from 2009 onwards posed a threat to both main parties. While the party never achieved a parliamentary breakthrough at the national level, largely as a result of the inhospitable Single Member Plurality system applied in UK general elections, its appeal was nevertheless obvious from 'second-order' European Parliament elections, in which it finished first in 2014 and 2019, securing more than a quarter of the vote each time. The Labour Party had initially assumed that UKIP's Euroscepticism would split the right-wing vote and inflict damage on the Tory party by opening up old divisions on Europe (Lynch and Whitaker 2013). However, as Sobolewska and Ford (2020) observe, UKIP's focus on immigration and border control mobilised 'identity conservatives' across the traditional left–right divide. Ultimately, the party was no less successful in appealing to voters in former Labour heartlands as it was in Tory strongholds. Despite attempts made by Ed Miliband, the Labour leader from 2010 to 2015, to discuss immigration and consider re-evaluating the party's position, the Labour government's record on immigration was a source of much discontent among working class voters in northern England (Bale 2014). Insofar as UKIP took votes away from both main parties, it effectively weakened the link between the pro-EU consensus and voters; it connected identity conservatives from diverse backgrounds with a party that was proudly pro-Leave and prepared to openly debate immigration (Ford et al. 2012). In other words, it broke the permissive consensus whereby the two main parties peddled a largely pro-EU membership narrative despite relatively low levels of support for the EU among the electorate.

In many respects, UKIP's electoral fortunes mattered less than the party's impact on the political discourse. In the run-up to the 2015 general election, Ofcom, the UK regulator for communications services, took the decision to award UKIP 'major party' status. This meant that it would receive significantly more broadcast time and media coverage than in previous elections. To a large extent, Ofcom's decision simply formalised what was already the reality: UKIP was now a major player in UK politics. Its primary impact was to frame leaving the EU in terms of controlling immigration and regaining sovereignty – a fusion that stuck and became a significant part of the *leitmotif* of the Brexit campaign (Clarke et al. 2017). This linkage became the key to winning support among voters in working class areas in the north of England as well as among disaffected Tory voters in the South East and elsewhere. The willingness of UKIP and its most prominent politician, Nigel Farage,[2] to openly discuss limiting immigration was hugely significant, with a narrative that resonated among an electorate that had become increasingly concerned about the number of workers from the new member states of Central and Eastern Europe who had settled in Britain after 2004 (Ford and Goodwin 2010). UKIP's framing of the debate in terms of 'giving away our country' combined with a direct call to halt immigration from the EU was the discourse that pro-Remain activists found themselves having to confront on street stalls and that they struggled to contest or challenge in the referendum campaign and beyond.

However, the relationship between media coverage of UKIP, support for the party, and support for Leave is complex. Despite a surge in the party's popularity from 2010 onwards and a growth in new members, UKIP's appeal remained limited to a minority segment of the UK population. Recent scholarly analysis suggests that increased media attention received by the party and its leader delivered a dividend in terms of popular support (Murphy and Devine 2020): Farage was effective at appealing to confirmed Eurosceptics and disaffected voters across all parts of England (Mason et al. 2014). This mattered, given that the referendum pivoted on undecided voters and that the eventual outcome, though decisive, was close. But others were put off by what Douglas Carswell – an MP who defected from the Tories to UKIP before switching back again – referred to as Farage's 'angry nativism' (Evans and Menon 2017, 52). In terms of framing leaving the EU as limiting the number of immigrants, UKIP provided hardline Eurosceptics with a political party that was prepared to amplify that viewpoint; more respectable than other far-right parties such as the British National Party, UKIP galvanised the Leave vote among those who were never likely to support Remain. What is hard to quantify is the extent to which Farage and the UKIP rhetoric alienated undecided voters and encouraged them to vote for Remain.

Most Brexit-supporting Tory politicians steered clear of an overt radical-right framing of the EU. In terms of winning over floating voters and the genuinely undecided, it was the framing of support for Leave in terms of regaining democratic control and the loss of sovereignty – an angle adopted by the likes of Michael Gove, secretary of state for justice in the Cameron government – that probably impacted most (Heuser 2019, 2). The Leave referendum campaign was notably split between the official, more 'respectable', Vote Leave campaign and the Leave.EU campaign of Farage and his friend and funder Arron Banks (Clarke et al. 2017). Endorsing Vote Leave, prominent Tories, including then backbench MP Boris Johnson, did much to frame the Leave narrative and campaign using less explicit anti-immigration messages (Evans and Menon 2017, 53) – including the dubious claim that the National Health Service (NHS) would get an extra £350 million per week after Brexit.

It is certainly the case that UKIP's prevalence in the media and its capacity to capture popular support reconfigured the political opportunity structure in terms of the prevailing discourse. However, as Sobolowska and Ford (2020) illustrate, the growing number of university graduates since the mid-1990s had swollen the ranks of the 'conviction liberals' – those valuing highly individual freedom and social diversity, supportive of migration, and defensive of minorities. It was the young graduates living in cities among ethnic minorities and supportive of EU membership who were in the ascendancy, not the identity conservatives clinging on to an ethnically and culturally homogeneous Britain. It is important, therefore, to place any analysis of UKIP's impact in this broader context.

The Remain referendum campaign: enabling or obstructing local activism?

Thus far, our analysis of the political context in which the anti-Brexit movement operated both before and after the June 2016 referendum has focused on the political parties and their positioning on the issue of EU membership. Our discussion of elite alignments and allies that shaped the emergence and efficacy of the grassroots Remain campaign has emphasised fluctuations and shifting positions within the Conservative and Labour parties between the 1975 referendum and the vote four decades later. The rise of UKIP and, to a lesser extent, the electoral decline of the Liberal Democrats were identified as factors that had an impact on the capacity of pro-Remain activists to galvanise popular support.

For any potential pro-European activists across the United Kingdom, access to elites was, to a large extent, conditioned by the infrastructure of the official Remain campaign that developed prior to the referendum. A full discussion and analysis of the anti-Brexit movement – its mobilising strategies, resources, and internal divisions – is included in the next chapter. Here, we explore the official Remain campaign in terms of how it contributed both to the presence or absence of elite allies and to the discursive opportunity structure in which the grassroots anti-Brexit movement operated after the referendum vote. Indeed, from the perspective of local community-based activists seeking to mobilise in their towns and cities in the months and years after the June 2016 referendum, the link with the remnants of the national Remain campaign proved a source of significant frustration.

Unsurprisingly, perhaps, the United Kingdom has never successfully established a permanent or standing pro-EEC/EU broad-based movement with an institutional infrastructure of grassroots organisations. Nor has there existed an effective pro-European advocacy coalition with influence at the very heart of Westminster, with the only exception being the short-lived Britain in Europe group (1999–2005) launched by Tony Blair and a host of senior politicians from across the political spectrum (Fella 2006). When it has occurred, pro-European activism at the local and national levels has emerged hastily in response to referendums on membership, or in the context of separatist or regional politics (Gifford 2010). Indeed, in the period between 1975 and 2016, a pro-European campaign simply did not exist. The European Movement (EM), which had been established in London in 1949 and had played a role in the 'Yes' campaign in the 1975 referendum, was still formally in existence in the run-up to the 2016 referendum. However, its membership had dwindled in the intervening years, local branches were largely dormant, and its capacity to campaign and mobilise a wide demographic was limited. Moreover, as discussed in the next chapter, the EM functioned more as a social and cultural organisation than as a political advocacy group.

In terms of a popular movement and a national movement, the pro-EEC membership campaign of 1975 was more extensive and reached more deeply into civil society than was the case forty years later. A key difference between the two periods was that in 1975 there was a groundswell of support for the United Kingdom remaining in the EEC among the leading trade unions, the established churches, and the labyrinth of women's organisations that punctuated much of life in Britain (Saunders 2018). Compared with 2016, Britain in the seventies was far more unionised, church attendance was significantly higher, and organisations such as the Women's Institute, the Mothers' Unions, and a host of other guilds and groups held sway over a significant number of Britons.

The origins of the movement and the organisational infrastructure that emerged in the run-up to the referendum in 2016 can be traced back to business- and industry-initiated pressure groups. These included Business for New Europe, founded in 2006 by Labour-supporting PR entrepreneur Roland Rudd, and British Influence, which emerged several years later. Funded by David Sainsbury, a businessman, philanthropist, and Labour peer, and led by the triumvirate of New Labour stalwart Peter Mandelson, the Liberal Democrat Danny Alexander, and Tory grandee Ken Clarke, the intention was to oppose the United Kingdom leaving the EU, a prospect that became ever more likely after David Cameron's 'Bloomberg speech' of January 2013, when he first committed to a referendum on EU membership.

On 13 April 2016, the electoral commission designated Britain Stronger In Europe (which was largely built on the foundations of Business for New Europe) as the official Remain campaign. In many respects this boded well, insofar as it was a genuinely cross-party advocacy coalition including high-profile politicians from the main parties and pledges of support from smaller parties across the United Kingdom, as well as engaging a former general secretary of the Trades Union Congress. The Stronger In campaign was successful in terms of its internal coherence and in framing the discourse of the Remain campaign. Indeed, bringing together a team of senior Remainer politicians from across the party spectrum against a backdrop of divisions within Corbyn's Labour Party and Cameron's Tories was no mean feat. As one senior figure in the campaign observed, 'we were the pluralist, liberal, centrist force in British politics' (Behr 2016). Stronger In established the underpinning narrative of the Remain referendum campaign: economic and social liberalism, a defence of the status quo, fused with rather prosaic references to security and future prosperity. Apart from rather tepid endorsement of Cameron's negotiated reform deal with Brussels, Stronger In did not engage with notions of a reformed EU, nor did it address the issue of border control and immigration.

However, the cross-party nature and the seniority and eminence of the Stronger In leadership were somewhat chimeric. The main parties were represented by a previous generation of political grandees who had fallen foul of the current leadership and were now residing at the fringes of their respective parties. Mandelson was a particularly divisive figure both within the Labour party and among the electorate. Clarke, on the other hand, was popular among the voting public, but he was very much an older-generation Tory and was seen as the standard bearer of the narrow band of pro-EU Tories from the 1990s. These politicians had little leverage within their respective parties. Politically, therefore, Stronger In was a mirage. Cameron and his chancellor and ally, George Osborne, were wary and concerned about the 'metropolitan Europhilia' image and the quality of the campaign's leadership (Behr 2016). Without the full commitment of either Cameron – who had to be cautious not to aggravate divisions in his party – or indeed the Labour leadership, Stronger In was the worst of all worlds: synonymous with the Westminster-based establishment elite but not really anchored within it or inclusive of its key figures. At the same time, the endorsements of various business leaders, academics, and foreign leaders were not necessarily helpful, as these people embodied the London-centric or internationalist pro-EU consensus that the 'Leave' campaign was largely rallying against (Clarke et al. 2017).

For the limited number of pro-European and anti-Brexit activists trying to mobilise in communities, furthermore, Stronger In was remote and somewhat irrelevant. As the national debate became more polarised, the campaign seemed increasingly anchored to a narrow core of pro-Remain elites and to be synonymous with a metropolitan liberal establishment position that ultimately defined the referendum campaign. As discussed in more detail in the next chapter, the aftermath of the referendum saw a host of new or invigorated London-based (umbrella) organisations and initiatives emerge. These included, inter alia, Britain for Europe, the European Movement, Best for Britain, and Open Britain (a relaunch of the Stronger In campaign), plus a host of campaign networks and organisations such as Stand of Defiance European Movement (SODEM), and the youth-led For our Future's Sake (FFS) and Our Future Our Choice (OFOC). The local organisations that mushroomed in the months after the referendum were encouraged to affiliate to one or more of these aspiringly nationwide networks. Although there was a degree of cooperation (sharing know-how, preparing joint protests, etc.), it was not until April 2018 and the launch of the People's Vote campaign that a concerted effort was made to bring together the major anti-Brexit organisations and deliver a degree of coordination and unity. However, from the perspective of grassroots organisations, mobilising in local communities against Brexit, the coalition of elite actors supposedly representing their position at a national level continued to appear divided, introspective, and detached from the concerns of the activists on the ground.

CONCLUSION

The grassroots anti-Brexit movement that emerged in the aftermath of the June 2016 referendum was a reaction to the fact that neither of the two main parties in the United Kingdom unequivocally defended the idea of EU membership. The political opportunity structure was therefore conducive to the initial emergence of the movement but, as argued above, not to its subsequent efficacy. The core argument of this chapter has been that notwithstanding significant mobilisation and a United Kingdom-wide network of local campaign organisations, the relative closure and centralised nature of the political system, the instability of elite alignments, the absence of elite allies, the particular configuration of actors, and the prevailing discourse all worked in conjunction to limit the political efficacy of the anti-Brexit campaign that emerged after the referendum. For any individual or group of British citizens attempting to influence the Brexit debate – whether it be challenging the referendum result or campaigning for a second vote – the political opportunity structure was more inhospitable in and after 2016 than it had been forty years earlier. The pervasive political discourse was Eurosceptic, and the referendum result itself bestowed democratic legitimacy on the decision to leave the EU.

As will be shown in chapter 5, moreover, even among those persuaded by the merits of Britain's continued membership, support for the pre-referendum status quo was expressed mostly in instrumental and somewhat insipid terms. The emergence of UKIP, and the media coverage that the party and its leader received, had amplified the pro-Leave position beyond the actual support base of the party, and had placed pressure on the Conservatives, in particular, to adopt more Eurosceptic and anti-immigration positions. This enabled the fusion of EU membership and questions of sovereignty (not least regarding immigration) to become a mainstream *zeitgeist* – a discourse that framed the public debate in the months prior to, and immediately after, the referendum of June 2016. Indeed, the notion that the United Kingdom needed to leave the EU in order to reclaim lost sovereignty, restore democracy, and control its borders – the *lingua franca* of the Leave movement – became as much the battle cry of the Eurosceptic Tory right as it was of Nigel Farage. Despite Prime Minister Cameron's pro-Remain stance and his attempt to negotiate certain reforms with Brussels, a significant and vocal proportion of the Tory party he led was pro-Leave. Whereas in 1975, despite internal divisions, the Conservative party (in opposition) had been led by a pro-EEC corps of senior front-bench politicians, the pro-Remain Tories in 2016 were outmanoeuvred by the likes of Michael Gove and Boris Johnson.

Had any contender for the leadership of the Labour Party other than Jeremy Corbyn won in 2015, the party may well have been at the heart of the pro-Remain campaign, working across party lines and galvanising support in the country for the United Kingdom to stay in the EU. As it transpired, Corbyn showed a tangible lack of enthusiasm for the EU and was reluctant to be drawn into the referendum campaign. This meant that despite the majority of Labour MPs favouring Remain, the party was divided and embroiled in infighting on an issue that may otherwise have united it. With the Liberal Democrats bereft of electoral support and parliamentary seats, there was effectively no strident and unequivocally pro-Remain party with whom activists could connect or align if they so wished. The pro-European cross-party breakaway group Change UK proved too weak to make a difference in this regard. Time and again, activists interviewed for this research articulated their frustration with the ambiguity of Labour's position, their sense that the party was not fully behind the Remain movement, and their irritation with the reluctance of Corbyn to publicly commit to a second referendum.

While the changed stance of the main parties on Europe between 1975 and 2016 and the rise of UKIP meant greater instability of elite alignments, there had also taken place in this forty-year period a fundamental weakening of the link between voters and political parties (Sobolewska and Ford 2020, 121–53). Referred to as 'partisan dealignment' (Crewe 1983), both Labour and the Conservatives had, in a post-industrial economy, become increasingly 'catch-all', competing for the growing number of white-collar, university-educated middle-class voters. However, there had also occurred a decline of deference to elites and an erosion of trust in politicians and political parties (Pattie and Johnston 2001). In terms of anti-Brexit activism this mattered because it meant greater instability of elite alignments and the weakened functioning of parties to link citizens with power and elites.

While the connection between anti-Brexit activists and the mainstream political parties was weaker in 2016 than it had been in 1975, the pro-Remain referendum campaign was also less effective and rooted in civil society than it had been forty years earlier. Stronger In, the official pro-Remain campaign, remained centralised, and it hardly nurtured the development of a grassroots movement with local anti-Brexit activists. As the next chapter shows, the emergence of the anti-Brexit movement after the referendum was largely driven by local initiatives that initially had little help from any national campaign organisation.

4

Mapping Anti-Brexit Activism in the United Kingdom

Grievances and political opportunities alone are not sufficient to explain the emergence and fate of a social movement: the agency of social movement actors themselves must also be considered. This includes their ability to create sufficiently enduring organisational structures to sustain collective action. Approaches derived from resource mobilisation theory have tended to emphasise the role of social movement organisations (SMOs) that consciously mobilise on the basis of available resources (see, for example, Oberschall 1973; McCarthy and Zald 1977), and scholars in the tradition of the political process model (Tilly 1978) have placed emphasis on informal, grassroots structures. Synthesising the various studies that emerged in this area, McAdam, McCarthy, and Zald (1996, 3) use the term 'mobilizing structures' to refer to 'those collective vehicles, informal as well as formal, through which people mobilize and engage in collective action'.

In this chapter, the mobilising structures of the anti-Brexit movement are central. We consider how various anti-Brexit organisations were created, and we look at their efforts and ability to sustain collective action. Referring to Rucht's (1996) different dimensions of the 'context structure' in which social movements operate, the previous chapter demonstrated how the *political* context influenced the anti-Brexit movement's mobilising capacities. This chapter will consider in more detail the evolution of the movement, including the variety of anti-Brexit organisations and their underlying social milieus and networks (which are part of the movement's *social* context). The discussion will then consider the characteristics and attitudes of activists (which are part of the movement's *cultural* context), their repertoires, and their motivations to action (Klandermans 2015). We consider the extent to which the movement has tried and been able to attract a diverse core of activists, and we assess whether their values and actions were likely to resonate beyond a narrow ideological constituency. In addition to information from organisations' websites and from media coverage, our arguments and observations in this chapter rely mostly on original survey and interview data. Several representatives we interviewed from central UK-wide organisations are mentioned by name. We generally chose to anonymise interviewees from local groups to prevent an excess of names throughout the chapter. This is not at all to suggest that local activists were any less important in the mobilisation of the anti-Brexit movement.

After a brief reflection on the concept of mobilising structures and its operationalisation, the chapter provides an overview of the anti-Brexit movement's evolution into SMOs and other actors, including their interaction and development across time. It subsequently moves to the individual level and discusses local activists' demographic characteristics, their motivations to action, and the various types of organised action and repertoires. We note the movement's remarkable achievement in organising large demonstrations that attracted considerable attention, but we also highlight its limitations: the local organisations were typically built from scratch and lacked a pre-existing infrastructure of activists and resources. Their rather traditional repertoires of action were geared more at mobilising support than at swaying opinion. The movement was also hampered by fragmentation and disagreements about the key objective – an issue that will be further discussed in the next chapter. The emergence of the national People's Vote (PV) campaign focused minds, but it also fuelled a considerable degree of factionalism that ultimately weakened the efficacy of the broader movement. The collapse of PV due to strategic and personal conflicts in the central organisation was a final blow to the movement in the run-up to the December 2019 general election – the outcome of which erased any hopes of averting Brexit.

MAPPING MOBILISATION STRUCTURES

Following Rucht (1996, 186), mobilisation structures serve 'to collect and use the movement's resources' and are explicitly 'designed for mobilisation' (as opposed to mere information dissemination

Table 4.1 Typology of mobilising agents.

	SMOs	Interest groups	Political parties
Mode of operation	Protest actions	Representation of members in polities	Occupation of political offices
Main resources	Committed adherents	Expertise, money, access to decision-makers	Voters
Structural features	Networks of groups and organisations	Formal organisation	Formal organisation

Source: adapted from Rucht (1996, 187).

or identity formation). 'Mobilisation', in turn, can be understood as 'the process of creating movement structures and preparing and carrying out *protest actions* which are visible movement "products" addressed to actors and publics outside the movement' (Rucht 1996, 186; original emphasis). In analysing mobilising structures, it is key to consider the movement's various composite organisational forms, yet also the more general 'agreed upon ways of engaging in collective action', which include its activities, tactics, and repertoires (McCarthy 1996, 141).

It is important to keep in mind that social movements are not organisations as such (della Porta and Diani 2020, 25–7); instead, they consist of networks of groups and organisations characterised by various degrees of formalisation and different modes of operation. The structures of social movements are usually fluid, with organisational forms being quite amorphous; some organisations will require formal membership, others rely instead on casual supporters and a reserve of activists (see table 4.1). As this chapter will demonstrate, key 'mobilising agents' of the anti-Brexit movement were grassroots SMOs, as well as a number of specialised interest groups with a more formal organisational structure. Protest actions, albeit not particularly disruptive ones, were central to the movement's activities.

Social movements do not consist of only more-or-less formal organisations, however, but also of 'individuals who attend protest activities or contribute resources without necessarily being attached to movement groups or organizations' (Rucht 1996, 186). It is therefore also important to consider the identity and motivations of activists (Giugni and Grasso 2019), and how they aim to reach out to 'bystanders' and turn them into 'adherents' or even resource-providing 'constituents' of the movement (McCarthy and Zald 1977, 1,221). The means to achieve this can include messages and claims – key to the process of 'framing', as will be discussed in the next chapter – but also 'repertoires of contention', a term coined by Charles Tilly (1978). Repertoires are understood here as 'specific routines of claim making that are selected and acted out by people in their pursuit of shared interests and change during contentious interactions with others' (Alimi 2015, 1). In applying this concept, we consider the activities of social movement activists, but also the way these were *performed* in order to attract attention and convince the wider public. While more traditional forms of protest activities, such as street stalls, leafletting, and marches, were key to anti-Brexit actions, we also consider the movement's 'electronic repertoires of contention' (Rolfe 2005). In the second decade of the twenty-first century, online or 'digital' activism was naturally also part of the campaign (Usherwood and Wright 2017; Brändle et al. 2022).

This study is specifically interested in the movement's contribution to the politicisation of 'Europe' within the UK context. Our main focus is therefore on the movement's efforts to convince the wider public – *consensus mobilisation*, in the words of Klandermans (1988) – and less on the process of transforming sympathisers into activists (*action mobilisation*). While an ability to recruit activists is important for successful consensus mobilisation, the primary aim of our analysis is to make judgements about the movement's efficacy in attracting attention, generating mass support, and, ultimately, influencing decision makers.

THE EVOLUTION OF THE ANTI-BREXIT MOVEMENT

From the announcement of the referendum to the point at which the United Kingdom formally left the EU in January 2020, the country's anti-Brexit movement was continuously evolving into a complex network of various affiliated groups. Typical for a social movement, interactions within the anti-Brexit campaign have been marked by a considerable degree of contingency and fluidity (Diani and Mische 2015). Informal interpersonal and localised exchanges developed into more institutionalised forms of social organisation at the national level. Alliances were formed between the different organisations that emerged and defined themselves as part of the movement. Eventually, networks grew into more formal 'social movement coalitions' when distinct groups decided to cooperate more closely (Zald and Ash 1966; McCammon and Moon 2015), with the People's Vote initiative being the most notable result of this process. Yet not all activists were satisfied with the asymmetrical exchanges that materialised between the central PV organisation and local grassroots branches. Infighting within the central PV organisation ultimately resulted in its implosion in November 2019, just before the crucial parliamentary election one month later. In what follows, we discuss the evolution of the movement in more detail, revealing the experiences of campaigners at the national and grassroots levels.

The referendum campaign and its aftermath: limited grassroots mobilisation

When the referendum was announced, the only overtly pro-European organisation in the United Kingdom with a long history was the European Movement (EM). With origins dating back to 1947, the EM is a pan-European network of pro-European organisations supporting the aim of an 'ever closer union'. Its UK chapter played an active role in the 1975 referendum (see the previous chapter). At the time the 2016 referendum was announced, however, its local branches were largely dormant, and the organisation's capacity to campaign and mobilise a wide demographic was limited. Several of our interviewees described the EM as a rather inward-looking and inactive organisation, with an ageing and predominantly higher-educated membership. As long-standing EM member Nick Hopkinson explained in early 2019:

> When the referendum campaign started, we were actually quite weak. Most of our members were veterans of the 1975 campaign who really hadn't moved on or those with professional or personal interests in the EU. We only had about fifteen national branches nationwide. We almost were starting from scratch. We had a membership list; we had about, I think, only 700 members. Now, today, we are about ten times that.
> Interview 1: European Movement/London4Europe
> (4 February 2019)

Several other pro-European organisations in the United Kingdom also existed in the years prior to the referendum but they took the form of interest groups rather than grassroots SMOs. Business for New Europe was a pressure group set up in 2006 by PR businessperson and political activist Roland Rudd. Seeking to make the case for continued British EU membership in a similar way was British Influence, a London-based pro-single market think tank founded in early 2013. Scientists for EU was founded after the referendum was announced. This sectoral interest group, which initially started out as Scientists for Labour, rebranded itself in May 2015 and shifted its attention to campaigning for continued EU membership. As described in the previous chapter, *the* key organisation that emerged after the announcement of the referendum was Britain Stronger in Europe (or Stronger In). It was launched in October 2015 and built primarily on the foundations of Business for New Europe. Another Europe is Possible was founded in February 2016 as a left-wing alternative to the cross-party yet mainly centrist/liberal Stronger In. Another Europe is Possible was partly rooted in the Jeremy Corbyn-supporting Momentum movement, but it also drew on members of the Green Party.

Stronger In was designated the official 'Remain' campaign by the Electoral Commission in April 2016. Its pragmatic yet hardly inspiring key message that the United Kingdom was better off under the status quo, not least in economic terms, came to dominate the Remain camp's discourse (Clarke et al. 2017). The campaign was supported by pro-Remain politicians from most political parties, including the newly established Labour In for Britain and Conservatives In groups. A plethora of other sectoral interest campaigns, such as Lawyers In for Britain, and advocacy groups, such as Environmentalists for Europe, also rallied behind Stronger In. In terms of its public messaging, the campaign also relied on the more ad hoc engagement of various celebrity Remain supporters as well as business leaders, academics, and civil service reports outlining the predicted economic harm of leaving the EU.

At the grassroots level, various local groups were active under the Stronger In banner, yet their number and scope were insignificant in comparison with the movement that would emerge after the referendum. In some parts of the country – typically more urban and affluent areas – a core of local activists got involved in the referendum campaign. Yet especially in heavily Leave-supporting parts of the country pre-existing resources and networks were lacking. In the words of an activist in one of these regions:

> Certainly in an area like this, in deepest rural Lincolnshire, there really was nothing happening. There were no local groups active. It really was a matter of starting things absolutely from scratch.
> Interview 13: Lincolnshire for Europe (15 April 2019)

Yet even in most parts of the United Kingdom where support for EU membership has traditionally been high, grassroots mobilisation during the referendum campaign was virtually non-existent. This activist, for instance, blamed the inactivity in Scotland on both complacency and local political idiosyncrasies that dampened the salience of 'Europe':

> I think it was almost taken for granted in Scotland. Scotland feels European, I think that's reflected in the vote by and large; I think it still feels a European country … So I think that's very, very deep within the national psyche. But I think the other thing is, you know, [Scottish] independence even now is still perceived as the central issue. And actually trying to communicate to people that the most pressing issue currently isn't independence … [but] that the biggest issue overwhelmingly is Brexit is still a battle. And we struggle quite hard to untangle these two issues.
> Interview 23: Stirling for Europe (25 October 2019)

In our interviews, several activists who were involved in the referendum campaign criticised the national Stronger In organisation for being centralised and London-centric, and for lacking engagement with local campaigners. An erstwhile representative from Wales recalls:

> I have to say, that was one of the more painful experiences of my life, because it was a fantastically centralised campaign. I mean, I used to go to meetings of Stronger In

in London every few weeks and basically Craig Oliver [the prime minister's director of communications] would turn up from Number 10 and just tell us, you know, what was going to happen. There was no real discussion about it.

Interview 16: Wales for Europe (25 July 2019)

Evidently, the Stronger In campaign was ultimately unsuccessful in securing a Remain vote. Scientists for EU's co-founder Mike Galsworthy described the frustration among local activists after the referendum as follows:

> There was anger on the Remain side because they felt the campaign had been badly run, they felt that it was arrogant, they felt that it was top-down, didn't make the right arguments ... And so all over the country local groups decided to sort of take it into their own hands, to sort of campaign against what just happened.
>
> Interview 28: Scientists for EU/March for Change (22 June 2020)

The mobilisation of local anti-Brexit protests thus mainly occurred in response to the referendum result. A notable example of such grassroots activity was The 48% (the name refers to the percentage of 'Remain' voters in the referendum), which constituted a more-or-less immediate online reaction to the referendum outcome. Across the country various local 48% Facebook groups sprung up in the referendum's aftermath, providing a means for pro-European citizens to form a network that gradually expanded. Such online networks would prove key to the development of the local campaign groups that later engaged in more traditional street campaigning.

Frustration with the central pro-Remain campaign did not wane when, in August 2016, Stronger In continued as Open Britain. The organisation was widely seen by local activists as too accepting of the referendum outcome given that its primary aim was to retain access to the single market instead of full EU membership (Lynskey 2018). At the same time, there was a recognition among activists that the failure of the Remain campaign had to be placed in a wider historical and structural context. London-based activist Nick Hopkinson emphasised the more general lack of pro-European infrastructure and preparedness for the referendum campaign:

> In spite of the many valid reasons for criticisms about the campaign, it achieved a lot in a short time ... There was no way the pro-European movement was prepared. You know, the Brexiteers had been gearing up for this since 1975, whereas we just sat on our laurels, or just were fairly complacent. A lot of the European Movement groupings were effectively 'wine and cheese clubs' rather than political activist groups.
> Interview 1: European Movement/London4Europe
> (4 February 2019).

The notion of the EM being a solidarity club or a social network rather than a cohesive political actor was an issue raised in several interviews. For example, this member of the Northern Ireland branch acknowledged the lack of activism characterising the organisation in the run-up to the referendum:

> Perhaps that helps explain why we got into the mess that we did. There wasn't a proper narrative here about what the European Union did ... There was a vacuum then filled unfortunately, which is easily filled by *The Sun* and the bendy banana story and things like that, which feeds into people's sort of consciousness.
> Interview 6: European Movement Northern Ireland
> (28 February 2019)

Prior to the referendum, then, there were no pro-European organisations that attracted an audience beyond a small group of ardent EU enthusiasts; the EM was the only long-standing organisational structure, but it was largely dormant. In the years that followed, however, an anti-Brexit movement emerged that was largely grassroots driven (see figure 4.1). One notable turning point was August 2016, when Britain for Europe (BfE) was established as a more grassroots-based and more explicitly anti-Brexit response to Open Britain. Both the EM and BfE would see their networks of local organisations grow gradually and significantly in the subsequent months.

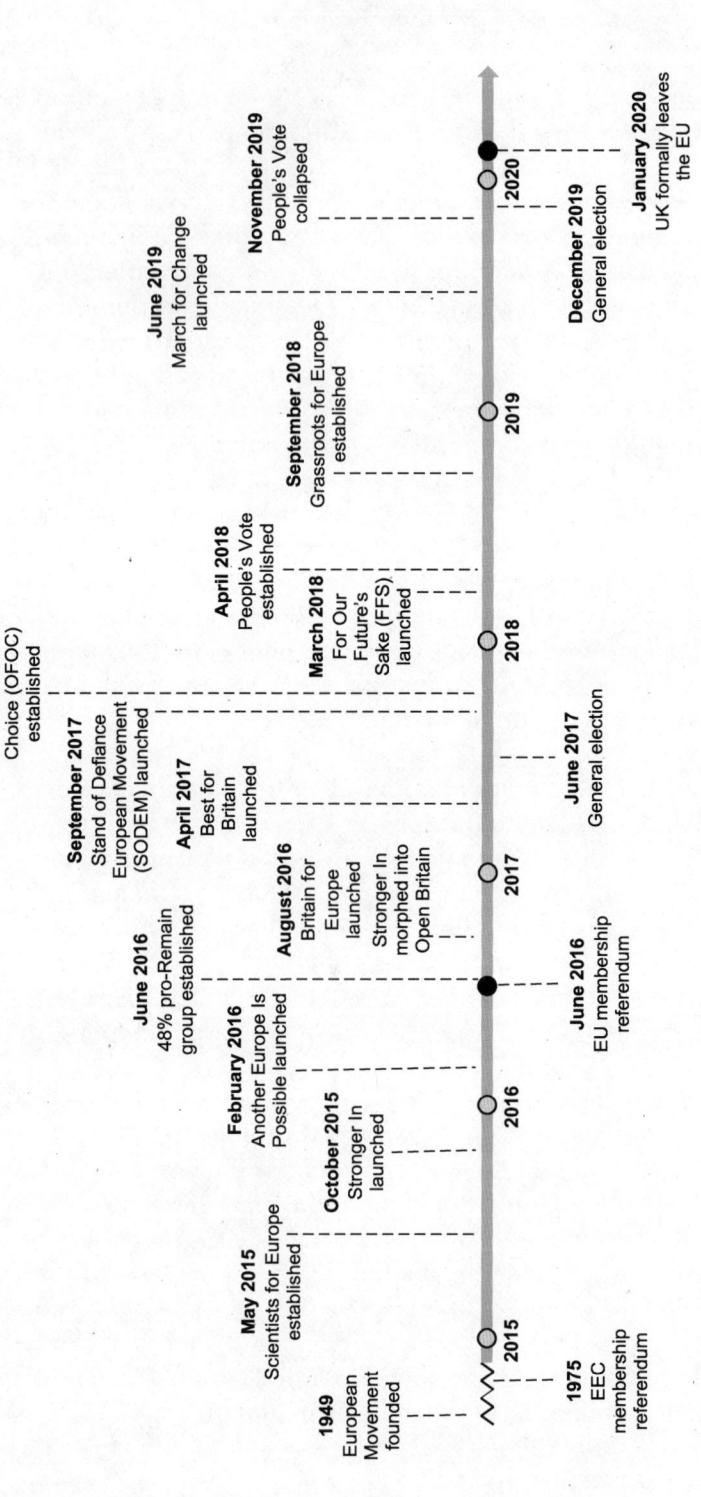

Figure 4.1 Timeline of anti-Brexit mobilisation in the United Kingdom.

The emergence of an anti-Brexit social movement

Throughout the remainder of 2016 and much of 2017 the post-referendum movement lacked a dominant overarching national organisation: a raft of anti-Brexit initiatives emerged that did not unite behind a common objective or message. The experience of this Lincolnshire activist is typical across our interviews:

> I think that an awful lot of the people who ended up being campaigners, like myself, had not been involved in campaigning before the referendum. We weren't members of the European Movement or any of the other groups. It was the result of the referendum that pushed us into doing something. So it took a while for that to coalesce into any kind of organisation. And even when it did, it was spread across any number of small local groups and several sort of national or international organisations. So coordinating that into an organised movement, yeah, did take some considerable time.
> Interview 25: Lincolnshire for Europe (28 May 2020)

Despite the lack of a coordinated campaign, local grassroots groups continued to emerge, and many of them associated themselves with the nationwide BfE network, the EM, or indeed both. Pioneering local organisations – typically in more cosmopolitan and left-leaning cities – such as Bath for Europe and Bristol for Europe were created in the first months after the referendum. Groups in parts of the United Kingdom with weaker public support for EU membership, such as more rural areas in the Midlands and Yorkshire, were less numerous and typically took longer to form. The steady growth of the movement coincided with the organisation of numerous local marches; this form of action became a major feature of the anti-Brexit campaign. Gradually, the EM shed its 'wine and cheese club' character, developing into an organisation facilitating local activism and collaborating with the more recently established BfE and other anti-Brexit initiatives. In the words of one Leeds activist:

> The movement, the way it's developed since 2017, has created a huge number of groups like ours, and a lot

of those groups have looked to national organisations
to become connected with. And European Movement
have welcomed that, actually. They've welcomed that
and they've adapted and changed in response to that. So
they're a very different type of organisation now from what
they were in 2015.
Interview 27: Leeds for Europe/Grassroots for Europe
(5 June 2020)

In terms of formal organisation, BfE and the EM also became increasingly intertwined. The London4Europe umbrella organisation, for example, was effectively a rebranded version of the previously dormant London EM branch. Gradually, the leadership and personnel on the boards of the central BfE and EM organisations were largely integrated, to the extent that the distinction between the two organisations became somewhat opaque in practice. On the ground, furthermore, it was typical for local activists with different organisational affiliations to cooperate closely with one another. Formal organisational allegiances were often not very relevant in combined efforts to protest Brexit, particularly in the context of organising and participating in demonstrations and other anti-Brexit actions. In our survey it was very common for respondents to list several organisations to which they were affiliated.[1] Nonetheless, divisions and tensions remained in specific areas, for instance between more activist-oriented local BfE groups and ostensibly more elite-focused EM branches. One Liverpool for Europe activist articulated the situation thus:

There was certainly a cultural difference opening up
between European Movement Merseyside and Liverpool
for Europe. And it's to do with: 'are we going to run
workshops where essentially we are preaching to the
converted, sitting in a room with twenty people talking
about trade policy, or are we going to be out on the street
talking to citizens of Liverpool and engaging with MPs, and
also putting on events?'
Interview 4: Liverpool for Europe (26 February 2019)

Ideological divisions, not least between supporters and opponents of the Labour leader Jeremy Corbyn, also sometimes hampered effective coordination of activities and distribution of resources. At the same time, however, many activists spoke positively about the camaraderie and mutual support that existed within groups. Links with groups in other parts of the country, typically facilitated through Facebook, also promoted the sharing of ideas, resources, and knowledge. There were notable differences between local groups in terms of both the number of activists and their levels of experience, not least regarding the use of social media. BfE branches in urban strongholds such as Bristol, Bath, and Manchester, which benefited from greater numbers of activists as well as IT know-how, shared expertise with more recently formed local groups. Information was most effectively exchanged horizontally between local branches rather than vertically between national umbrella organisations and local groups. As one Lincolnshire activist explains:

> It was largely a grassroots sort of campaign, and the small local groups really had very little contact with any kind of central organisation. And what central organisation there was tended to be pretty opaque. So knowing what was being done at the top of the tree was pretty much impossible for people at the bottom.
> Interview 25: Lincolnshire for Europe (28 May 2020)

Previously existing organisations (including Another Europe is Possible and Scientists for EU) continued to operate alongside the local groups, whereas Open Britain's engagement with grassroots activism was limited. While it was Open Britain that had inherited the large email database of supporters from the Stronger In campaign, the organisation centred its activities more on lobbying politicians and the media. Meanwhile, a variety of other initiatives sprung up, and there also emerged a few media outlets publishing explicit anti-Brexit content. *The New European* (TNE) appeared as a weekly pro-European print newspaper and online platform. According to its website, TNE 'was launched days after the June 2016 EU referendum result in an attempt to rebalance the right-wing extremes of much of the UK national press' (TNE 2021). Journalist and entrepreneur Hugo Dixon set up the website InFacts as soon as the referendum was announced, with the aim of publishing fact-checking articles holding both sides to account. After the referendum, the website developed into a more unambiguously anti-Brexit platform.

One prominent new pressure group was Best for Britain, which was created in April 2017. Acting as an organisation seeking to enable various anti-Brexit activities and campaigns, its planned launch fell in the period in which Theresa May announced the June 2017 snap general election (Lynskey 2018). Consequently, the organisation's priority shifted to encouraging tactical voting for pro-Remain candidates. The organisation was briefly co-fronted by entrepreneur Gina Miller, who was already a notable figure in the anti-Brexit campaign due to her previous legal challenge against the British government for its intention to invoke Article 50 by means of prerogative powers. After the 2017 election, Best for Britain continued with a range of activities, including media campaigns, fund raising, public opinion polling, the lobbying of politicians, and supporting other anti-Brexit initiatives through funding and training activities.

Several months after the June 2017 vote, which left the United Kingdom with a 'hung parliament' and eventually a Conservative minority government supported by the Northern Irish Democratic Unionist Party, two additional organisations with a clearer grassroots SMO profile were founded. The first, Stand of Defiance European Movement (SODEM), was started by Steven Bray in September 2017. Bray's straightforward protest action was captured by the 'Bollocks to Brexit' slogan, and his demonstrations in front of the Houses of Parliament in Westminster attracted considerable attention and a nationwide following. One month later, Our Future Our Choice (OFOC) was created. Supported by Best for Britain, it was an initiative of young people, aiming its anti-Brexit messages and activities at this specific age cohort. One key OFOC activist explained the group's lack of affinity with existing pro-European political actors:

> There wasn't anything new. I saw London4Europe and Britain for Europe, and the Lib Dems as well, as people who hadn't really accepted and processed the result of 2016 ... There was no sense of energy; I didn't see any young people speaking about the EU or about Brexit. There was nothing for someone like me to get involved with.
> Interview 12: Our Future Our Choice (26 March 2019)

In March 2018, a student-led initiative with yet another mischievous acronym emerged: For our Future's Sake (FFS). It was founded by members of the National Union of Students (NUS), and it called for another referendum on the negotiated Brexit deal.

The above description of anti-Brexit organisations is hardly exhaustive: the movement included a wide variety of further initiatives (Led by Donkeys, EU Flag Mafia, Veterans for Europe, and so on) and personalities, such as performing artist Madeleina Kay (aka EU Super Girl).[2] As one London4Europe member recalls from the first meeting they attended:

> One of the points that was made at that meeting was how fragmented the whole pro-European movement was, and is. And I think something like roundabout 200 different organisations were quoted, and some of them named, that were active. Now I think ... there's a certain amount of coalescence that is taking place in the intervening two-and-a-half years. So we are now sort of seeing some meaningful groups, but they still haven't entirely coalesced into one.
> Interview 11: London/Watford for Europe (12 March 2019)

The various initiatives formulated their own specific aims, used a variety of action repertoires, and reached out to different audiences. As is typical for social movements, the anti-Brexit movement was also characterised by overlapping affiliations and cooperation, not least in terms of organising rallies and marches. As will be discussed in more detail in the next chapter, different organisations, despite sharing a distaste for Brexit in a general sense, were also notably divided on the question of what the eventual outcome should be. After the referendum, for instance, Another Europe is Possible essentially settled for a 'soft Brexit', aiming to save the 'progressive aspects' of EU membership such as freedom of movement and citizenship rights. Other organisations primarily emphasised the need for a second referendum – a cause that Another Europe is Possible did eventually rally behind later. SODEM and many grassroots BfE-allied activists were, for their part, more attracted to the idea of revoking Article 50 and stopping Brexit altogether. It was not until the launch of the People's Vote (PV) campaign that a concerted effort was made to bring together major pro-European organisations and to unite them behind a single goal.

The People's Vote campaign

The disjointed nature of the anti-Brexit campaign was widely considered to have harmed its chances of success. Former Liberal Democrat leader Nick Clegg, for instance, lamented that 'it is frankly a gift to the Brexiters the way so much anti-Brexit energy is being dissipated in so many disorganised ways' (cited in Lynskey (2018)). In late 2017 and early 2018, various figures voiced their ambition to bring together the variety of anti-Brexit organisations and pursue a clearer strategy. These included Mark Malloch-Brown, the then chair of Best for Britain and a former diplomat and cabinet minister (Wintour 2017), and Chukka Umunna, who was then a Labour MP, who collaborated in Parliament with fellow anti-Brexit MPs from various parties: notably, Anna Soubry (then Conservatives), Caroline Lucas (Greens), and Jo Swinson (Liberal Democrats) (Mason 2018). Ultimately, however, it was Open Britain that became the key organisation coordinating collaboration between various initiatives, joining forces with five other groups in March 2018: the central EM and BfE organisations, Scientists for EU, Healthier IN the EU, and InFacts (EM 2018). Crucially, the groups started to share office space in London's Millbank Tower. Close to the Houses of Parliament, this site would become the new de facto national headquarters of the movement. The move further intensified the organisational and operational integration of EM and BfE. Other organisations, including OFOC and FFS, would later also move into Millbank Tower.

On the basis of this collaboration, the PV campaign was launched in April 2018, serving both as an umbrella organisation and as a common platform for various anti-Brexit initiatives. With PV's inception, the focus of the anti-Brexit campaign would markedly shift towards the aim of forcing a People's Vote on the outcome of the government's Brexit negotiations – the term 'second referendum', which might have suggested the desire to overturn a democratic decision, was avoided for strategic reasons.

Among the notable organisations that did not formally join or endorse the PV campaign were the Labour Party – which continued to be marked by internal divisions on Brexit – Best for Britain, and Another Europe is Possible. Best for Britain continued its activities independently on the basis of a more explicit pro-EU message, even though it supported the idea of a new referendum as a democratic means to stop Brexit from happening. This was also true for Another Europe is Possible, which was, however, reluctant to collaborate with individuals from the 'Labour Right', in the words of its national organiser (Interview 29: Another Europe is Possible, 25 February 2021). The people in question here included former figures from the New Labour governments, such as Peter Mandelson and former director of communications Alistair Campbell, who played influential roles in Open Britain. The urge to retain autonomy as a more broadly oriented organisation was also relevant:

> In terms of our personnel, and our background and our kind of instincts, we were the activist left doing Remain campaigning, rather than being the Remain campaign that was left-wing.
> Interview 29: Another Europe is Possible
> (25 February 2021)

Meanwhile, the more direct action-oriented SODEM was shunned by the central PV organisers, as its message (to revoke the decision to leave) was at odds with the new aim of campaigning for a new referendum. SODEM's Steve Bray, for his part, lamented the internal politics of the PV campaign:

> We all want that one aim. Let's all just agree on the one thing and get that, without all the pettiness in between. That's what is fracturing Remain. People's Vote ... They don't invite me. I'm not given a voice to speak. Because they don't like my 'Stop Brexit' message.
> Interview 17: SODEM (25 July 2019)

While the PV initiative was thus met with considerable scepticism in certain parts of the movement, many local activists at the time of its launch subscribed to the idea that more national coordination and a clearer message were required. One Bristol for Europe activist argued:

> The reason why the People's Vote happened was because everyone accepted that it didn't work having lots of different ideas, people pushing for different things. One thing that everyone could agree on – which was a bit of a compromise, it's not ideal – was to have a People's Vote.

> You don't even have to agree what's on the ballot paper yet, we were just all agreeing that we want a People's Vote ... It was a good development for the time.
> Interview 15: Bristol for Europe (6 June 2019)

Through their affiliation with BfE and the EM, many local organisations were thus brought under the umbrella of the PV campaign. Activists typically saw the added value of PV in terms of financial support, campaign resources, and (media) training activities. They also commented positively on its ability to attract celebrity endorsement and send out a positive message: *for* a People's Vote, instead of *against* Brexit. In the words of two of these activists:

> There's a national organiser who will get us equipment if we need something. So, for example, we wanted a whiteboard to use and we were able to ask for that, and get that. If we needed more leaflets or anything we can ask for that. So yeah, it's pretty well-organised.
> Interview 24: Falkirk for Europe (25 November 2019)

> There is no question that most groups certainly saw the imperative of ... getting a People's Vote, and they saw that the People's Vote campaign was being quite effective in some regards, particularly at the top level. In national media and in dealing with politicians and lobbying MPs and all that kind of thing. So there was certainly a strong support for that function of the People's Vote campaign.
> Interview 27: Leeds for Europe/Grassroots for Europe (5 June 2020)

Tom Brufatto, previously BfE's chair and later a leading figure in PV's campaigns and local branch development, similarly saw the value of the organisation's ability to pull resources and appeal to an audience beyond ardent pro-European Remainers:

> It went really well whilst the People's Vote campaign was growing demonstrably at a very fast pace. And we benefited hugely from the bringing together of the organisations, political connections, media operations, grassroots operations, polling, messaging, for quite a lot of time.
> Interview 30: BfE/EM/PV/March for Change (18 June 2021)

As will be discussed in more detail in the next chapter, many activists privately desired more than simply a second referendum; namely, they wanted to stop Brexit altogether. Yet many could live with the PV's key messages and strategy even if they were defensive of their autonomy and reluctant to follow directives from above very strictly. In the words of one Sunderland activist:

> Inasmuch as they don't tell us what to do, because we agree with probably 95 per cent of what they say, but there's, like, probably 5 per cent where we'd like to keep our autonomy. Like, they don't like the 'Bollocks to Brexit' stickers whereas we find it really works up here, so we like to keep our own autonomy.
> Interview 9: North East/Angels for Europe (7 March 2019)

Still, for other activists the PV campaign ultimately failed to deliver enough in terms of resources and support. They also criticised the central organisation for being London-centric, aloof, and politicised. Indeed, several interviewees voiced considerable scepticism and distrust:

> There has been a gulf opening up between the centre and people like ourselves ... I think various groups working with People's Vote on the marches were having a really hard time coping with the dysfunctionality of this kind of corporate [organisation] and being left to do it all at the last minute, having march routes imposed on us, you know, all these sorts of things.
> Interview 4: Liverpool for Europe (26 February 2019)

> One of the things that has been frustrating me is all these different groups [within PV]. I've read a horrible article about, you know, the warring between these factions ... I mean, I'm really not keen to get too embroiled under any of them, because I think they all want to use us for their own ends ... Because I think what they want is, they want to say 'well, we can mobilise all these groups and therefore we should get the money for the Remain campaign'. And I find that really cynical and I hate it.
> Interview 22: anonymous (22 October 2019)

Such grievances triggered the establishment of the Grassroots for Europe network in September 2018, which sought to support the needs of local anti-Brexit organisations. Richard Wilson, one of the network's initiators, explained the shortcoming of the PV campaign as follows:

> A lot of groups, tens of thousands of people, some of those people extremely skilled and experienced professionally. All of those people are very passionate and got a lot of time to give to the campaign. So I think it is pretty important that we use those tens of thousands of people to the best potential. And People's Vote were not very good at that. They really operated in a different way. They were in an office in Westminster and they thought that they could do everything or control everything. And they didn't really understand the capabilities and resource that they had at their disposal in the grassroots. Historically, Britain for Europe would have served that purpose, but because they'd gone in with the People's Vote they'd lost that capability.
> Interview 27: Leeds for Europe/Grassroots for Europe
> (5 June 2020)

Best for Britain's CEO Naomi Smith voiced very similar frustration with the way the PV campaign was run from the centre:

> It was top-down when it needed to be bottom-up. And the groups around the country wanted leadership, they wanted guidance. This incredible movement had been built from nothing; in June 2016 none of these groups existed around the country apart from a handful of European Movement ones that really were 'wine and cheese parties' ... You suddenly had these activists, all these people that came from nowhere, that were prepared to go out in the rain and stand on a street stall and at a farmer's market on a Saturday morning handing out leaflets or, you know, door-knocking and things like this. What happened was that you suddenly started having this very authoritarian grip from the People's Vote campaign over this unwieldy enormous movement around the country. And while these

groups were looking to central national campaign for some guidance, they didn't want to be dictated to. They wanted to be listened to and they wanted to have that 'feedback loop' where they could give messages up from what they'd heard in their local community, what they thought was working, what wouldn't work. [But] rather like the 2016 campaign, doors [of the central PV organisation] were closed: 'What do you know, you're just a lay person that wears an EU beret and waves flags. We're the serious campaigners, we're the political communicators, we're the hot shot former journalists. We know what we're doing, and you need to do this.' And leaflets would be sent to these groups, and they'd be told to put them out, and they were completely tone deaf to the local situation, the local area etcetera.

Interview 31: Best for Britain (29 June 2021)

Within the central PV campaign tensions also existed between the more activist-oriented organisations (notably EM and BfE) and Open Britain, which controlled PV's finances and focused mainly on the campaign's PR and media activities. These tensions surfaced for instance during the organisation of large marches in central London. As expressed by Galsworthy:

There was this tension between the activist-organising half of the People's Vote campaign and the media half of the People's Vote campaign, which was Open Britain. And so that's why there was that awkward balance and there were disagreements about the marches and about who would get on stage ... There were some real political games about who they were trying to bring into the fold, which we felt was very much a political hijack.

Interview 28: Scientists for EU/March for Change (22 June 2020)

Towards the summer of 2019, furthermore, progress had stalled, in terms of both trends in public opinion and the battle in the parliamentary arena. The replacement of Prime Minister Theresa May by Boris Johnson in July, furthermore, was seen to undermine the chances of securing a new referendum. According to PV's Brufatto:

> And that started causing frustration at every level, but particularly with the local groups ... With the growing animosity and the advent of the removal of Theresa May and the likely imposition of Boris Johnson, that changed everything. We knew that the prospects for negotiation were far reduced at that point, and that the shift in the power base of the Conservative Party meant that, ultimately, the battle lines had shifted ... And we knew that that meant there was going to be a general election. And if a general election was to be held, I think it is very fair to say that we knew that it was very unlikely ... we would be able to prevail. If there was a referendum, we would, and if there was a general election, we wouldn't.
>
> Interview 30: BfE/EM/PV/March for Change
> (18 June 2021)

Given these circumstances, Brufatto and Galsworthy were motivated to create an organisation with a more overtly pro-EU message, which would operate alongside the PV campaign: March for Change was launched in June 2019 and organised a large London march one month later (an event that was notably not supported by Open Britain).

Several months later, the PV campaign would collapse as a direct result of strategic and personal conflicts within Open Britain itself (Mance 2020). While sources of tension were multifaceted and not always related to substance, one notable conflict pertained to the campaign's key message. Open Britain's chair, Roland Rudd, was in favour of a more explicit 'pro-Remain' course, and he found an ally in long-term friend Hugo Dixon. Campaign director James McGrory, director of communications Tom Baldwin, and former New Labour figures Mandelson and Campbell instead favoured the existing People's Vote strategy, which ostensibly had the potential of attracting both Remainers and Leavers dissatisfied with the unfolding of events. The rift between Open Britain's corporate structure and its day-to-day operations team reached a climax when Rudd fired McGrory and Baldwin in October 2019, not long before the general election in December. PV's campaign staff overwhelmingly took sides against Rudd, which spelled the end of the organisation in practice.

From the perspective of many local activists, the internal politics of the PV organisation were something of a mystery, and they erupted at a considerable distance from their day-to-day campaigning experience:

> Certainly from my point of view, and I think I probably speak for most on-the-ground campaigners, we were looking at each other and thinking: 'What the hell is going on? Where is all this internal politics suddenly coming from? We're supposed to be focusing on the campaign and that's what we need these people to be doing – and they're just fighting with each other!'
> Interview 25: Lincolnshire for Europe (28 May 2020)

While it is clear that the collapse of PV was ill-timed and a major blow to the anti-Brexit efforts, there is still a conviction among many activists that the campaign was the right choice at the time. Brufatto, for instance, denies that, with hindsight, the PV campaign was a mistake:

> I think it was essential to get us to where we did. If you look at the change of the size of the movement, the voices that we brought in, and how the campaign was run, it was absolutely the right thing to do ... [The campaign strategy explains] why we got so close: it did appeal in some way to people who were centre ground for some time.
> Interview 30: BfE/EM/PV/March for Change (18 June 2021)

An exclusive focus on the failures of PV also distracts from other areas of contention within the broader movement. Interpersonal rivalries and the tensions within the PV campaign, in other words, were not the only factors hampering the movement's unity of direction. As a case in point, prominent individuals within the movement had different opinions about the extent to which the anti-Brexit campaign ought to be unified and focused. Mike Galsworthy, for instance, favoured a more decentralised campaign:

> What I always wanted to do was represent and nurture different sectoral campaigns and different geographically located campaigns, because I felt that different spokespeople and different campaigns speak to different

audiences. And I wanted to get away from one brand.
Because then you completely limit your flexibility like that.
Interview 28: Scientists for EU/March for Change
(22 June 2020)

The chair of the Wales for Europe umbrella organisation, on the other hand, was more inclined towards a less fragmented campaign, preferably under a single banner:

One thing that worries me about the rest of the UK is ... the current fragmentation of efforts across the UK. There is now a blizzard of brand names, you know: Open Britain, People's Vote, Best for Britain, Best for Europe, Another Europe, you know, you could list probably hundreds of brand names. And I'm quite pleased with the fact that in Wales I think it is more unified than anywhere else.
Interview 16: Wales for Europe (25 July 2019)

These examples indicate that the movement remained divided up until the critical December 2019 general election, both in terms of organisational structures and when it came to primary aims and strategies to reach those aims. To obtain a fuller picture of the ultimate failure of the movement, we also need to consider the individuals involved in anti-Brexit activism and the efficacy of their repertoires. The second part of this chapter is concerned with these themes.

ACTIVISTS AND THEIR COLLECTIVE EFFORTS

Demographics and motives for action

Who were the activists involved in local organisations campaigning against Brexit, and what were their motives? Our findings show that they tended to be educated professionals, some of them involved in prior party-political activities. They generally conformed to the typical profile of people who engage in protest activities: politically interested, critical, and confident (Giugni and Grasso 2019). Yet many were new to social movement activism. While some were already active during the 2016 referendum campaign, most of the individuals we interviewed described how they had been jolted into action through shock at the result, a desire for solidarity, and a determination to try to shape the course of events. Many expressed regret and a degree of remorse for not having been active during the referendum campaign. In line with this, our survey data suggest that many activists became more politically involved after the referendum. Just over a third of respondents indicated they were 'very interested' in British politics prior to the Brexit vote, and another 57 per cent described themselves as '(fairly) interested'. While these numbers indicate that the surveyed activists were already reasonably politically engaged, the percentage of 'very interested' notably rose to 90 per cent for the period after the referendum. When asked about specific interest in EU politics, the trend was even more noticeable: 16.5 per cent of respondents indicated they were 'very interested' prior to the referendum, compared with almost three-quarters after.

Activists typically had a sense that Brexit was compromising their identity, their values, and their beliefs. While activists evidently shared an instrumental aim to revert the political decision to leave the EU, seeking connection with like-minded people (identification) and sharing views and feelings about the Brexit vote (expressiveness) were also important motivations to action (Klandermans 2015). From the outset, local groups acted as a support and solidarity network for their key activists. Some interviewees expressed relief at having 'discovered' others in their area or city, with several describing a similar sense of desperation and anxiety in the immediate aftermath of the referendum being assuaged by their participation in the network. In the words of one Liverpool activist:

> We were all so damaged by the referendum ... We lost,
> we got absolutely shafted! ... There was a healing process,
> there was a collegiality to it. We shared our pain, we shared
> our different life experiences. That was very important.
> Interview 4: Liverpool for Europe (26 February 2019)

When we asked activists in our survey about their motivations to become involved, many indicated that a raft of different preselected motivations were of importance (see figure 4.2). Among the strongest motivations were 'Safeguarding the well-being of future generations', 'Travelling freely within the EU', 'Protecting my European identity', 'Concern about growing nationalism',

'Preserving peace in Europe', 'Support for the EU', and 'Concern about the UK's economy' – more than 90 per cent of respondents indicated that these were (very) important motivations. Such motivations suggest pragmatic as well as more idealistic perspectives on the benefits of EU membership. A considerable number of respondents added as additional reasons for becoming involved the specific concern about growing xenophobic or far-right politics, a fear of worsening legal and environmental standards, or anger with dishonest Brexit-supporting politicians. Indeed, many survey respondents added that they considered the grounds for leaving the EU to be illegitimate, given the large amount of misinformation disseminated during the referendum campaign, for which they blamed not only politicians but also private media corporations. Motivations that apparently played less of a crucial role included 'Concern about my local area' and 'Concern about developments in other countries'. The latter finding suggests that activists were mainly concerned about the *domestic* effects of Brexit. Indeed, the surveyed activists also seemed more concerned about the economy, safety, and security in the United Kingdom as opposed to in Europe as a whole.

As far as political orientation is concerned, some organisations, such as Another Europe is Possible, had a clear ideological profile, but most local groups were careful to retain their non-partisan character. Having said that, most activists tended to feel most affinity with left-wing or liberal parties, and many held the Tories responsible for fanning Euroscepticism in the most recent decades (see also chapter 5).

Looking at our survey results, self-reported party membership is well above the typical average for West European countries (van Biezen et al. 2021): almost 60 per cent of respondents indicated they were a party member, mostly of the Liberal Democrats (33.3 percent) and Labour (13.9 per cent). These figures again suggest that anti-Brexit activists were considerably more politically involved than the average UK citizen. When asked which party they voted for in the 2017 general election, 42.6 per cent of respondents in our survey answered Liberal Democrats, 40.3 per cent indicated that they voted for Labour, and only 2.3 per cent reported that they voted Conservative. In the 2019 European Parliament election, which operates under a proportional representation system, the Liberal Democrats (58.0 per cent of respondents) and the Green

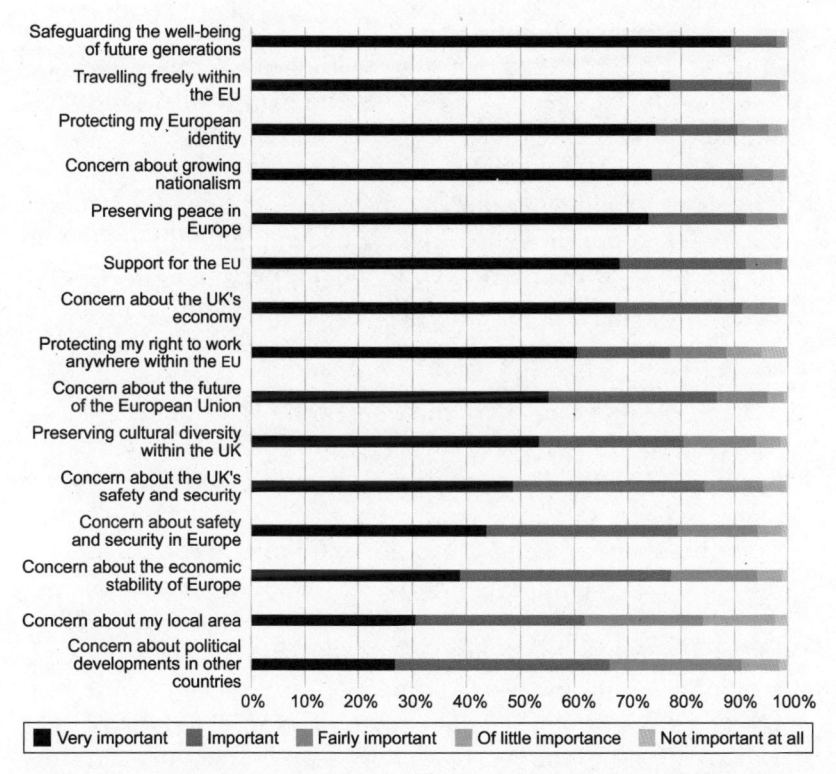

[Bar chart showing personal reasons for becoming involved in the anti-Brexit movement, with categories listed from top to bottom:
- Safeguarding the well-being of future generations
- Travelling freely within the EU
- Protecting my European identity
- Concern about growing nationalism
- Preserving peace in Europe
- Support for the EU
- Concern about the UK's economy
- Protecting my right to work anywhere within the EU
- Concern about the future of the European Union
- Preserving cultural diversity within the UK
- Concern about the UK's safety and security
- Concern about safety and security in Europe
- Concern about the economic stability of Europe
- Concern about my local area
- Concern about political developments in other countries

Legend: Very important, Important, Fairly important, Of little importance, Not important at all]

Figure 4.2 Personal reasons for becoming involved in the anti-Brexit movement. (*Notes.* Question wording: 'Please indicate how important the given reasons were for you becoming active.' $N = 562$.)

Party (21.7 per cent) were the top two choices – just one of the 562 activists reported voting Conservative. This masks the likely fact, of course, that some activists used to be Conservative supporters but became disgruntled with the party precisely because of Brexit.

In terms of activists' demographic characteristics, there appears to be gender balance alongside a clear overrepresentation of higher-educated, middle-aged, and older people from a white ethnic background. This was evident in our pool of interviewees as well as in survey results – even if sample size and self-selection may distort the figures to a certain extent. More than 87 per cent of our survey's respondents reported to be aged 45 and over, with 41.4 per cent reporting that they were 65 or older. A clear majority (58.1 per cent) indicated they had a postgraduate qualification, a further 32.2 per cent reported that they were graduates, while less than 10 per cent answered that they had finished formal education at 18 or under. This general picture is also confirmed by the activists we interviewed:

> The activists still tend to be ... 'male, pale and stale' as it were. It's sort of the retired people or semi-retired people who tend to be the ones who are the most activist.
> Interview 1: European Movement/London4Europe
> (4 February 2019)

> The whole problem about the whole pro-EU movement is: it is middle class, generally older and generally whiter people. The only thing you can say in its favour is: there's a lot of women, so a good gender balance.
> Interview 27: Leeds for Europe/Grassroots for Europe
> (5 June 2020)

These characteristics have been associated not only with core activists, but also with the wider population of movement adherents who frequented the large PV marches in London. This Lincolnshire activist recalls a humorous association between marchers and the clientele of a high-end UK supermarket:

> Somebody described it as being the longest Waitrose queue in history ... There is a tendency for it to look very white and very middle class.
> Interview 13: Lincolnshire for Europe (15 April 2019)

A widely shared concern among key activists was the lack of engagement of young people in local groups. Some activists even showed considerable frustration with the apparent passivity among younger age cohorts:

> We do have a huge number of students in Leeds, we've got about five universities. We've done lots of events that were specifically targeted at students and young people, including our marches. And very little, you know, traction there to be honest. And I don't think that's unique to Leeds, I've heard that story all across the country.

That getting young people fired up about this is very, very difficult.
>> Interview 27: Leeds for Europe/Grassroots for Europe (5 June 2020)

I was just going to say: the youth are noticeable by their absence. And not just in our group, but even when you're out campaigning on the streets. The apathy of the young people, that's what makes me angry. Because they're the ones who are supposed to be up in arms; it's their future and they just couldn't care less. Most of them anyway.
>> Interview 2: Liverpool for Europe (25 February 2019)

While the difficulties with engaging younger people was generally seen as a challenge, and as a weakness in terms of the movement's efficacy, some interviewees also noted optimistic trends. Take the observations of this Northern Irish EM member, for instance:

Since the referendum I think the demographic has changed very much and we've seen a lot more young people getting engaged. And that's quite interesting to me, because politics in Northern Ireland is not something you step into lightly.
>> Interview 6: European Movement Northern Ireland (28 February 2019)

As described above, young people did indeed mobilise by means of their own organisations, most notably OFOC and FFS, and the anti-Brexit artist-activist Madeleina Kay was also part of a younger cohort. Yet even within these organisations there was a recognition of the difficulty of enthusing young people:

I think it's challenging wherever you are to engage young people in politics in general, because many young people have the attitude of politics that it doesn't work for them; 'It's nothing to do with me, it doesn't affect my life.'
>> Interview 8: OFOC Northern Ireland (1 March 2019)

Considering limited efforts to engage 'black, Asian, and minority ethnic' (BAME) communities during the 2016 referendum campaign, it remained similarly difficult for the PV campaign to gain traction with them. London-based youth organisations, however, were considerably more diverse than most local BfE and EM branches. Whereas the leadership of the various anti-Brexit organisations was primarily drawn from a relatively narrow social demographic of people who tended to be more politically active in general (white, middle-class, middle-aged and older), OFOC was fronted by Femi Oluwole, a young, Black British activist of Nigerian descent. Furthermore, a specific Ethnic Minorities for a People's Vote group was set up to create awareness of the potential negative consequences of Brexit for ethnic minority groups, including an increase in hate crimes and disproportionally adverse economic and health impacts. According to its campaign manager, the main aim was not to praise the accomplishments of the EU as such:

> We don't really do anything where we're trying to make a point to other people. It's more ... to engage with ethnic minorities who aren't necessarily involved, and let them know how Brexit is impacting them.
> Interview 19: Ethnic Minorities for a PV/LGBT+ for a PV (30 August 2019)

Many activists acknowledged that mobilising and reaching out to those who were disengaged and seemingly ambivalent about the issue of European integration was a real challenge. Referring to the anti-Trump rallies that were held during the US president's visit to London in June 2019, Best for Britain's Naomi Smith recalled:

> They would have babies, toddlers, children, black people, white people, Asian people. And I just would always say to the team: 'Until the People's Vote marches look like this march, we're not winning.' And the over-60s, home-owning wealthy boomers that were the grassroots movement around the country were wonderful, wonderful people. But we weren't cutting through, we weren't persuading and getting that younger generation fired up about why this matters and why it is part of a broader culture war that is going to hurt them.
> Interview 31: Best for Britain (29 June 2021)

As the following discussion shows, part of the movement's difficulties in reaching out to a wider audience can also be related back to its rather traditional forms of action.

Activities and repertoires

The concrete activities employed by the individual anti-Brexit organisations partly depended on whether they were an interest group or an SMO. Best for Britain, for instance, fitted more neatly in the former category as it lacked an activist base as such, and instead facilitated the work of other anti-Brexit initiatives. To this end, it notably benefited from a particularly large donation from the Open Society Foundation (OSF) of billionaire investor George Soros (Elgot 2018). Open Britain, later in conjunction with central organisations in Millbank Tower, was another organisation that concentrated on attracting funds from donors and on lobbying, in addition to coordinating national campaigns and events. Local groups, on the other hand, had a more unmistakable SMO profile and relied predominantly on small groups of committed volunteers. While they could draw on leaflets and advice provided by central BfE and EM organisations, and later by the PV campaign, local groups were still largely self-funded. As one London-based activist put it:

> Most of us are volunteers and we are contributing when we have the time, in areas where we either have skills or interests.
> Interview 1: European Movement/London4Europe
> (4 February 2019)

Focusing on the activities of local grassroots organisations, it is clear that they engaged in similar initiatives across the country, which indicates that there was sharing of good practices and coordination between local groups. The most typical activities included regular street stalls in city and town centres, marches and demonstrations, leafleting, canvassing during election campaigns, and writing letters to (local) MPs, councillors, and media outlets. Some activists wrote blogs, commented on news website articles, called in to talk radio shows, or gave media interviews themselves. Small-scale events with high-profile pro-European speakers were also organised, but these mainly attracted an already Remain-supporting audience. The large national demonstrations in London clearly formed the most extensive form of collective action and attracted most public attention. While predominantly organised by the central anti-Brexit organisations, these marches also required local groups to invest effort and resources into promoting the events via leafleting and social media, and into arranging transport and sometimes accommodation.

In terms of concrete repertoires, the 'Brexitometer' was a particularly widespread phenomenon, forming part of street stalls across the country. It consisted of a whiteboard with statements about Brexit on which passers-by could indicate their (dis)agreement by means of colourful stickers. Responses were overwhelmingly skewed against Brexit, which provided good material for social media posts featuring images of the Brexitometers. More importantly, the Brexitometer was seen as an effective means of attracting attention and starting conversations, including with supporters of Brexit. According to one activist from the North East:

> We use a Brexitometer because it is useful with the People's Vote campaign. We tend to ask, 'Is Brexit going well?' People just laugh and it is a good tactic for engaging people who may be Brexiteers. Gets us away from telling people what we think – ask people for their views and not tell them they're wrong.
> Interview 10: North East for Europe (8 March 2019)

Besides setting up street stalls in their own hometowns, groups also visited targeted locations. A 'Bollocks to Brexit' bus – a parody of the red Vote Leave referendum campaign bus – was driven to the constituencies of Theresa May, Boris Johnson, and Jeremy Corbyn (Heal 2018). OFOC had its own 'Battle Bus' that called at university campuses and schools, including in areas marked by overwhelming support for Brexit. The youth organisations, in particular, also engaged in various direct-action demonstrations in and around Parliament, using visually striking materials in the hope that these would 'go viral' online. Groups also invested in advertisements and billboards criticising the Brexit process and UK politicians. Led By Donkeys was one notable group leading such campaigns, with one tactic being to erect billboards featuring past tweets of politicians that revealed their supposed hypocrisy, untrustworthiness, or U-turns (Sherwood 2019).

In general, actions remained relatively non-disruptive. Local anti-Brexit groups affiliated with BfE and EM, in particular, mainly relied on conventional means of action, such as marches, street stalls, and leafletting. Among the more unruly forms of action mentioned in our survey were 'Chalking "Stop Brexit" on pavements', 'Standing on motorway bridges with pro Remain banner', and 'Blocking Lambeth Bridge'. SODEM was among the organisations that employed more radical forms of action. The group's founder, Steve Bray, became something of a cult figure, appearing in front of Parliament on a daily basis, usually joined by fellow protesters. Sporting a large blue-and-yellow hat with 'Stop Brexit' written on it, Bray shouted anti-Brexit slogans and was often visible and audible in news broadcasts. Yet the repertoires of the movements did not get much more unruly than that. When asked about the disruptive nature of his actions, Bray commented:

> Well, unfortunately for the news teams, yes. But we try to keep it to a minimum, we do not want to alienate people.
> Interview 17: SODEM (25 July 2019)

Several interviewees lamented the lack of concerted and effective anti-Brexit online action during the referendum campaign. One London activist referred to social media as 'the undefended battle ground that cost the June 2016 referendum' (Interview 11: London/Watford for Europe (12 March 2019); see also Usherwood and Wright 2017). In the immediate period after the referendum, a genuinely effective online campaign again failed to materialise. Yet, as mentioned before, the internet did play a prominent role in the movement's evolution as well as its actions. More traditional forms of social movement action were advertised and documented online, not least through the various (local) organisations' Facebook pages and Twitter feeds. The groups also used social media to spread campaign messages, to share and comment on news stories, and to call out misinformation (Brändle et al. 2022). On Twitter, the '#FBPE' (Follow Back, Pro-EU) community emerged.

The social media platforms were thus used as means 'to supplement and even displace mass media in terms of reaching broad publics', but also 'to create organizational networks among populations that lack more conventional institutional forms of political organization' (Bennett and Segerberg 2015, 3; see also Bennett and Segerberg 2013). As described previously, Facebook in particular functioned as a platform for connecting local groups and allowing them to communicate with each other. Social media platforms were also important to mobilise potential activists and to spread information about events. As Brändle et al. (2022) found, more than a quarter of all posts on anti-Brexit Facebook pages included 'calls to action', including requests to sign petitions, write to MPs, and join protests. Local groups were successful in signing up hundreds of thousands of people to their mailing lists, and by the end of 2019 considerable investments had been made to coordinate online engagement, networking, and advertising activities (Manthorpe 2019).

It remains difficult to gauge, however, how much impact these online activities genuinely had in terms of swaying public opinion or mobilising adherents in a meaningful and durable way. One notable example of ephemeral and low-cost online activism – or 'slacktivism' – was the petition to Parliament in March 2019 asking to 'Revoke Article 50 and to remain in the EU', which attracted more than six million signatures. Despite attracting considerable support and attention, this action did little to alter the course of events.

Finally, it is important to consider whom the organisations sought to target strategically with their actions and messages. There was a considerable degree of discrepancy between organisations and individuals in this regard. Most interviewees agreed that there was little point in getting into heated debates with convinced Leavers. Here is a description from one activist about their lack of motivation to engage in conversation with those who believed Brexit would in the end be beneficial to the United Kingdom:

> Some really believe that everything will be better, as promised, and they don't want to even discuss this. Why should you discuss this with them and waste my time and their time? Because you see that they are not approachable, and I don't want to go into a fight ... These people have their own experiences and they will have their own reasons, and I won't convince them. I know this.
> Interview 3, anonymous (26 February 2019)

Many activists did indeed argue that their actions were geared at building support and enlisting pro-Remain adherents more than swaying opinion. Not all interviewees, however, thought this was a sufficient strategy in the longer run. In the words of one Bristol activist:

> Streets stalls are a means not an end. A street stall is a means to hoover up Remainers ... to come and volunteer with us when we do the thing that we actually have to do, which is to go and find and talk to some 'soft Leavers'. I know it's hard, people don't like doing it. Remainers don't want to have to go and do that. But we're not going to win a second referendum if we don't go and talk to some people that don't agree with us. Isn't that nakedly obvious, right?
> Interview 15: Bristol for Europe (6 June 2019)

This Lincolnshire activist agreed that changing people's opinions was necessary to prevent Brexit from happening, but reckoned the process of convincing them had to happen in the more personal sphere:

> That's how you change people's minds. Not by shouting at them from a pulpit. Though shouting out from a pulpit has to happen, because it rallies the troops; it frightens politicians. It has its place. But in terms of actually changing minds at the grassroots level, you need to engage a group of activists who then engage with their own social circles; that's how you get a change.
> Interview 13: Lincolnshire for Europe (15 April 2019)

Some organisations, including FFS and OFOC, spent considerable time and resources visiting Leave areas and engaging with disenfranchised groups – 'Why preach to the converted?' in the words of one FFS activist (Interview 21: For Future's Sake (9 September 2019). Yet, attesting to the varied strategies that could be discerned across groups and individuals, one OFOC member told us that victory could ultimately be achieved precisely by mobilising the convinced Remainers:

> If we are going to run a [new referendum] campaign in 2019, it's almost certainly for us, from an Our Future

Our Choice perspective, going to be a turnout campaign rather than a changing-minds campaign. Because we want to mobilise as many young people as possible, and the marginal cost of changing a mind versus the marginal cost of getting one young person more out who already agrees with you ... the balance just doesn't make sense.
Interview 12: Our Future Our Choice (26 March 2019)

As we know, however, attempts to force a second referendum failed, as did any endeavour to stop Brexit from happening altogether. Before concluding this chapter on mobilising structures, we turn briefly to the question of the movement's future after the United Kingdom's formal departure from the EU.

A future for a pro-European movement?

When we consider our survey data, most activists were clearly appalled by the prospect of any form of Brexit, and many expressed the desire to keep campaigning after the United Kingdom's potential departure (see figure 4.3). More than three-quarters disagreed that a 'soft' Brexit would be acceptable (close to half *strongly* disagreed). A very large majority supported a new referendum, while around 60 per cent of respondents reckoned they would keep campaigning even after another 'Leave' result. What is more, three-quarters agreed that, irrespective of public opinion, Brexit must be stopped and the United Kingdom must remain (over half *strongly* agreed).

Follow-up conversations with activists in the course of 2020 revealed that, while many had given up and resumed their ordinary lives, there was still a core group of activists determined to keep the pro-European cause alive. The quest for rejoining was widely considered a 'long game', though, and the Covid-19 crisis made impossible the typical street-based activities that characterised the movement. The main aim, according to many, was to keep the United Kingdom as closely aligned as possible to the EU's legal framework. New strategies included destabilising the Conservative government by highlighting its more general policy errors – not least in regard to dealing with the Covid-19 pandemic. Organisations such as Best for Britain and March for Change accepted the reality of Brexit and broadened their scope to safeguarding rights and standards and promoting international cooperation and a close relationship with

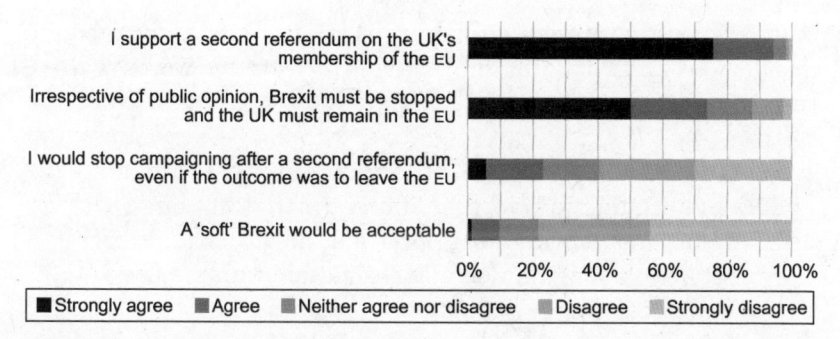

Figure 4.3 Activists' perspectives on the Brexit process. (*Notes*. Question wording: 'This question is about your personal views on the referendum and Brexit process. Please read the following statements and say whether you agree or disagree.' $N = 563$.)

the EU. The EM and Grassroots for Europe remained committed to re-joining the EU, albeit in a 'step by step' fashion.

While the post-Brexit pro-European movement in the United Kingdom is certainly stronger than it was prior to the 2016 referendum – EM's membership, for instance, has grown considerably – it remains to be seen what form it will take in the longer term. Judging from what interviewees said in interviews prior to the United Kingdom's departure from the EU, it seems obvious that the energy around the large marches in London cannot be structurally retained. Understandably, activists were focused more on the imminent threat of Brexit than they were on planning to sustain their organisation in the long run. Asked whether there is scope for a more permanent pro-European movement, this Newcastle activist tellingly answered:

> I think people would agree, in principle. But how [do] we achieve that? I don't know. Maybe we could achieve that, but I don't know. What you actually centre it around is difficult to see. People have got other things to do with their lives.
> Interview 10: North East for Europe (8 March 2019)

The urge to keep the pro-European struggle alive appeared particularly muted among the younger activists we interviewed. For them, a People's Vote appeared to be the main goal: a new campaign marked by less misinformation on the basis of which citizens could, this time around, make an informed decision. In the words of these young activists:

> If we were to have a vote between Remain and a specific Brexit deal, that for me, even if that Brexit deal won: fantastic. You know, at least politicians get a kick to do that thing. People have democratically chosen, with the facts available to them.
> Interview 12: Our Future Our Choice (26 March 2019)

> If there was a People's Vote and it was, say, specifically on a 'no deal' or specifically on a deal that Johnson had negotiated, and that won, then I would accept that as people knew roughly what Brexit is going to look like.
> Interview 19: Ethnic Minorities for a PV/LGBT+ for a PV (30 August 2019)

> Personally, I would be upset [in the event of another referendum vote favouring Brexit]. I worked on this campaign for so long. I've put in many a night, you know, reading up and just everything. I would be very, very upset personally. But at the end of the day, we as the People's Vote campaign, we as FFS have done absolutely everything we can to correct that fault in our political system. And if we end up not getting what we want, you know, we can't continue this for the rest of our lives, you know ... a third vote, a fourth vote, a fifth vote ...
> Interview: 21 For Future's Sake (9 September 2019)

These quotes suggest that a fair share of the activists who were part of the anti-Brexit movement – and perhaps particularly those of a younger generation – were likely to withdraw from pro-European activism after the United Kingdom had finally left.

CONCLUSION

This chapter has described the virtual lack of a pro-European movement infrastructure prior to the Brexit referendum vote. The European Movement, a key actor in the 1975 referendum, was by this time a largely dormant organisation with a small and older group of EU enthusiasts. The Stronger In referendum campaign in 2016 was often criticised by local campaigners for its aloofness and its top-down nature. The grassroots movement that gradually emerged in the referendum's aftermath was thus largely new; most activists we interviewed admitted and regretted their lack of engagement in any campaigning activities in the run-up to the Brexit referendum. It was the result that shook a considerable number of people into activism.

Despite an augmented capacity to organise demonstrations and other quite large actions, local networks often remained relatively small in terms of their numbers of core activists and strategists. Driven by an apparent absence of an effective pro-European movement organisation, they mobilised their neighbours, colleagues, and friends via social media. Notwithstanding the emergence of groups specifically targeting young and BAME citizens, anti-Brexit activists were typically middle-aged and older, white, middle class, and highly educated. While local groups and individuals affiliated themselves with emerging or reinvigorated national organisations, which provided them with advice, materials, and some financial resources, informal networks remained crucial to campaigning initiatives and activities.

Given the deep-seated nature of Euroscepticism in the UK media and in party politics, the late mobilisation of the movement meant that it faced an uphill battle from the outset. Yet there were also important weaknesses in the anti-Brexit coalition that hampered its efficacy. Local groups typically functioned as a support network for grieving pro-European citizens, and relationships between local groups were largely collegial and constructive. There nevertheless existed ideological differences and disagreements about the strategy to follow that fed into the fragmentation of the movement. Even if specific organisational allegiances were not always relevant for the campaign 'on the ground', tensions materialised about how best to distribute and use resources. The emergence of the national People's Vote campaign focused minds, but also fuelled a considerable degree of factionalism. Some organisations chose to stay out, while others were not welcome under the PV umbrella. Akin to earlier complaints about Stronger In, many local activists criticised the top-down, London-centric, and centralised nature of the PV campaign, and they were reluctant to surrender their autonomy. The establishment of the Grassroots for Europe network was evidence of these grievances.

The existence of a range of different groups and initiatives is not a sign of weakness per se. Several activists in fact made the case for a decentralised anti-Brexit campaign, with a variety of organisations appealing to specific target audiences and sections of society. Yet, in practice, the campaign had a disjointed character: activists and groups expressed different views about whom to target with their messages, and about whether the campaign should mainly be about mobilising pro-Europeans or convincing ('soft') Leavers. As will be explored further in the next chapter, moreover, the emergence of the PV campaign contributed to discord about the actual goal and messaging of the movement: a second referendum or averting Brexit.

Finally, the repertoires of anti-Brexit organisations and activists were unlikely to convince many people beyond an already pro-Remain audience. Most activists were engaged in activities that were limited in terms of scope and reach: leafleting and operating street stalls, contacting politicians and media outlets, and commenting on and sharing information on social media. Local organisations tended to attract people from a fairly narrow demographic. In many cases, they could better be described as solidarity networks for impassioned and like-minded individuals than as practiced and savvy campaign organisations. While the central PV organisation was better placed to engage in larger-scale PR, lobbying, and media campaigns, its own internal divisions ultimately caused its downfall at a crucial point in time ahead of the December 2019 general election.

Given the adverse political conditions and the virtual lack of any pre-existing pro-European infrastructure, the accomplishments of the movement were no small feat. For the first time, large crowds of people came out, often draped in European flags, to defend EU membership. This was not enough, however, to fundamentally shift public or elite opinion, or to gain the required support from politicians to force a second referendum. The book's next chapter, which focuses on the movement's 'framing', argues that the strategic messaging of the movement was also insufficient to change the course of events in the short amount of time that was available.

5

Framing Leave and Remain

In this chapter we engage more fully with the conceptions of 'Europe' that are held by activists, and with the claims and messages that the movement used to rally support. This part of the book, in other words, shifts its focus to the role of 'framing'. Emphasising its strategic nature, McAdam et al. (1996, 6) define the act of framing as 'the conscious strategic efforts by groups of people to fashion shared understandings of the world and of themselves that legitimate and motivate collective action'. We consider the campaign messages addressed at the wider public, as well as the strategic considerations and debates underlying them. We ask how the individuals and (local) organisations that were part of the anti-Brexit movement interpreted the event of Brexit and the broader issue of European integration. Bearing in mind that 'the quality of the frames is one of the crucial factors which determine the success of the mobilization of social movements' (Gerhards and Rucht 1997, 226), we ask what specific dilemmas these organisations faced in constructing ideational frames and formulating their messages.

We begin by presenting results from our survey, which capture the personal views, perceptions, and interpretations of activists pertaining to the EU and the Brexit process. Analysing this data helps assess whether the movement's public messages were consistent with activists' private perceptions. The remainder of the chapter investigates the messages used in the campaign against Brexit. We do this, first, by presenting the results from a content analysis of campaign materials and social media posts. The analysis reveals which issues and frames prevailed within the movement's messaging. Second, we use data from our interviews to assess not only which frames were adopted, but also why. We focus specifically on how the activists problematised Brexit and who they blamed for the adverse outcome ('diagnostic' framing), and also whether and how they sought to mobilise support and sway Eurosceptic citizens by providing alternative solutions and ideas about (the United Kingdom's future in) the EU ('prognostic' framing) (see Benford and Snow 2000). The analysis of interview material also reveals the existing debates within the movement about the pursued objectives and framing strategies.

We conclude that although activists were committed supporters of EU membership, their messaging often lacked a positive vision and interpretation of European integration. While campaign materials outlined a range of pro-European messages, the emphasis in conversations in the streets, certainly in areas with weak public support for EU membership, centred largely on the dishonesty of Leave-supporting politicians and the negative consequences of Brexit for the United Kingdom. After the launch of the People's Vote campaign, the focus shifted to the prospect of a new referendum as a key objective, and as a consequence took the debate even further away from positive interpretations of the EU.

The emphasis on the problems of Brexit rather than the virtues of European integration is perhaps best explained in terms of how rapidly the grassroots movement formed and the short space of time it had to formulate its strategies and achieve its objectives. Furthermore, to avert Brexit by means of a potential People's Vote, a key necessity was to convince precisely those who did not come out to support Remain in the 2016 referendum, and who were probably not overly enthusiastic about the EU. Debates about strategy within the movement revealed the difficulty in formulating a positive message about the pre-referendum status quo, which was portrayed as imperfect at best and had come under repeated attack in the preceding years and decades. The dominant messaging of the movement was essentially similar to the failed Stronger In referendum campaign.

ACTIVISTS' ATTITUDES AND PERCEPTIONS CONCERNING EUROPE AND BREXIT

During anti-Brexit marches, many people draped themselves in the colours and insignia of the European flag. Yet is it the case that activists were also true Europeans at heart, or did they primarily come

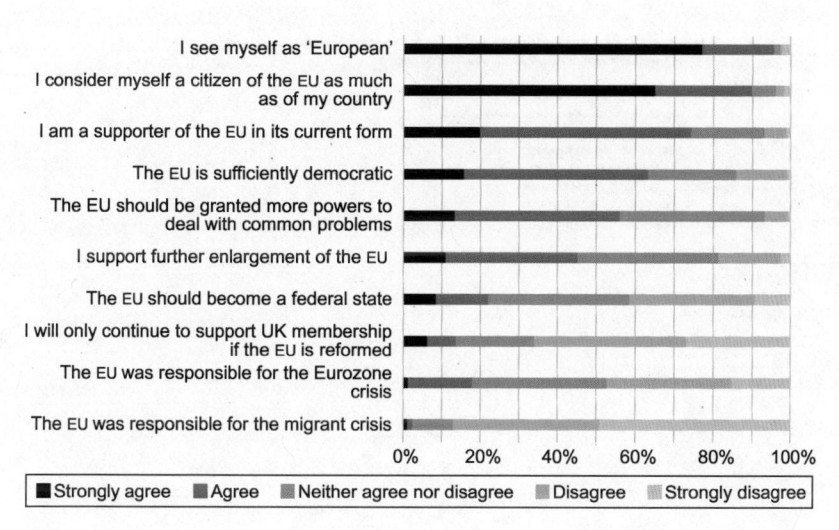

Figure 5.1 Personal views on the European Union. (*Notes.* Question wording: 'This question is about your personal views on the European Union. Please read the following statements and say whether you agree or disagree.' Answer categories in the figure are slightly abbreviated. $N = 562$.)

out to defend EU membership because of its presumed advantages for the United Kingdom (or the disadvantages of leaving)? In other words, were the frames deployed in the anti-Brexit campaign aligned with the personal views of activists? We start by presenting the results of our survey pertaining to activists' personal views on the EU and the Brexit process.

Figure 5.1 indicates that most grassroots activists were convinced supporters of the EU. A large majority self-identified as 'European' and as an EU citizen on par with their national citizenship. A large majority supported the EU in its current form; almost three-quarters of respondents (strongly) agreed with the related statement, whereas a small minority (less than 14 per cent) indicated they would only continue to support EU membership on the condition that the bloc would reform. Only a small minority of respondents held the EU responsible for the migrant and Eurozone crises. Almost two-thirds (strongly) agreed with the notion that the EU is sufficiently democratic, and a small majority expressed (tentative) support for granting the EU more powers to deal with cross-border problems. Respondents were somewhat less enthusiastic about further EU enlargements, and more disagreed than agreed with the

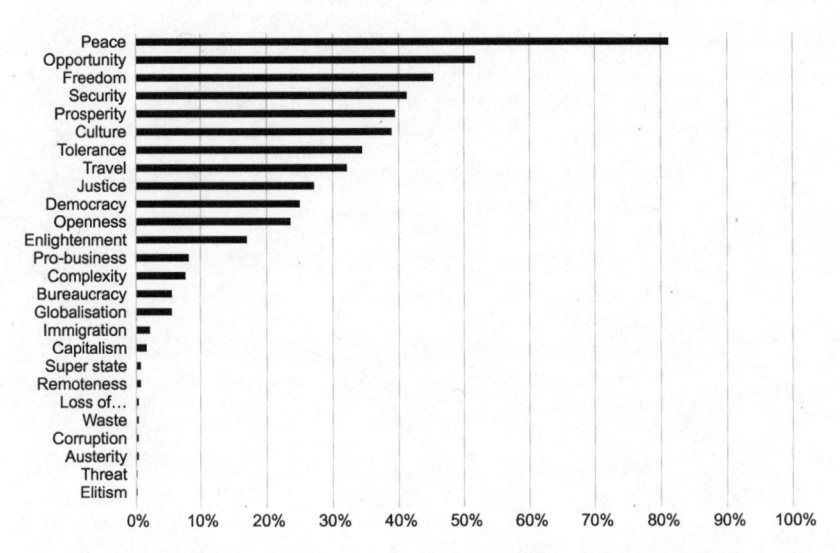

Figure 5.2 Pre-selected terms associated with membership of the European Union. (*Notes.* Question wording: 'From the following list of words and phrases, please select up to five that you most strongly associate with membership of the European Union.' *N* = 563.)

statement that the EU should become a federal state. Still, more than 20 per cent showed some degree of sympathy towards arguably the most far-reaching form of European integration.

Respondents were also asked to select up to five words and phrases they associated with membership of the EU (from a list of twenty-six randomly presented items). It is clear from figure 5.2 that most activists were inclined to choose concepts with a positive connotation: 'peace' was particularly popular (selected by more than 80 per cent of respondents), and 'opportunity', 'freedom', 'security', and 'prosperity' were also in the top five. 'Immigration', a key theme for the Leave campaign as well as for Brexit voters, was notably only chosen by 2 per cent of surveyed activists. Concepts often used by Eurosceptics with a more obvious negative connotation – such as 'super state', 'loss of sovereignty', 'corruption', and 'elitism' – were hardly ever chosen by our respondents. Perhaps unsurprisingly, it is clear that grassroots anti-Brexit activists were inclined to associate the EU with positive instead of negative concepts, related to a variety of socio-economic, socio-cultural, or postmaterialist themes. Judging from the presented data, anti-Brexit campaigners seemed more

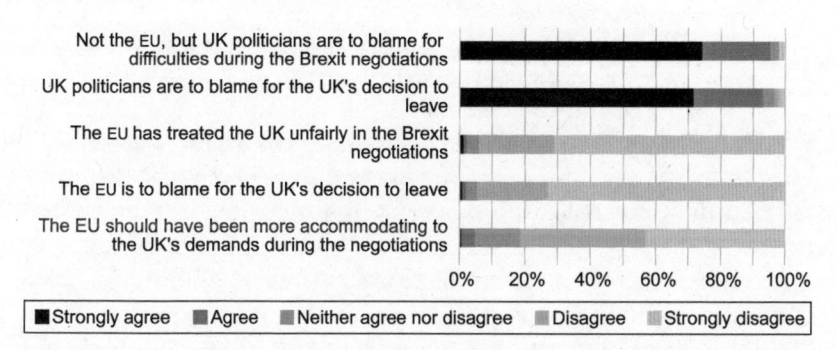

Figure 5.3 Personal views on the referendum and the Brexit process. (*Notes.* Question wording: 'This question is about your personal views on the referendum and Brexit process. Please read the following statements and say whether you agree or disagree.' N = 563.)

supportive of the EU in its current form than the more 'critical Europeanist' activists of left-wing movements that previously politicised the issue of European integration in other countries (della Porta and Caiani 2009; della Porta 2020a).

Turning to perceptions more directly related to the Brexit process, it is evident that activists viewed the EU with more sympathy than they had for their domestic politicians (see figure 5.3). As far as the attribution of blame is concerned (which is part of 'diagnostic framing'), UK politicians were widely held responsible for the referendum result as well as the difficult negotiation process. Only 5 per cent of respondents (strongly) agreed with the notion that the EU should have been more accommodating to the United Kingdom, with a little more than 2 per cent feeling that the EU had treated the United Kingdom unfairly.

Our survey data indicate that anti-Brexit activists were committed pro-Europeans who clearly saw more advantages than disadvantages in British EU membership. The EU was seen in a positive light, while UK politicians were blamed for the unfavourable referendum outcome and also for the troublesome negotiation process that followed. To what extent, and how, were such sentiments publicly conveyed in the campaign claims and messages of the anti-Brexit movement? The remainder of this chapter shifts from the personal perspectives of activists to claims and messages that were publicly conveyed in the campaign against Brexit.

FRAMING LEAVE AND REMAIN IN CAMPAIGN MATERIALS

Previous studies have identified various ways in which 'Europe' has been interpreted and perceived. On the basis of a comparative analysis of public and elite attitudes in Germany, Spain, and the United Kingdom, Diez Medrano (2003) highlighted how conceptions of European integration have been largely shaped by historical and cultural conditions. In comparison with the other countries, Diez Medrano found that attitudes towards the EU were more negative in the United Kingdom, and that European integration was associated, more than it was elsewhere, with a loss of national identity and sovereignty.

Other scholars have identified more concrete framing categories, whereby 'frames' are understood primarily in relation to the issues with which the EU is associated. In their studies on political party positions, Helbling et al. (2010) and Grande et al. (2016) distinguish 'cultural', 'economic', and 'other utilitarian' framing categories (see Della Porta and Caiani (2009) for an alternative set of categories). Cultural frames relate to questions concerning identity, sovereignty, migration, and multiculturalism. Economic frames relate to assumed economic benefits and disadvantages of European integration. The 'other utilitarian' category includes diverse matters such as the efficiency of European institutions, environmental policy, and international security. In their study of populist radical right parties, Pirro and van Kessel (2018) identify a similar set of frames used by Eurosceptic actors to criticise the EU in relation to specific policy areas (socio-economic and socio-cultural frames), and add categories related to questions of sovereignty and legitimacy.

To study the framing of the anti-Brexit organisations in terms of the specific issues and themes they associated with Europe and Brexit, we similarly adopt the 'culture' (including issues related to immigration, identity, and sovereignty) and 'economy' framing categories; both themes were evidently salient in the Brexit debate. Based on case-specific knowledge, we also identify several additional categories that we expected to be relevant in the context of the UK referendum campaign or the general political debate. These categories are 'security', related to matters such as war and peace, terrorism, and cyber crime; 'health', including statements about the National Health Service (NHS); the environment, including

European regulations and climate change; and 'legitimacy', which relates to arguments about the legitimacy of the referendum outcome, the (adverse) role of British politicians and media, and the more general state of democracy in the United Kingdom and the EU. We reserve the 'other' category for messages related to any other policy areas, and we create a final 'general' category for messages with no specific substantive content (such as 'Bollocks to Brexit'). We further divide each category to distinguish between messages that emphasise the negative consequences of Brexit ('Brexit neg', e.g. 'jobs will be lost') and those that stress the benefits and positive sides of EU membership ('EU pos', e.g. 'access to internal market'). For the legitimacy framing category we added two further subcategories pertaining to messages blaming national politicians ('UK pol neg', e.g. individuals, parties, or 'the establishment' as a whole) and national media ('UK media neg'), either for spreading misinformation or for taking inconsistent or ill-informed positions.

Figure 5.4 presents the results of our analysis of the messages we found in the campaign materials of the various anti-Brexit organisations (see chapter 1 for a discussion on the data collection). Such messages could come in the form of short slogans or longer statements, e.g. testimonials of Remain-supporting politicians or other public figures. Two categories stand out: frames related to socio-economic issues and those related to the legitimacy of the Brexit outcome and process. Both types of frame were used in just under a quarter of all messages (in combination in some cases).

The 'legitimacy' category included many messages alluding to the alleged shift in public opinion against the current direction of Brexit, or in favour of a new referendum or of simply remaining in the EU. Other recurring arguments were that the decision to leave lacked genuine legitimacy given the small margin of the vote, and that the parliamentary stalemate made a second referendum necessary. March for Change printed a leaflet with the text 'Reject Brexit. Defend Democracy', suggesting that the Brexit process was essentially lacking democratic legitimacy. 'Public wants People's Vote more than general election', a leaflet of the PV campaign proclaimed. The youth organisations OFOC and FFS emphasised that most young people were in favour of Remain, and they lamented the fact that Brexit had a detrimental effect on their future opportunities. One FFS leaflet proclaimed that: 'Two million young people didn't get a say last time. They wouldn't have voted for this shit show.'

The Failure of Remain

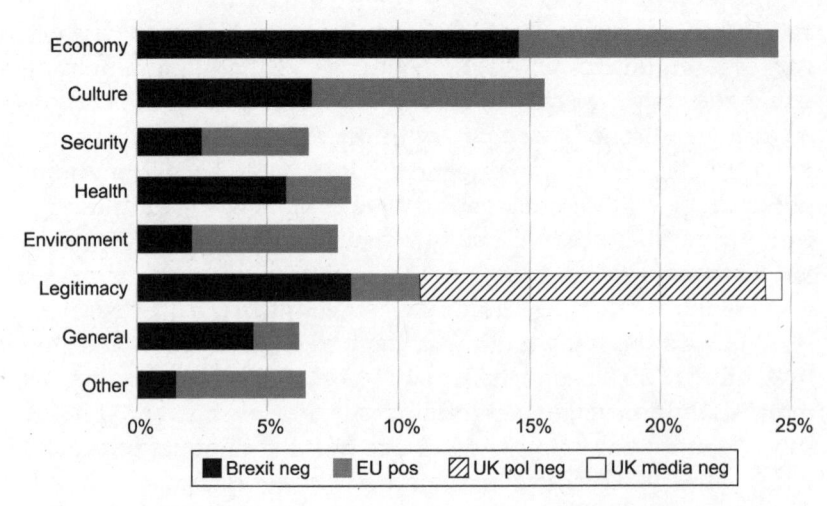

Figure 5.4 Prevalence of frame categories in the campaign materials of the anti-Brexit movement. (*Notes.* Analysis on the basis of 547 collected items, including flyers, posters, and edited photos/memes on social media. Categories are non-exclusive, as messages could refer to more than one category, e.g. when adverse socio-economic consequences of Brexit (economy frame) were blamed on elite failure (legitimacy frame). Given that single items could contain multiple messages, we identified 803 individual messages for our analysis, which form the basis for the percentages.)

More frequently, statements from across the various organisations expressed explicit criticism of UK politicians (more than half of the messages in the legitimacy category). Some messages criticised the government for acting irresponsibly or against the interests of the British people, while others were more aggressive and explicitly *ad hominem*. An item from the East Midlands prior to the 2019 European Parliament elections proclaimed: 'Put [Brexit Party leader] Farage out of Business. Defeat Fascism at the Ballot Box.' Campaign materials frequently accused (governing) Leave-supporting politicians of lying, of making false promises or breaking them, or of flip-flopping. Best for Britain, for instance, produced a series of leaflets comparing statements of Brexit-supporting politicians across time, inferring that Brexit was not quite as straightforward or beneficial as they had previously suggested. Upon becoming prime minister in July 2019, Boris Johnson became a prominent target. 'He's lying to you,' FFS claimed, 'Johnson's deal won't "get Brexit done" – it'll keep us stuck in chaotic negotiations for years.'

Unsurprisingly, the Conservatives were the target of disdain much more often than Labour or the other parties were. 'Use your vote to stop Tory Brexit' even became a central slogan of the left-wing Another Europe is Possible group prior to the 2017 general election. Interestingly, campaign materials only rarely targeted the Brexit-supporting press.

Socio-economic themes also featured prominently in the movement's messages. Almost two-thirds of the messages applying an economic frame referred to the presumed adverse socio-economic consequences of Brexit. These included damage to the United Kingdom's economy in general, a loss of jobs, a depreciation of the pound, threats to local businesses, and a predicted exodus of large companies. These arguments were found across all organisations that were part of the movement. Other messages from more left-leaning local branches or organisations such as Another Europe is Possible emphasised the threats to workers' rights and the quest for social justice. The latter organisation vocally argued that the EU was in need of reform but also that it was the EU that guaranteed workers' rights, paid holidays, and parental leave. Such positive messages about the EU were thus also part of the arguments expressed by the anti-Brexit organisations, which also spoke of the benefits of EU membership for the economic development of certain regions through European funds or trade. Wales for Europe, for instance, produced a leaflet with the statement: 'Europe. Welsh farming's biggest export market, supporting the backbone of rural Wales. #ThankyouEurope.'

During the referendum campaign it was mainly the pro-Brexit side, and the Leave.EU campaign in particular, that brought up themes related to immigration and identity. The Remain campaign focused mainly on economic arguments, and, judging from our sample of campaign materials, socio-economic themes were also more salient in the messaging of the anti-Brexit movement that appeared after the referendum. Nevertheless, cultural frames, for instance referring to the specific issue of migration, were also regularly employed. Fewer than half of the messages in this category alluded to negative consequences of the United Kingdom leaving the EU. A recurring argument was that Brexit would discourage EU healthcare workers from coming to the United Kingdom, which would in turn have an adverse effect on the NHS. Best for Britain, for instance, lamented that 'Since the 2016 referendum, the NHS has lost 26,000 staff members.' Restrictions on the freedom of movement for Britons (to work and study in mainland Europe) were also regularly evoked. Many of the 'positive' messages emphasised the opportunities the EU provided in this regard.

There was hardly any engagement with Leave's key claim about 'taking back control'. Few messages, in other words, touched on the theme of the United Kingdom's sovereignty in the area of immigration specifically, or in terms of the country's freedom to create its own laws more generally. Some items did refer to the United Kingdom's reduced international clout as a result of Brexit, such as the following extract from a leaflet from March for Change: 'The UK has greater global influence as a member of the EU.' Revealing that debates about sovereignty in the United Kingdom do not relate only to the international sphere, several Scottish leaflets argued that 'EU membership has strengthened Scotland's influence'.

In general, many of the messages in the 'culture' category emphasised rather pragmatic or utilitarian arguments related to freedom of movement and immigration. As already mentioned, such arguments included references to the loss of key (NHS) workers due to Brexit, the contribution of foreign workers to the United Kingdom's economy, and opportunities for UK citizens to travel and work abroad. Less frequent were messages that openly celebrated cultural diversity (through immigration) and European identity. In this sense, there seemed to be a reluctance of many groups to openly counter the culturally conservative – or even xenophobic – arguments of the Leave campaign. A case in point is a North East for Europe leaflet proclaiming that 'Brexit will not stop immigration'. This message seemed to reveal a tacit acknowledgement that immigration was generally perceived as a problem rather than as something positive, and that leaving the EU did not contribute to solving this 'problem'. A message spread by the PV campaign showed a similar implicit suggestion that immigration was something that needed to be 'controlled': '73% [of trade union members] say maintaining free trade is more important than controlling immigration.'

None of this is to say that cosmopolitan and pro-immigration messages were entirely absent from campaign materials. Another Europe is Possible produced stickers and other materials with the slogan 'migrants welcome', and more examples could certainly be found in parts of the country in which left-liberal and pro-European attitudes were more prevalent. Liverpool for Europe, for instance, proclaimed: 'Liverpool is a city that looks outward to the world. We are a proudly international place built on the ingenuity and hard work of people from all over the globe.' In Scotland, where 62 per cent of voters supported Remain in the 2016 referendum, leaflets featured the slogan 'We are European'. In Bristol, one item featured the text 'I will not be silenced by the Far-Right Anti-EU Propaganda Machine … I am not "Betraying" my country: I am concerned we are losing our values of tolerance, acceptance and diversity.'

A variety of further messages fell into other more specific framing categories. Arguments related to 'security' often alluded to the EU's presumed positive contribution to preserving peace and occasionally to Brexit's threat to the Northern Irish peace settlement. A leaflet from OFOC Belfast, for example, warned that 'Brexit threatens a generation who've grown up knowing only peace in [Northern Ireland].' As mentioned above, the supposed harm to the NHS was a recurring theme of messages placed in the 'health' category. The 'environment' category included references to EU regulations and the feared degradation of food standards. One PV leaflet, for instance, raised the prospect of post-Brexit cross-Atlantic trade deals and claimed that 'US food standards establish a maximum of one maggot per 250 millimetres of orange juice. That's 1.4 maggots per day for the average UK household.' The EU was also regularly lauded for measures to protect the environment and fight climate change, with various organisations, including Best for Britain and FFS, not confident that the UK government would try to save the planet with the same gusto after Brexit. There appears to be a positive correlation between the prevalence of post-materialist values in a particular area (typically urban areas, with relatively high levels of diversity and large numbers of students and graduates) and the frequency of messages related to the environment. In Oxford, for example, a series of leaflets focused on the EU's efforts to protect animal welfare. The same logic applies to some of the messages in the 'other' category: both Oxford and Bristol featured items focusing on women's rights and gender equality, for instance, and in Manchester a leaflet was distributed outlining the presumed negative consequences of Brexit for the LGBT+ community.

The examples outlined above indicate that some messages were tailored to the local context: campaign materials created by grassroots organisations regularly addressed concerns that were deemed to be widespread among the local population, or outlined economic benefits of EU membership for their particular region. In general, however, we found many of the same arguments across the various local groups and national organisations. This was partly because some materials – those produced by PV, for instance – were used across the country. Campaign materials thus touched on a wide variety of themes, and stressed the benefits of remaining in the EU and the illegitimacy of the Brexit process, as well as the disadvantages of leaving.

Several key observations can nevertheless be made. As was the case during the 2016 referendum campaign, socio-economic themes were prominent in the pro-Remain messaging. Of the materials that touched on the issue of immigration, the focus was often on pragmatic economic benefits too. While items celebrating cultural diversity and cosmopolitanism certainly existed, they were less common. As noted above, there was little engagement with the question of the United Kingdom's sovereignty, which was so central to the Leave referendum campaign. Anti-Brexit organisations in fact seemed to place more confidence in the EU than in their own politicians, and messages explicitly criticising UK politicians, especially Conservative members of government, did indeed form another important category. These messages typically blamed political elites for spreading misinformation, calling into question the arguments on the basis of which many people were presumed to have voted Leave.

DIAGNOSES AND PROGNOSES: PROBLEM IDENTIFICATION, AIMS, AND STRATEGIES

To corroborate the above findings but also to reveal underlying framing strategies, we now present data from our interviews with anti-Brexit activists. In interviewing activists across the United Kingdom, a key aim was to identify which arguments and claims were being made, and why. Interviewees reflected on why they chose certain slogans, messages, and campaign strategies; whether they were responding directly to specific local concerns; and the extent to which they were seeking to counter or challenge particular Eurosceptic perspectives. We begin this section by revealing how activists explain the levels of support for Brexit in their area and the United Kindom more generally – to gauge their starting premise and their understanding of the problem. We then go on to discuss how the activists problematised Brexit and whom they blamed for the adverse outcome in their public messages ('diagnostic' framing). Subsequently, the chapter interrogates what the activists proposed as a political solution, and which visions (if any) they offered in terms of European integration and the United Kingdom's future in Europe ('prognostic' framing). Particular attention will be given to the strategies underlying the choice of particular frames, to whether campaign messages were aligned with activists' personal attitudes and aims, and to the nature of debates or disagreements about aims and messages within the movement.

Explaining support for Brexit

Most activists involved in local campaign groups explained levels of support for Brexit in their area or region in terms of a mix of cultural and economic factors. They invariably highlighted a sustained negative discourse about the EU that was not properly countered either in political and media debates or as part of the education system. When activists identified perpetrators, these were typically the media and national politicians. In the words of one activist from London4Europe:

> I just foresaw this [Brexit] happening. I was one of the
> few people around who felt that we're going to lose this,
> you know, because I could just see the drip, drip, drip
> of 40 years of propaganda from the tabloids and the
> growth and activism of UKIP.
> Interview 1, London4Europe (4 February 2019)

Besides the printed media (usually the *Daily Mail*, the *Daily Express*, and *The Sun*) and far-right actors, national mainstream politicians were frequently blamed for spreading negative propaganda about Europe, and for using the EU as a convenient scapegoat for domestic problems. Many activists felt the EU was unfairly held responsible for social problems (ranging from social inequality to potholes) for which domestic politicians were to blame. At the same time, activists also reckoned that the Brexit vote could partly be interpreted as a vote against the British political establishment. When asked to explain why people backed Brexit in a city that has benefited greatly from EU Structural Funds, activists from Liverpool identified the impact of austerity and people wishing 'to kick the Tory government'.

Several activists also highlighted the failure of those who supported the United Kingdom's membership of the EU to speak out and to counter Euroscepticism within the media and in politics. As an activist from Wales for Europe observed:

> I think it's safe to say now that when you look back at the decades before the referendum, when even pro-European people in Britain largely took it for granted … they took the EU for granted and generally kept their heads down when the London press and the [*Daily*] *Mail* were savaging the EU; there was an assumption that it [Euroscepticism] would all go away.
> Interview 16, Wales for Europe (25 July 2019)

Alongside the role of the media and Eurosceptic politicians, the high levels of support for Brexit in the North East of England were also explained in terms of the local economy and distrust in political elites:

> These areas are run down. [There's] high unemployment and economic problems … [people] tend to think it's getting worse and worse. County Durham lost its pits which is strongly felt in these places. When we ask 'Do you trust the government to invest money in Hartlepool?' the response is along the lines of 'no', because we never get anything anyway … The Tories have never been popular in the North East and are pretty despised. And when you get rich people, Tory ministers standing up and telling you what to do, people will do the opposite. Simple as that.
> Interview 10, North East for Europe (8 March 2019)

As captured in the quote above, there was an overriding sense that the area would suffer regardless of the outcome: continued membership would not deliver benefits, but nor would leaving mean that the (Conservative) government would invest in the area.

Support for Brexit was thus understood as a reaction to years of economic decline and a sense of the region being forgotten by successive governments.

In many of the interviews, it was stated that people had voted for Brexit because they were unaware of the economic and cultural benefits of being part of the EU, or because this had not been made clear to them. In the words of this activist, for example:

> I was obviously always aware of the benefits of being part of Europe. I think others are not aware of the benefits the EU has given to us: no wars and it's kept people together. It is to me *that* which is the ultimate benefit. And I just find it bizarre [that] at a time like this we are actually leaving the organisation that actually prevents wars.
> Interview 24, Falkirk for Europe (25 November 2019)

What also became clear from the interviews is how local or regional idiosyncrasies influenced opinions and debates on EU membership. The previous chapter already alluded to the fact that support for Remain was generally high in Scotland, and also that the issue of Brexit was interwoven with the possibly more salient question of Scottish independence. In the debate about Brexit, support for EU membership was generally associated with a 'pro-indy' position. In Northern Ireland, meanwhile, the dominant cleavage between Republicans and Unionists influenced the debate around Brexit in complex ways: in both communities, Brexit was associated with both challenges and opportunities for their specific cause, in addition to being seen as a threat to the Northern Ireland peace process. This posed challenges to local anti-Brexit organisations. In the words of one activist:

> I think, if anything, it's probably one of the things that hinders us being more active than we actually are, because, my opinion is, trying to find strategies that could appeal across the political spectrum in Northern Ireland can be a challenge. Because no matter what you say, I think in Northern Ireland it will appear to be appealing to one community or another. And that's difficult.
> Interview 7: European Movement Northern Ireland (28 February 2019)

In what follows, we consider in more detail the strategies and messages used by the activists in their aim to mobilise support or sway opinion. The analysis first focuses on the arguments the activists used to convince people about the problems of Brexit (diagnostic framing); and then (debates about) solutions, goals, and visions of the future (prognostic framing) are discussed.

Problematising Brexit: diagnostic framing

Throughout our interviews, it was abundantly clear that the key issue that concerned UK activists was stopping or challenging Brexit; this was 'the problem' and the driver of activism. The anti-Brexit movement was essentially focused on the domestic context and on the immediate goal of remaining within the EU, while the challenges faced by the EU as a whole were all but absent from the movement's diagnostic framing. When activists were asked how they tried to convince people that Brexit was a bad idea, the answer was usually about the status quo (membership) being better than any alternative. In line with messages in many of the campaign materials, continued UK membership was often defended from the perspective of correcting misinformation and misapprehensions regarding the jurisdiction of the EU and the power that the Westminster government retained.

One thing that local activists agreed upon was that simply telling Brexit voters that they had been wrong was not an effective campaign strategy. Local activists described how they challenged pro-Brexit viewpoints carefully and somewhat indirectly, often by pointing out that the culprits of societal problems were national politicians rather than the EU:

> It's not easy and the way that you have to try and do it is kind of coming behind them rather than meeting them head on and saying, 'look, you are wrong', which is never going to go down well. You know, you've got to kind of understand where they're coming from and agree with their problems: 'Yeah, the state of the roads is dreadful; the fact that you can't get a doctor's appointment is dreadful. However, how about this: have you considered that actually, you know, Europe doesn't decide how much money gets spent on your local doctor's surgery. They're not responsible for roads. Who do you think is actually

making that decision?' You know, you've got to sort of acknowledge their pain, if you like, because it's genuine. And you take it from there.
> Interview 13: Lincolnshire for Europe (15 April 2019)

[Brexit supporters] are equating what's happening in society, what's happening in the UK, with us being in the EU and you try to explain: 'Well, we agree with you about the homelessness, absolutely. And all the issues ... we agree about all of those issues, and we're worried about them ourselves. But all these are the fault of our government, and our government has tried to blame the EU.' So we try and get that message out. We are fighting 40 years of indoctrination from the tabloids and the media. So it's hard.
> Interview 14: Stockport for Europe (17 April 2019)

The interviews also highlighted that there was considerable variation across the United Kingdom in terms of the arguments activists deployed in their quest to gain support. The predicted economic impact of Brexit was clearly a prominent theme. Support for Brexit was often strongest in areas that, due to high levels of social deprivation, received considerable EU subsidy. Local activists did broach the issue directly and tried to challenge the belief that the money saved through Brexit would be deployed locally, but this was not an easy argument to pursue:

There's been a lot of EU subsidy in terms of regional development grants. But most people aren't even aware of that kind of money. Where there is more knowledge, I suppose, is in terms of agricultural subsidies, which obviously is the case in an area like Lincolnshire. But the reaction you tend to get is: 'well, it's our money anyway'. You can understand how that mindset works. You know, if you don't recognise what that fifteen billion is buying us and everything we get back from it. If you're not seeing how that money is spent then it's actually seen just as a loss to your economy. To explain that this money would not otherwise go to the local area is a very difficult argument to actually put over.
> Interview 13, Lincolnshire for Europe (15 April 2019)

It was also complex to use an economic rationale for mobilising support against Brexit in Sunderland. Pro-Brexit sympathies remained strong despite concerns that the Nissan car plant, a major employer in the city, would potentially close if Britain left the EU without a trade deal covering the sector. Local activists did raise the issue as part of their campaigning efforts, but they did so with caution. Our interviewees were convinced that it was at best a neutral issue and at worst provoked a negative response from local people. As one Sunderland campaigner explained:

> Well, Nissan made statements over joining the Euro some years ago and this has caused a credibility issue for some people. People say [in response to the claim that Nissan would withdraw from the North East] that they cannot believe this would happen because Nissan are making money and therefore why wouldn't they continue? They say, 'we have such a skilled local workforce' – it provokes a survival instinct. People's eyes glaze over if you start talking about the supply chain ... So, it [the Nissan issue] is not the ace card you think it should be.
> Interview 9, North East/Angels for Europe (7 March 2019)

The same activist emphasised the stark difference with neighbouring Newcastle, which is a larger, more cosmopolitan urban area where it was possible to campaign on the basis of more unapologetically pro-European messages:

> You can easily wear all your EU regalia and be welcomed here, in Newcastle. Sunderland ... it's just basically: you can tell them all you like until you're blue in the face about the benefits of the EU and what they funded, and they just don't listen. But the nearest agreement you'll get is: 'You don't like the Tories, you don't like a "Tory Brexit"; we might have voted for it, but that's not the Brexit we voted for, so we may as well just have the status quo.' Which is basically an anti-Brexit stance, rather than a pro-EU one. I don't really care, so it's like, 'If that works, we'll just use that one.' ... It's just finding that common ground. 'You might have voted for Brexit but no one voted to be poorer.' Because there is no point lecturing someone;

they'll see you as the 'liberal elite' and they're not going to listen to you anyway.

> Interview 9, North East/Angels for Europe (7 March 2019)

One activist in Greater Manchester similarly argued that, in strongly Brexit-supporting areas, there was little point in referring to EU membership benefits such as visa-free travel, the freedom to study and work abroad, and enabling scientific collaboration:

> If you're in an area where people don't travel, that doesn't really mean anything to them. They're like: 'Well, so what? What have I lost then?' So you have to start talking about loss of investment and loss of jobs: ... 'A no deal would lose us jobs and that will impact on these areas more than any other areas. It's not going to impact on [Conservative MP] Jacob Rees-Mogg and Boris Johnson and people like that.' So you're coming [at] it from that angle. Talk about workers' rights, losing rights. You can also talk about losing environmental protection, but people don't seem to be as worried about that.
>
> Interview 14: Stockport for Europe (17 April 2019)

Unsurprisingly, given its proximity to mainland Europe and the cosmopolitan nature of the capital, London activists tended to emphasise travel and free movement more than activists elsewhere did. This London activist noted that these themes were often employed in conversations with younger people in particular:

> Different audiences will obviously have different buttons that will appeal to them ... [When speaking to young people] the appeal was usually, you know, free travel and the ability to work, live and study and opportunities in twenty-seven different countries and mobile roaming and apprenticeship opportunities and Erasmus and all this sort of stuff.
>
> Interview 1, London4Europe (4 February 2019)

Activists in London and other cities with a larger left-liberal community were clearly more prepared to emphasise positive messages about the EU and challenge a broader array of Eurosceptic positions. Messages were nevertheless tailored when speaking to more Eurosceptic fellow citizens. When asked how to defend the United Kingdom's membership and counter support for Brexit, one activist offered this rather pragmatic response:

> I think one ought to say: 'Look, these are our neighbours. We should cooperate with them just because they are. If we cooperate and pool our sovereignty, we get more.' Sovereignty is not something beautiful.
> Interview 11, London/Watford for Europe (12 March 2019)

Beyond arguments pertaining to the economy and the practical benefits of open borders, some activists from across the country also articulated their support for the EU and European integration in terms of what might broadly be referred to as 'the peace dividend'. This appeared to have particular resonance in some areas:

> I tell you the thing that's interesting. On the streets, when you talk to people on street stalls, the whole issue of international peace comes up, thankfully, surprisingly often and I think it was a message that was totally missed in the Remain campaign.
> Interview 16, Wales for Europe (25 July 2019)

Unsurprisingly, peace also had salience in Northern Ireland. As previously referred to, activists emphasised that Brexit would lead to a 'hard border' between Northern Ireland and the Irish Republic, which in turn would aggravate tensions between Republicans and Unionists.

Notably, the vast majority of local activists interviewed did not seem confident about trying to highlight the problems of ending free movement. They typically avoided framing the issue of immigration in a positive manner, and most expressed reservations about raising it as part of their campaigning. While privately convinced about the merits of open borders and free movement, many of our interviewees accepted that defending immigration was potentially problematic in terms of winning over Brexit supporters. When the issue was raised, it was typically approached from the perspective of correcting misinformation and misapprehensions rather than by making the case for open borders per se. In the words of one activist:

> For a start, you point out to them [Brexit supporters] all the half-truths that are talked about immigration. So, the fact that, for example, most immigration comes from outside the EU, we can already control that but we choose not to, or choose not to do it as strongly as some people would like. Nothing to do with the EU, and the EU doesn't cause it. Because that tends to be the assumption that, you know, 'we get all this immigration from the EU and the EU makes us do that'; no, it doesn't. That's entirely our choice. You talk to them about the safeguards that we could put in place now under the EU law.
> Interview 13, Lincolnshire for Europe (15 April 2019)

What becomes clear from the discussion thus far is that, especially when confronted with a Eurosceptic audience, activists' messages about the problems of Brexit tended to focus more on the disadvantages of the United Kingdom leaving the EU than on the merits of the EU as an organisation or the principle of European integration. This was evidently the case in Brexit-leaning areas, but even in more cosmopolitan parts of the country activists saw the need to strategically moderate their private enthusiasm for the EU. As this activist in one of such areas explained:

> Probably the most difficult emotional dynamic I have to deal with as current chair of Bristol for Europe [relates to] the volunteer base, who want to stand on a street corner wrapping themselves in an EU flag, shouting to everyone 'how much I love the EU', and tell people factually why they are incorrect. Because they [the volunteers] are people that care about facts, and they find people that don't know the facts incredibly frustrating. They get angry that people don't know these facts. But we also know that that is exactly the wrong tactic, if we want to win a referendum when it comes along.
> Interview 15: Bristol for Europe (6 June 2019)

To the extent that they were enthusiastic about European integration, younger activists operating from London-based organisations similarly indicated their caution in expressing praise for the EU in conversations with Eurosceptic people. In the words of one OFOC campaigner, for instance:

> I generally start by saying: 'Listen, I am what used to be called "somewhat of a Eurosceptic", and I don't think this is a perfect institution. The lack of transparency on lobbying, for example, is something that really really really frustrates me about the EU.' … I'd say, 'I don't think it's a perfect institution, but the future that we were all promised outside of it is not real, and the reality is far worse.' I make the case that, on balance, it's better to stay in.
>
> Interview 12: Our Future Our Choice (26 March 2019)

Another prominent challenge that activists struggled with was that factual arguments about specific issues or policy areas were often ineffective in terms of convincing Eurosceptic people that Brexit was problematic. One London activist expressed it as follows:

> The challenge is always boiling it down into simple, readily understood messages. And that is extremely difficult … I think, at the end of the day, many of them just won't go for the economic arguments. I think the crux of it is that their perception [is] that their sovereignty is being taken away from them. And then you have to go into the complex arguments about how, you know, pooling sovereignty makes us punch above our weight in the world, and it all gets a bit wonky. The obvious difficulty we have is, you know, how do we rebut the simplistic and misleading arguments of the Leavers that are, on the surface of it, seemingly seductive and true, when what we believe is the truth is a complicated explanation which they may not readily relate to?
>
> Interview 1: European Movement/London4Europe (4 February 2019)

Activists in other parts of the country similarly lamented the difficulty the anti-Brexit campaign faced with formulating arguments that resonated with Brexit supporters. There was a widespread conviction that merely listing facts was insufficient and that arguments also needed to make an impact at an emotional level:

> It doesn't involve bullet-point lists, for sure. Because facts are not effective on the target audience. We've got to use

rhetoric. The logical argument is not what's going to win this ... You might use some facts, but you've got to get the person who's reading your literature to be like: 'Oh, I actually feel like the EU is something I want.'
Interview 15: Bristol for Europe (6 June 2019)

And that has always been a problem for the pro-European campaign: to try and mobilise people at an emotive level, rather than at a cerebral level.
Interview 25: Lincolnshire for Europe (28 May 2020)

Overall, the data suggest a preparedness to adapt campaign strategies to suit local contexts. However, in terms of countering Eurosceptic narratives, explaining why Brexit was problematic, and mobilising support for both Remain and the EU, the majority of local campaigns relied heavily on diagnostic frames that highlighted the adverse effects of Brexit and that shifted blame or rectifed misinformation rather than presenting a positive vision of the EU and the United Kingdom's role within it. Much of the campaigning via street stalls and through face-to-face contact was about defending the status quo. There was evident difficulty in formulating a convincing economic case for the United Kingdom's continued membership or in defending the EU as it existed (i.e. the single market and open borders for people, goods, and services), and especially doing so in a way that did not sound like 'project fear'.

One salient finding from the interview data was the reluctance of many local activists to engage with the issue of immigration in positive ways. If it were talked about at all, it was often in terms of the necessity of having migrant workers to support the UK economy or the NHS, or by trying to point out that leaving the EU would not necessarily reduce numbers entering the United Kingdom. The next section will move from analysing the messages that focused on diagnosing the current situation and problematising Brexit to looking at the movement's publicly proposed solutions and visions, i.e. prognostic frames, and debates about those solutions and visions within the movement.

Campaign objectives and visions of the future: prognostic framing

What were the aims and visions that anti-Brexit campaigners presented to their audience? While we have already seen that activists were often careful not to come across as too Europhile, there was an overt commitment from most of those involved in local campaigns to remain inside the EU and to cancel Brexit altogether. The response of this activist from Bristol captures the prevailing view among the majority of local activists interviewed:

> Open Britain were initially peddling the idea of a soft Brexit which we didn't support at all. Bristol for Europe is basically [committed] to keeping Britain in the European Union. It's not about a Norway style relationship. We want to stay in the European Union and we think that is a feasible goal which is worth fighting for. And we're not really considering the alternatives until that becomes a goal that has been ruled out.
> Interview 15, Bristol for Europe (6 June 2019)

Amongst activists, 'keeping Britian in the EU' meant retaining the status quo rather than any notion of a different relationship or a reformed union. There was a general consensus across interviews that the EU as it existed and functioned was not perfect and required reform, but few activists came up with concrete plans to improve its performance or legitimacy. In many cases, part of this reluctance was ostensibly fed by a lack of genuine in-depth knowledge about the EU and its institutions. Indeed, many activists were not afraid to admit they knew little about the EU prior to the referendum, and that they had previously hardly followed EU-related news and developments. Without exception, activists answered with a 'no' when asked whether the functioning of the EU was a prominent discussion topic within their organisations or whether ideas about the EU's future played a role within their public messaging. It was clear that activists were reluctant to be drawn on these issues and did not consider the time ripe for such discussions, given that averting Brexit was the more pressing task at hand:

> We do have it in our constitution that we are, you know, we're Remainers and we keep a watching brief over reform of the European Union. But, I mean, with Brexit the rest of the world has fallen off the edge. And so we're not particularly interested in reforming the EU at the moment.
> Interview 1: European Movement/London4Europe (4 February 2019)

> We tend not to have those discussions. I was involved with a London-based group that talked about European democracy and citizenship. I think it's a bit too abstract to have traction in the debates we're going to have in the next ninety days to twelve months.
> Interview 4, Liverpool for Europe (26 February 2019)

> I don't think now's the time [to discuss reforming the EU]. I mean, one risk you have to avoid is 'remain and reform', which is what some people want to campaign for. I think it's absolutely right the EU should be reformed and it will reform. But what you can't do is say 'the following ten reforms are going to happen if you vote Remain', because you can't deliver that. So I think there is a danger in going down identifying desirable reforms.
> Interview 11, London/Watford for Europe (12 March 2019)

Despite a clear desire to overturn the 2016 referendum decision and for the United Kingdom to remain within the EU, the vast majority of local organisations campaigned for the so-called People's Vote once the PV campaign was launched in April 2018 (see chapter 4). The campaign for a People's Vote thus became the main focus and the dominant mantra of local activism across the country. There was a widespread recognition among activists that the movement needed to be clearer about its ultimate goal. Evaluating the merits of the PV campaign strategy, this activist was unsure about any feasible alternative to the People's Vote message:

> You can only campaign *against* something for so long, before you have to start campaigning *for* something. Because, quite rightly, the people you are talking to are going to start asking you: 'Well, what is it you want? You don't want that, what is it you do want?' And so you have to actually have something positive to be able to tell people.
> Interview 25: Lincolnshire for Europe (28 May 2020)

The demand for a People's Vote, presented as a democratic means to avert Brexit, also served to retort the claim that anti-Brexit campaigners failed to admit to their loss and tried to overturn the 'will of the people'. In light of this, the term 'second referendum', which could suggest the desire to overturn a democratic decision, was avoided for strategic reasons. As this activist explained, moreover, the focus on another public vote as an objective enabled campaigners to reach out to some Leave voters and those who were having doubts about how Brexit was taking form in practice:

> I say to people [on a stall or while leafleting], we want the People's Vote. If they say they voted to leave I say, 'OK, but do you think it's going well?' I ask them, 'Why do you think we haven't left yet?' And then, 'Do you think it [Theresa May's proposed deal] is a good deal?' Quite a lot of people say, 'No, it isn't.' And you then say: 'Well, do you think we need another vote so we can compare May's deal with what we have now?'
> Interview 14, Stockport for Europe (17 April 2019)

As discussed in the previous chapter, however, the PV campaign would ultimately be marked by serious organisational schisms and conflicts about strategy and campaign resources. The campaign's messaging similarly attracted controversy. Some of the more radical organisations, such as SODEM, continued to operate independently from the PV umbrella, persisting to campaign with the decisive message to 'Stop Brexit'. Best for Britain similarly felt the need to continue campaigning on the basis of an unequivocal pro-European message. As the group's CEO Naomi Smith explained:

> It came back to the mission. Because the People's Vote campaign was always about just trying to secure the referendum, we were worried that if we had gone in with them, nobody would have been doing the work to make sure we won it, if we ever got it. So we had to keep separate, because there had to be a different organisation talking about why Europe is a good thing. No one had done that for forty years, no one had tried to combat the Murdoch press being anti-Europe. Even the pro-European parties like, for instance, the Liberal Democrats [did not sufficiently acknowledge the benefits of the EU].
> Interview 31: Best for Britain (29 June 2021)

Furthermore, while many local activists appropriated PV messaging, they were very clear that they continued to want Brexit stopped. As expressed by the following activist and organiser, this caused a level of tension within the movement as well as between local activists and national campaign organisers:

> I think there's an interesting dynamic happening. I think some of the London-based organisations, who are very into the whole sort of Westminster thing, their argument would be: 'Look, we still haven't won a referendum yet; the argument has got to be about the referendum.' But if you go out into the grassroots ... the local groups are now desperate to get on to the front foot and say: 'We want to stop Brexit and we want to stay in Europe for positive reasons.'
> Interview 16: Wales for Europe (25 July 2019)

Former PV head of campaigns Tom Brufatto also spoke of the tensions that emerged within the movement precisely because it managed to attract both committed pro-Europeans and those who were primarily concerned with the democratic process or the practical execution of Brexit:

> The tent became a lot broader very quickly. And so of course that meant that within the demographics of the movement there started to be more tensions, especially at the grassroots levels. There were local groups that were more in favour of 'we don't want to talk about the EU, we are here because we want to do democracy right', and there were groups that were completely uninterested in talking about the democracy side and were totally focused on re-joining.
> Interview 30: BfE/EM/PV/March for Change
> (18 June 2021)

Recognising that, in the end, most activists wanted to stay in the EU, Brufatto also emphasised the challenging balancing act of campaigning on the basis of a single message while still making sure the messaging resonated with local sentiments towards EU membership:

> Most people in the movement, the activists, were there to
> stop Brexit. I don't think there's a huge amount of debate
> about that. But in terms of the progression of the groups,
> lots of the local groups in the Remain areas obviously
> felt the frustration more than anyone else, because they
> were effectively going with a message that was 'softer'
> than their target audience. However, the ones that were
> outside of the Remain areas, that really wanted to stop
> Brexit but were pushing against the grain, they're the
> ones that really benefited from the PV message because it
> did give them some form of support. Otherwise they were
> switching people off … But the tension was always there,
> and it wasn't easy. You know, ideologically, people come to
> politics to fight for what they believe in, and it's a big ask
> sometimes to say 'Well, we need to soften the message to
> make inroads.'
>
> Interview 30: BfE/EM/PV/March for Change
> (18 June 2021)

Frustration with the 'soft' lukewarm messaging was voiced by many, such as the following activist who was not particularly convinced about the PV aim to appeal to a constituency beyond Remainers:

> I would personally rather be more committed. I mean,
> PV are trying to take a line that they're not a Remain
> campaign; they're just trying campaigning for people
> to have the option. To me, I don't see the point in that,
> because the reality is that's what we're trying to do
> [campaigning to Remain], so you may as well be honest
> about it.
>
> Interview 5: Anonymous (26 February 2019)

Several activists went further and saw the focus on a People's Vote as an error in terms of a campaign strategy. The following quote from a London activist sums up the concerns:

> There is no Remain campaign because People's Vote has
> quite explicitly made itself not a Remain campaign, and no
> one else is doing it. And PV sucks up all the money and all

the enthusiasm. People who want to prevent [Brexit] are
demoralised by the People's Vote.
Interview 11, London/Watford for Europe (12 March 2019)

Richard Wilson, the co-founder of Grassroots for Europe, which was set up as a reaction against the centralised PV campaign, was equally dismissive of the strategic focus on a new referendum. According to Wilson, PV's campaign distracted from voicing powerful arguments in favour of EU membership:

> Fundamentally, this concept of having a campaign where you try and persuade people 'what we need is another vote', to me was fundamentally flawed. The public were not interested in having another vote for the sake of it. They were sick of the whole thing. You had to give them a reason for wanting to revisit the question of Brexit, and that reason had to be on the fundamentals of, you know, ripping apart 'Europe is not a good thing'. Being part of Europe is the greatest peace project in history, it's great for our economy, for our freedoms, for spreading democracy across the continent, ending wars. Perhaps I'm idealistic. I probably am, but I think you'd hear that a lot from the grassroots, that type of thing. We wanted the powerful, emotional messages. Because the Leave side, they won it – we know this – on emotional knee-jerk messaging, not on technicalities, not on facts. Everyone will say this. It's not about bombarding people with facts and figures, because we know perfectly well that doesn't work.
> Interview 28: Leeds for Europe/Grassroots for Europe (5 June 2020)

Ultimately, however, most local groups remained broadly committed to following PV's lead. Despite widespread acceptance of the People's Vote as a campaign focus and strategy, there was no coherent strategy among activists about how the case for remaining in the EU would be made as part of any such future referendum campaign. For example, when asked about free movement of people and migration, we gained no sense of a clear and cogent position having been formulated. The response below from an activist in North East for Europe reflects the lack of a prognostic perspective:

> We would all agree that you need to say something about freedom of movement and immigration. We can't just ignore it. I'm not sure what we would say but we can't get away with just saying that Theresa May's deal doesn't stop freedom of movement. I don't know how ... We've concentrated more on campaigning rather than what are solutions to some of these future problems. Because the big problem is staying in Europe and staying in the European Union.
> Interview 10, North East/Angels for Europe (7 March 2019)

When asked specifically about how free movement would be addressed as part of a future referendum campaign, the same activist responded, after a long pause: 'Don't know, is the answer.' Similarly, when asked about what issues besides the economy should be central during a second referendum campaign in favour of EU membership, one OFOC activist answered:

> That's very hard to say. It has not actually been something we have been able to spend that much time thinking about. We've mostly been on the idea of 'we need to secure a People's Vote'. And the message that we are going to try and spread once we've got it, is something that we haven't had that much time to think and talk about.
> Interview 12: Our Future Our Choice (26 March 2019)

When pressed, most activists seemed to imply that any such campaign would focus on defending the status quo, highlighting the risks of leaving, and exposing the inaccuracies of the pro-Brexit campaign. Yet it was clear that a coherent campaign strategy had not been worked out. Months after the collapse of PV, this Liverpool activist reflected on the detrimental impact of the movement's lack of a clear aim:

> The messaging and branding was completely confused. I don't mean just not sort of elegantly worded and all that. I mean, actually there were some fundamental contradictions between People's Vote and the broader Remainer campaign, which were never resolved and

which were obvious to everyone and obvious to us as street campaigners. People's Vote was: 'Well, we're not really campaigning either to remain or to leave, we just want a People's Vote.' Of course that had no credibility at all with, you know, 'Liverpool for Europe' splashed all over our t-shirts. We never really did resolve that. And unfortunately there were so many campaigns ... So there was just total incoherence in the messages, which was one of the principal reasons it failed.
>
> Interview 26: Liverpool for Europe (28 May 2020)

Overall, in terms of the activism that became ubiquitous in the aftermath of the referendum, our data suggest that while the greater clarity and certainty often expressed in campaign materials was reflected in the personal opinions of anti-Brexit activists, this was not always evident when activists spoke to Eurosceptic people on the street. After the launch of the PV campaign, the primary focus became the quest for a second referendum, with little room for prognostic frames related to the future of European integration or the United Kingdom's place in the EU.

CONCLUSION

By deciphering the claims and messages used by a wide variety of anti-Brexit organisations, this chapter has captured and analysed how 'Europe' was conceptualised among activists and groups. What we have revealed is that despite being overwhelmingly supportive of a new referendum, most activists first and foremost privately wanted to stop Brexit. While activists were generally pro-EU, they were prepared to concede criticism of the European Union as it currently functions. However, during the course of interviews we were rarely presented with any concrete ideas about institutional reform or a different kind of 'Europe'. This lack of a clear 'critical Europeanist' vision was further reflected both in the survey data and in the analysis of the campaign materials. Local activists individually expressed visions of Europe that conjured their experiences of travelling and expressed a strong sense of Europe as a cultural identity.

However, in expressing the objectives of their campaign or organisation in public, a much more parsimonious vision of the EU was offered. Apart from the occasional utterance about the need for reform, on the key issues of immigration and the single market there were few genuinely robust endorsements of the free movement of goods, people, services, and capital. Visions of 'Europe', the EU, and the United Kingdom's position within it were framed predominantly in terms of the status quo; membership was seen as better than any possible alternative that Brexit might deliver. Activists' strong personal expression of support for the United Kingdom remaining in the EU thus contrasted with the more cautious and measured strategic messaging they deployed in the course of their activism and during interactions with local citizens. Especially when interacting with Eurosceptics on the front line, activists emphasised misinformation, reapportioned blame, and mainly highlighted the harm of leaving the EU.

Immigration, despite its salience within the Leave campaign, was usually avoided. When the issue did come up, it was often discussed through a socio-economic frame or from the perspective of migrants being needed to sustain the NHS or other local industries. With the exception of activists within particularly cosmopolitan urban areas (e.g. Bristol, London, and Liverpool), there was relatively little celebration of cultural diversity in the movement's messages, and no strong defence of free movement. The Leave campaign's central 'Take Back Control' slogan was not genuinely rebutted. What was particularly noteworthy was the lack of any concerted attempt to challenge the notion that the United Kingdom's membership of the EU represented a compromise of sovereignty. The closest that local campaigns seemed to get to the issue of sovereignty was to stress how EU membership had delivered a peace dividend and had augmented the United Kingdom's security and its international clout. The overarching focus on a People's Vote as the aim of local anti-Brexit organisations obfuscated the fundamental and strong 'Remain' commitment of these activists. The People's Vote objective further removed the incentive to really think about positive arguments for continued EU membership, as the focus was placed so much on the means (referendum instrument) rather than the end (staying in the EU).

In terms of the movement's framing of 'Europe', therefore, our data reveal a high degree of pragmatism, some variation according to local contexts, and an overriding emphasis on correcting perceived untruths and misinformation. Certainly in heavily Leave-supporting areas, local campaigns focused primarily on the deleterious economic impact of Brexit, and messaging was usually underpinned by the claim that the status quo was better than any post-Brexit scenario. Considering the need to sway undecided voters and 'soft Leavers' in a potential second referendum, such a cautious defence of EU membership was entirely understandable. Yet given the activists' often-gloomy portrayal of the current domestic political situation, the movement's framing amounted to a rather awkward and half-hearted defence of the pre-referendum status quo (i.e. the status quo ante). The difficult challenge for the anti-Brexit movement was to strike a balance between criticising the status quo ante just enough to acknowledge that there was a problem requiring a solution, while at the same time bolstering support for the existing arrangements. The EU had been given so much negative attention in political discussions and media coverage over the years that the anti-Brexit movement faced a very difficult task in terms of formulating resonant messages. Despite the considerable mobilisation of people across the country in the aftermath of the June 2016 vote, the grassroots movement's approach and rhetoric was ultimately all too similar to the failed Stronger In referendum campaign.

6

Conclusion

The provocation for writing this book and for conducting the underpinning research was twofold. First, we were triggered by watching the anti-Brexit movement as a remarkable phenomenon in and of itself. Witnessing citizens openly, noisily, and enthusiastically defending 'Europe' was unprecedented not just in the United Kingdom, but is a rarity across the European Union. Second, such politicisation 'from below' has implications for academic theories across the fields of EU studies and social movement research. The anti-Brexit movement, emerging rapidly, generally without direct linkage to political parties or national elites, appearing to gain momentum against a backdrop of several large London demonstrations but ultimately failing, is surely a phenomenon worthy of sustained and careful analysis. We undertook this study to discover why the anti-Brexit movement did not manage to galvanise sufficient support and influence to stop Brexit, or at least to shape the terms of the United Kingdom's departure. This concluding chapter seeks to bring together the various parts of the preceding analysis and to highlight implications for further research on the 'politicisation of Europe' as well as for social movements that exist not to challenge but to defend the status quo.

THE EMERGENCE AND THE EFFICACY OF THE ANTI-BREXIT MOVEMENT

In designing the research and undertaking this study, our aim has been to offer a comprehensive evaluation of the emergence and efficacy of the anti-Brexit movement as a case study of a pro-European grassroots movement. We deployed the framework proposed by social movement scholars McAdam, McCarthy, and Zald (1996) to analyse whether the rise and the ultimate failure of the movement to alter the course of events was a consequence of three dynamic and interrelated conditions: (i) systemic and institutional constraints (political opportunity structure), (ii) the movement's organisation and use of resources (mobilising structures), and (iii) the way activists articulated their cause (framing processes).

Though unprecedented in scale and intensity, the anti-Brexit movement was not the first expression of pro-European political activity in the United Kingdom. The most obvious comparison was with the 1975 campaign to keep Britain in the EEC – a mobilisation that arguably realised a measure of quite considerable success (Smedley 2020). In seeking to identify what was different about the post-2016 campaign and why a grassroots movement emerged, chapter 3 focused on the political opportunity structure within which the movement emerged and operated in the period between the referendum campaign in 2016 and the United Kingdom's formal departure from the EU in January 2020. We argued that it was necessary not only to place the anti-Brexit movement in historical context, but also to capture how the political opportunity structure explained both the type of activism and the ultimate efficacy of its action.

We described the growing predominance of Eurosceptic sentiment in the United Kingdom, a media environment that actively fuelled anti-EU attitudes, and the presence of two dominant mainstream parties, Labour and the Conservatives, that have been internally divided about the merits of European integration. In the most recent decades, the rise of the UK Independence Party (UKIP), whose original founding purpose was urging the United Kingdom to leave the EU, transformed party-political dynamics. While support for UKIP in national elections remained limited, the party pushed the case for leaving the EU up the political agenda and emboldened the Eurosceptic wing of the Conservative Party. The ensuing political pressure was instrumental to Prime Minister David Cameron's decision to call the referendum on the United Kingdom's membership of the EU.

At first sight, it appears surprising that a pro-European grassroots movement would develop in such a hostile political environment. Indeed, prior to the referendum of June 2016 there was no network of pro-European organisations to speak of. The official Stronger In

Remain campaign only had a short history, it was London-based, and it lacked a developed activist base in local communities. The UK chapter of the European Movement (EM), which had played an active role prior to the EEC membership referendum of 1975, subsequently turned into a rather dormant 'wine and cheese club', with little capacity to campaign and mobilise a wide demographic. After the referendum, however, a labyrinth of anti-Brexit initiatives emerged, and local groups across the country were established that affiliated themselves with new or revamped national umbrella organisations, including the EM and Britain for Europe (BfE).

The mobilisation of grassroots anti-Brexit opposition after the referendum vote was a consequence of pro-European positions being left insufficiently represented at the party-political level. The pro-European Liberal Democrats, the main 'third party' in recent decades, was going through an electoral slump, and the Scottish National Party had both limited geographical appeal and other priorities (namely, Scottish independence). At the same time, the referendum outcome itself placed considerable pressure on politicians of the two main parties to support some form of Brexit, given that overturning an ostensibly democratic decision carried political risks. Meanwhile, Open Britain, the successor of the official Stronger In campaign, initially set a 'soft' Brexit as its aim. In the immediate aftermath of the referendum there were, in other words, insufficient elite allies that pro-Remain citizens could rely on, which in turn explains the mobilisation of a network of grassroots anti-Brexit organisations and initiatives.

As discussed in chapter 4, most of the citizens involved in anti-Brexit activism had been inactive during the referendum campaign. Our interviewees typically described how they had been jolted into action through shock at the result and a desire for solidarity and determination to try to shape the subsequent course of events. Many had not foreseen the referendum outcome and expressed regret and a degree of remorse for not having been active during the referendum campaign. In the absence of an existing infrastructure for pro-European activism, it is no surprise that the mobilisation of local groups and initiatives occurred in an ad hoc fashion, with little direction from any central organisation. The movement continued to be fragmented throughout its existence. While BfE and the EM began to act as national umbrellas for the local groups, there continued to be a variety of initiatives and organisations (including Open Britain, Scientists for EU, Another Europe is Possible, and Best for Britain, to name several prominent examples). Even though there existed collaboration and synergy between these initiatives, with individual activists often being affiliated with a variety of organisations, the anti-Brexit movement as a whole remained heterogeneous in terms of strategies, priorities, ideology, and eventual goals.

Towards the end of 2017 and in the early months of 2018, efforts were made to integrate various initiatives and concentrate on a clearer aim. Eventually, some of the key organisations joined forces and launched the People's Vote (PV) campaign in April 2018. Not only was this initiative relevant in terms of the movement's organisational evolution, but it also had a large impact on the key messaging of the campaign. Not least to broaden the appeal beyond ardent Remainers and EU-enthusiasts, the central focus of the campaign became forcing a public vote on the outcome of UK–EU negotiations (as we have said before, the term 'second referendum', which could suggest the desire to overturn a democratic decision, was avoided for strategic reasons). While some organisations remained unaffiliated and chose to continue their more unambiguous campaign to stop Brexit (e.g. SODEM, Best for Britain), many local groups were effectively folded under the PV initiative due to their affiliation with BfE and the EM. This process came to an abrupt end when the central PV organisation imploded in October 2019, just ahead of the general election of December 2019 – an election that saw a large victory for Boris Johnson's Conservatives, which in turn erased any hope of halting the Brexit process.

This leads us on from the emergence and evolution of the movement to the question of why the movement failed to stop Brexit, to force a People's Vote, or even to secure a 'soft' version of Brexit by means of 'damage limitation'. While the collapse of PV as an organisation certainly played a role here, the 'failure to remain' is explained by an interplay of factors related to political opportunities, mobilising structures, and framing strategies. As became clear from chapter 3, while the *emergence* and growth of the movement were largely driven by a disconnect between pro-European citizens and political elites, the political opportunity structure was ultimately hostile to its chances of *success*. To succeed, the movement needed the linkage to power and elites that political parties are normally able to provide. Yet that linkage proved tenuous at best and non-existent at worst. In the aftermath of the 2016 referendum, the Conservative government sought to honour the plebiscite's outcome, and the Tories increasingly became a 'hard Brexit' party under Boris Johnson's leadership (Hayton 2021). Labour's position on future UK–EU relations was ambiguous, and the leadership of Corbyn intensified ideological divisions on this issue as well as others – between representatives, but also between Labour's leadership and the party's support base.

Particularly important was the malign *discursive* opportunity structure and how it had developed over a longer period. The EU as a project had few vocal proponents in the decades leading up to the referendum, while popular tabloid print media sustained a long tradition of Eurosceptic and Europhobic editorial stances that were echoed in particular by UKIP and the Eurosceptic wing of the Conservative Party. The prevailing discourse and norms about 'Europe' made it extremely difficult for potential pro-European activists wishing to mobilise either in defence of the status quo or for further European integration.

This discursive context also had a clear impact on the way anti-Brexit groups mobilised, and particularly on their messaging. As discussed in chapter 5, the local groups that formed more or less spontaneously in the aftermath of the referendum consisted of convinced Remainers who were keen to highlight the advantages of EU membership – typically in combination with the perceived disingenuousness of Leave-supporting politicians – and to stop the Brexit process altogether. Yet within certain parts of the anti-Brexit camp there also existed the conviction that mobilising pro-European segments of the population was insufficient to alter the outcome of the Brexit process. Formulating a single key message that defended continued EU membership and resonated with an audience beyond Remainers was a genuine challenge. First, there was a widespread acknowledgement of the difficulty of convincing Eurosceptic citizens in the short span of time that was available prior to the United Kingdom 'Brexiting', precisely because of the enduring negative coverage the EU had received over the past decades. Second, campaigners faced the reality of great geographical differences in terms of support for Leave or Remain. Understandably, messages were tailored to the local context, with pro-European claims being very subdued in heavily Leave-supporting areas.

Reflecting the lack of consensus about the best 'framing strategy', but also actual disagreements about the United Kingdom's future in Europe, the multitude of anti-Brexit organisations and initiatives for a long time presented a variety of messages and aims – varying between acceptance of a 'soft Brexit' at one end of the spectrum and revoking Article 50 at the other. The PV campaign that emerged in April 2018 was an attempt not only to campaign based on a single 'positive' message (*for* a People's Vote), but also to bring into the fray those who may have supported Brexit at the time of the referendum but had grown disappointed with the way the process was evolving. Many pro-European activists, however, desired a more unambiguous pro-European message. This was certainly the case in larger metropolitan settings with a university population and a relatively high level of social and cultural diversity. In such areas endorsement of EU membership was strong, and local groups continued to show overt support for the EU even if this was strictly speaking against the line of the PV campaign. This led to an awkward tension in terms of campaign rhetoric, certainly considering that the EU flag and insignia were omnipresent at the large marches in the capital and elsewhere. What is more, with the focus shifting so decisively towards the goal of securing a second public vote, much less energy was expended on devising campaign strategies for a potential new referendum campaign. Even if a second referendum were to be held, what would the pro-EU/anti-Brexit arguments and messaging be? Most activists interviewed could not provide an answer to such a fundamental question.

What became clear throughout chapters 4 and 5 was how different views about the best strategy – either mobilising pro-European citizens or swaying (soft) Leavers – continued to exist. What activists generally acknowledged and regretted, however, was the difficulty of enthusing and mobilising ethnic minorities and, in particular, a younger generation of citizens. This was a source of frustration, given that younger people overwhelmingly voted in favour of Remain during the 2016 referendum, albeit that they came out in lower numbers than did older voters (Moore 2016). Post-referendum anti-Brexit local grassroots groups were largely run by activists from a narrow demographic (white, more highly educated, and middle aged or older), who typically engaged in traditional forms of action (street stalls, marches). It is true that specific organisations (OFOC, FFS) emerged that were led by and engaged with young people, but many interviewees expressed their frustration with the apparent apathy of the younger generation concerning the issue of EU membership. It is indeed notable that the focus of OFOC and FFS activists we interviewed was more on securing a People's Vote than on defending the EU – a finding that stands in contrast with the pro-integration idealism that was found among young campaigners prior to the 1975 referendum (Smedley 2020).

This does not take away from the fact that the mobilisation and achievements of the newly founded and largely grassroots-driven anti-Brexit initiatives were remarkable. Over the course of many months, Britain had the most proactive pro-European grassroots movement in Europe, capable of mobilising hundreds of thousands to demonstrate and protest. Never before had large crowds marched through the streets across the United Kingdom in defence of EU membership. A People's Vote was for some time a potential scenario largely due to the combined efforts of local activists and national umbrella organisations. Ultimately, however, there were a variety of interacting conditions that made a successful outcome for the anti-Brexit movement increasingly unlikely. Without the active allegiance of elite allies (particularly the leadership of the Labour Party) and an effective organisation capable of reaching new constituencies of support via resonant messaging, the movement's chances of overturning the 2016 referendum vote – generally respected as a democratic decision – were always slim.

In terms of post-Brexit Britain, the government of Boris Johnson left the EU with a 'hard' Brexit deal and the United Kingdom has remained embroiled in what are likely to be long and bitter negotiations with 'Brussels' regarding the Northern Ireland protocol and other contentious issues. An imminent re-accession is extremely unlikely, and the main objective of many of the United Kingdom's remaining pro-European organisations has consequently been to secure the closest possible relationship with the bloc. Organisations such as Another Europe is Possible and Best for Britain have made the case that various international challenges – including security threats, the climate crisis, and the impact of the Covid-19 pandemic – necessitate pan-European and global cooperation (see, for example, Smith 2021). The anti-Brexit movement has therefore certainly left a legacy in the shape of a network of organisations that strive for European and international cooperation. If and when the issue of EU membership appears back on the UK political agenda, it remains to be seen whether this potentially enables pro-European activists to widen their support base and make a cogent and renewed case for 'Europe' with a clear set of arguments.

IMPLICATIONS FOR PRO-EUROPEAN ACTIVISM AND THE POLITICISATION OF EUROPE

The case of the anti-Brexit movement presents us with a rare but pertinent example of how politicisation of European integration can also be driven by grassroots movements with an explicit pro-European agenda. As discussed in chapter 2, the extant literature focuses mainly on Eurosceptic political parties as key drivers of politicisation (see, for example, Hutter and Grande 2014; Kriesi 2016; Dolezal and Hellström 2016). While there are various studies that consider the way in which the EU and its institutions are perceived and approached by a variety of social movement organisations (see, for example, Reising 1999; Marks and McAdam 1999; Imig and Tarrow 2001; della Porta and Caiani 2009), this literature is interested primarily in how various social movements have used the political opportunities afforded them by the EU to further their campaigns. What barely exist are studies concentrating on the general course of European integration as the *subject* of politicisation in the protest arena (see, for example, Brändle et al. 2018; FitzGibbon 2013; van Kessel and Fagan 2022b).

The fact that such protests have remained relatively uncommon is one obvious explanation; the issue of European integration has been more salient in the electoral arena than in the protest arena (see, for example, Dolezal et al. 2016). Only a limited number of studies have described the 'critical Europeanist' positions of radical left SMOs (della Porta and Caiani 2009; della Porta 2020a) or the EU-sceptic 'Europe of sovereign nations' vision of far-right movements (Caiani and Weisskircher 2019). While some grassroots organisations have thus taken an explicit stance on the EU and the future of European integration, these themes are usually only a (minor) part of their broader agenda. While rarely rejecting any form of European integration outright, SMOs on both the radical left and the radical right tend to be critical of current institutional arrangements, processes, and outcomes (Caiani and Weisskircher 2022).

The anti-Brexit movement that emerged in the United Kingdom is different in two key respects. First, its exclusive focus was the issue of EU membership, and the movement lacked a broader agreed-upon ideological agenda. Second, the movement did not formulate an 'alternative vision' of Europe, but instead defended the pre-referendum status quo. During its campaign, there was virtually no place for discussing EU reform, certainly when the main focus shifted to a People's Vote as the movement's primary aim. This makes the movement interesting from an academic perspective: while the extant literature tells us a great deal about left-wing movements demanding social justice and change, on the one hand, and conservative counter-mobilisations, on the other, we know very little about activism defending a liberal-cosmopolitan status quo.

Indeed, the anti-Brexit movement differed from two other recent pan-European initiatives – the radical left Democracy in Europe Movement 2025 (DiEM25) and the liberal Volt – that presented clear and far-reaching plans for the future of Europe. Both organisations favoured closer European cooperation and EU reform, albeit from very different ideological perspectives. DiEM25 is an example of a left-wing exponent of 'critical Europeanism', and it launched a transnational alliance for the 2019 European Parliament elections – though its affiliated parties failed to win seats at the European level. Co-founded and fronted by former Greek finance minister Yanis Varoufakis, the movement called for a radical democratisation of Europe (de Cleen et al. 2020) and espoused radical ideas about institutional reform: 'We must replace the current structure, serving the rich and powerful, with a union of all European countries under an independent parliament, operating based on a Constitution that protects all Europeans as equal citizens, and is designed to ensure their welfare and happiness' (DiEM25 n.d.). Volt, which did not share the radical left positions and populist rhetoric of DiEM25, also formulated far-reaching proposals in terms of institutional renewal and proposals for a 'federal Europe' (Volt 2018). Its proposals included, inter alia, majority voting on all issues, abolishing the European Council, and direct election of the Council of Ministers. As its participation in European and various other elections in individual member states attests, Volt has grown to become more than a grassroots movement and has essentially entered the conventional political arena.

Lacking these ambitions and refraining from presenting ideas about the future of Europe, the anti-Brexit movement was more akin to the organisation Pulse of Europe (PoE), which we introduced in chapter 2. PoE has defended European cooperation, values, and identity without reservation – 'Peace, Freedom, Cohesion' (*Frieden, Freiheit, Zusammenhalt*) was its key slogan ahead of the 2019 European Parliament elections. Its messages typically suggested a celebration of European identity and a desire to make

European integration a project that appealed to citizens on an emotional level – one illustrative message was: 'Europe must bring joy again' (*Europa muss wieder Freude Machen*). As is evident from the previous chapter, this approach contrasted with the framing strategies of the anti-Brexit organisations, which often focused primarily on the problems of Brexit rather than explicitly celebrating the virtues of the EU.

Both movements, however, were similar in refraining from formulating clear 'prognostic frames' about EU reform or their ideal direction of European integration (van Kessel and Fagan 2022a). The anti-Brexit movement was primarily occupied with halting a domestic political process for which it had very limited time, whereas PoE saw policy formulation as the responsibility of politicians in the conventional political arena. Prior to the 2019 European Parliament elections, for instance, all broadly defined 'pro-European' political parties (i.e. all but the radical right and Eurosceptic Alternative für Deutschland) were provided a platform during PoE manifestations. One key PoE message at this time was: 'Whatever you vote, vote Europe' (*Was immer du wählst, wähl Europa*).

As theorised in chapter 2 and demonstrated in chapter 5, the formulation of campaign messages and more general frame construction are complex for pro-European movements that essentially defend a status quo that has become subject to so much criticism. While conservative 'counter-movements' can refer back to a more desirable situation in the past, the *raison d'être* of movements with a culturally liberal character is normally to strive for a fairer future and the winning of new rights, especially for those who lack privilege and power (Schradie 2019, 157–8). This puts liberal-cosmopolitan pro-European movements in a difficult position. In terms of their 'diagnostic framing', how much criticism of the current situation can be articulated without calling into question the merits of the status quo? Regarding their 'prognostic framing', to what extent can a vision of the future be promoted without sowing the seeds of discontent with the current state of affairs?

This study has shown that, in terms of its messaging, the anti-Brexit movement has to a large extent focused on apportioning blame: lambasting those who have enabled the current adversarial situation to happen. Brexit-supporting politicians and media were criticised for spreading untruths about the reality of the United Kingdom's EU membership. It was clear that activists tried to acknowledge the 'pain' felt by Brexit-supporting fellow citizens as the result of the adversities they faced in daily life. As part of their diagnostic framing, activists' messages often centred on the argument that the EU was used as a scapegoat for social problems for which domestic politicians were in fact to blame. The main vision espoused by activists was that the pre-referendum status quo may be highly flawed, but it was at least better than the scenario of the United Kingdom suffering the adverse consequences of Brexit. What was lacking was an identification of potentially legitimate reasons why citizens did not support the idea of European integration.

Following on from this, our case reveals how the prognostic and diagnostic frame types are intrinsically linked, and how the weaknesses and limitations of one directly curtail the other (see Smith 2020). For pro-European movements, diagnostic frame construction involves attempting to strike a balance between criticising the status quo just enough to acknowledge that there is a problem requiring a solution while at the same time bolstering support for the existing arrangements and not further weakening public support. Prognostic frame construction then becomes particularly challenging: it involves articulating a vision for the way ahead that cannot veer too far from the status quo lest it inadvertently conjures further discontent. In this sense, it is hardly surprising that the prognostic framing of the anti-Brexit movement essentially remained undeveloped.

Referring to the dimensions of politicisation as identified by Hutter and Grande (2014), it is evident that the anti-Brexit movement has contributed to the 'politicisation of Europe' in the UK context. Not only have activists contributed to the *salience* of the issue by means of their mobilisation and the considerable attention they received, e.g. through the large anti-Brexit marches. The movement also signified an *expansion of actors and audiences* involved in EU issues given the unprecedented mobilisation of citizen initiatives and grassroots groups. Finally, this mobilisation clearly reflected, and contributed to, the *polarisation of attitudes* concerning the United Kingdom's membership of the EU. Anti-Brexit initiatives and local activists have reinvigorated political contestation around European integration, and their mobilisation underlines the salience of the 'integration vs demarcation' (Kriesi et al. 2006) or 'cosmopolitanism vs parochialism' (de Vries 2018b) cleavage.

The ability of the movement to alter the terms of the political debate has nevertheless been limited. One of the main reasons for this is that grassroots activists, despite their capacity to mobilise, failed to reach out beyond their own camp. As Sobolewska and Ford (2020, 11) observe: 'Britain woke up [the day after the 2016 vote] to a referendum result which demonstrated to everyone that they lived in a country evenly divided into two opposing tribes: "Leave" and "Remain".' This new political cleavage was subsequently described as a divide between 'identity liberals' and 'identity conservatives', or 'anywheres' and 'somewheres' (Goodhart 2017). Brexit consolidated and calcified emerging political cleavages that are not unique to the United Kingdom. To succeed, the anti-Brexit movement needed to challenge this broad divide, and to win over more of those who felt 'left behind' and who thought London and Brussels were in cahoots. As anyone who attended one of the large anti-Brexit London demonstrations will attest, it failed to do these things.

What our research has revealed is that none of the activism – the tactics, slogans, framing – were sufficiently targeted to reach across the political divide. While many have interpreted Brexit as being less about 'Europe' and more about a political clamour for change, the anti-Brexit movement called for the restoration of the status quo; activists told the public who ventured to their stalls that the EU was not as bad as they thought, and that we were better off remaining within it. Questions about sovereignty and immigration went largely unanswered. The conscious choice to campaign on the basis of a broad anti-Brexit or People's Vote message may have been effective in terms of mobilising activists and supporters with diverging party-political allegiances (see Aslanidis 2018), but it did little to reach across a more fundamental, bitter, and polarising political divide.

What does all this mean for the future of pro-EU activism in the United Kingdom and, indeed, elsewhere in Europe? What our research reveals is that if pro-European social movements wish to counter Euroscepticism effectively as well as to set the agenda on European integration, they first and foremost need to articulate a cogent vision of a future Europe that at least addresses Eurosceptic concerns. If pro-European movements fail to do this, it is likely that grassroots-driven politicisation of Europe will remain a temporary endeavour that is orchestrated mainly around critical events such as EU referendums or Treaty change (Grande and Kriesi 2016).

One thing our analysis has revealed is that anti-Brexit activists fit the typical profile of people participating in demonstrations, in that they 'stand out for their particularly high interest in politics, their critical stance towards political institutions as well as towards conventional politics and how democracy works in their country, and [for] a heightened sense of political efficacy' (Giugni and Grasso 2019, 159). A key challenge for these activists is to reach out and convince not only some of those who are critical but also those who are politically disengaged and disillusioned, and who are unlikely to be convinced by long lists of the advantages and achievements of the EU. While the most disengaged citizens and ardent opponents of European integration are unlikely ever to be swayed, there appears to be more potential in embedding 'Europe' in a broader programme for dealing with contemporary (global) challenges, specifying the roles and responsibilities the EU ought to have.

In contemporary European political arenas, we do in fact see various organisations that place considerable emphasis on the EU both as part of the problem as well as being part of the solution. In the words of della Porta (2021, 2), 'research on social movements points at a broad range of variegated and nuanced visions of Europe, as it is and as it should be'. The previously mentioned DiEM25 and Volt are examples of this, but various other movements on the radical left and the radical right have also moved beyond clear-cut anti- or pro-European positions (Caiani and Weisskircher 2022). These 'anti-nationalist Europeans' and 'pro-European nativists' are highly critical of the EU in its current form (for very different reasons), but they acknowledge that there is an inevitable place for 'Europe' in dealing with the political problems they identify and prioritise.

As noted above, some of the remaining organisations of the erstwhile anti-Brexit movement have also attempted to broaden the scope of their campaigns, signalling how European cooperation may be an answer to current (cross-national) problems. Indeed, now that the highly polarising question of EU membership as such has essentially been resolved (for now), there is potentially more scope for more substantive reflections and debates about the future of the United Kingdom in Europe. Future research should continue to assess what role grassroots organisations and other social movement actors play in this regard, and to what extent there is scope for a continued politicisation of Europe 'from below' in the United Kingdom and in the remaining EU member states.

APPENDICES

Appendix A: List of Interviews

Interview #	Date	Organisation	# of interviewees
1	04/02/2019	European Movement UK/London4Europe	1
2	25/02/2019	Liverpool for Europe	5
3	26/02/2019	Anonymous	1
4	26/02/2019	Liverpool for Europe	1
5	26/02/2019	Anonymous	1
6	28/02/2019	European Movement Northern Ireland	2
7	28/02/2019	European Movement Northern Ireland	1
8	01/03/2019	Our Future Our Choice (OFOC) Northern Ireland	2
9	07/03/2019	North East/Angels for Europe	2
10	08/03/2019	North East for Europe	1
11	12/03/2019	London/Watford for Europe	3
12	26/03/2019	Our Future Our Choice (OFOC)	1
13	15/04/2019	Lincolnshire for Europe*	1
14	17/04/2019	Stockport for Europe*	1
15	06/06/2019	Bristol for Europe	2
16	25/07/2019	Wales for Europe*	1
17	25/07/2019	SODEM (Stand of Defiance European Movement)	2
18	15/07/2019	Determined to Rejoin the EU Facebook Group*	1
19	30/08/2019	Ethnic Minorities for a PV/LGBT+ for a PV	1
20	30/08/2019	Our Future Our Choice (OFOC)	1
21	09/09/2019	For our Future's Sake (FFS)	1
22	22/10/2019	Anonymous	1
23	25/10/2019	Stirling4Europe*	1
24	25/11/2019	Falkirk for Europe*	1
25	28/05/2020	Lincolnshire for Europe*	1
26	28/05/2020	Liverpool for Europe*	3
27	05/06/2020	Leeds for Europe/Grassroots for Europe*	1
28	22/06/2020	Scientists for EU/March for Change*	1
29	25/02/2021	Another Europe is Possible*	1
30	18/06/2021	BfE/EM/PV/March for Change*	1
31	29/06/2021	Best for Britain*	1

All interviews were conducted face to face except the ones with an asterisk, which were conducted via Skype/Zoom.

Appendix B: Survey Questionnaire

The questions and the answer categories of the survey are listed below. Answers were collected by means of five-point Likert scales (questions 1, 7, 9, 10, and 12), predefined answer categories (questions 2, 5, 6, 11, and 13–24), and/or free text boxes (questions 3–5, 8, 13–18, 24, and 25).

(Q1) Please indicate how interested you were in ...

- » British politics PRIOR TO the Brexit vote on June 23rd 2016
- » British politics AFTER the Brexit vote on June 23rd 2016
- » European Union politics PRIOR TO the Brexit vote on June 23rd 2016
- » European Union politics AFTER the Brexit vote on June 23rd 2016

(Q2) When did you become involved in pro-European/anti-Brexit activism?

- Before the referendum campaign
- During the referendum campaign
- After the referendum (i.e. after June 23rd 2016)

(Q3) With which pro-European/anti-Brexit organisation(s) or group(s) are you primarily affiliated? (More than one answer possible.)

(Q4) Please list up to five other pro-European/anti-Brexit organisations or groups you have been in contact with (if any).

(Q5) Which pro-European/anti-Brexit activities have you engaged in? (Multiple answers possible.)

- Attending public meetings/marches
- Organising public meetings/marches
- Distributing leaflets/operating stalls
- Writing letters to print/online media
- Posting personal contributions on social media
- Sharing messages of others on social media
- Writing letters to politicians
- Other activities (please specify)

(Q6) Excluding use of social media, how often have you engaged in pro-European/anti-Brexit activities

- At least once a day
- At least once a week
- At least once a month
- Less than once a month

(Q7) Please indicate how important the given reasons were for you becoming active.

- Support for the European Union
- Protecting my European identity
- Concern about growing nationalism
- Preserving peace in Europe
- Concern about political developments in other countries
- Preserving cultural diversity within the UK
- Travelling freely within the European Union
- Protecting my right to work anywhere within the European Union
- Safeguarding the well-being of future generations
- Concern about the UK's economy
- Concern about the economic stability of Europe
- Concern about the UK's safety and security

- » Concern about safety and security in Europe
- » Concern about my local area
- » Concern about the future of the European Union

(Q8) Did you have other reasons to become involved (which are not listed above)?

(Q9) This question is about your personal views on the European Union. Please read the following statements and say whether you agree or disagree.

- » I see myself as 'European'
- » I consider myself a citizen of the European Union as much as a citizen of my country
- » I have good knowledge of the European Union and how it makes decisions
- » The European Union was responsible for the migrant crisis
- » The European Union was responsible for the Eurozone crisis
- » I am a supporter of the European Union in its current form
- » I will only continue to support UK membership in the future if the European Union is reformed
- » The European Union is sufficiently democratic
- » The European Union should be granted more powers to effectively deal with common European problems
- » The European Union should become a federal state
- » I support further enlargement of the European Union

(Q10) This question is about your personal views on the referendum and Brexit process. Please read the following statements and say whether you agree or disagree.

- » The European Union is to blame for the UK's decision to leave
- » UK politicians are to blame for the UK's decision to leave
- » The European Union should have been more accommodating to the UK's demands during the negotiations
- » The European Union has treated the UK unfairly in the Brexit negotiations
- » Not the European Union, but UK politicians are to blame for difficulties during the Brexit negotiations

- » A 'soft' Brexit would be acceptable
- » I support a second referendum on the UK's membership of the European Union
- » I would stop campaigning after a second referendum, even if the outcome was to leave the European Union
- » Irrespective of public opinion, Brexit must be stopped and the UK must remain in the European Union

(Q11) From the following list of words and phrases, please select up to five that you most strongly associate with membership of the European Union.

Peace	Democracy	Remoteness
Opportunity	Openness	Super state
Freedom	Enlightenment	Corruption
Security	Pro-business	Waste
Prosperity	Complexity	Austerity
Culture	Globalisation	Loss of sovereignty
Tolerance	Bureaucracy	Threat
Travel	Immigration	Elitism
Justice	Capitalism	

(Q12) This question is about your personal views on (the relationship between) politicians and the people. Please read the following statements and say whether you agree or disagree.

- » Politicians need to follow the will of the people
- » The people, and not politicians, should make our most important policy decisions
- » The political differences between the elite and the people are larger than the differences among the people
- » I would rather be represented by a citizen than by a specialised politician
- » Elected officials talk too much and take too little action
- » What people call 'compromises' in politics are really just selling out one's principles
- » The particular interests of the political class negatively affect the welfare of the people
- » Politicians always end up agreeing when it comes to protecting their privileges

(Q13) Are you a member of a political party? (If so, which?)

- I am not a member of any party
- Conservatives
- Labour
- Liberal Democrats
- Green Party
- Other (please specify)

(Q14) Which party or parties best reflect your political views? (Select up to three parties, if any.)

- There is no party that reflects my political views well
- Conservatives
- Labour
- Liberal Democrats
- Green Party
- Change UK/The Independent Group
- Brexit Party
- Other (please specify)

(Q15) Which political party did you vote for in the last general election (2017)? (If any.)

- I did not vote
- Conservatives
- Labour
- Liberal Democrats
- Green Party
- Other (please specify)

(Q16) Which political party did you vote for in the last European Parliament election (2019)? (If any.)

- I did not vote
- Conservatives
- Labour
- Liberal Democrats
- Green Party
- Change UK/The Independent Group

- Brexit Party
- Other (please specify)

(Q17) Which political party or parties would you never consider voting for, because of their political stance? (Select up to three parties, if any.)

- There is no such party
- Conservatives
- Labour
- Liberal Democrats
- Green Party
- UK Independence Party
- Change UK/The Independent Group
- Brexit Party
- Other (please specify)

(Q18) Region of residence.

England: North East	England: South West
England: North West	England: South East
England: Yorkshire/Humber	Northern Ireland
England: East Midlands	Scotland
England: West Midlands	Wales
England: East	Other (please specify)
England: London	

(Q19) Age: which age bracket do you fit in?

Under 18	45–54
18–24	55–64
25–34	65–74
35–44	75+

(Q20) Gender: how do you identify yourself?

- Male
- Female
- Other
- Prefer not to say

(Q21) Education.

- I finished formal education at 18 or under
- I am a graduate
- I have a post-graduate qualification

(Q22) Employment status.

- Employed
- Self-employed
- Out of work and looking for work
- Out of work but not currently looking for work
- Carer (of home, family, etc.)
- A full time student
- Retired
- Unable to work

(Q23) Ethnicity: how do you identify yourself?

- Asian or Asian British
- Black or Black British
- Mixed
- White British
- White Irish
- White: any other background
- Any other ethnic group
- Prefer not to say

(Q24) Nationality/identity: how do you identify yourself? (Multiple answers possible.)

- English
- Scottish
- Welsh
- Irish
- British
- European
- Other (please specify)

(Q25) Do you have any further comments prior to finishing the survey?

Notes

CHAPTER ONE

1. Throughout the book we use 'anti-Brexit' rather than 'Remain' or 'pro-EU' to refer to the grassroots movement that emerged in the aftermath of the referendum. As we argue, the mobilisation was first and foremost a reaction to Brexit and the outcome of the June 2016 referendum. Although the activists invariably supported 'Remain', their primary focus after the referendum was to challenge the United Kingdom's impending departure. As our data suggest, their commitment to the EU in its current form varied, particularly on the basis of age and ideological orientation. We thus prefer not to use 'pro-EU' or 'pro-Europe' to describe the activism. However, when we are referring more broadly to movements that exist to defend the EU or European integration (chapter 2), or, as in chapter 3 when we are taking a longer view of support for 'Europe' in the United Kingdom during the post-war period, we refer to 'pro-Europe'/'pro-European'.
2. In using this term we draw on the definition offered by liberal cosmopolitan theorists such as Mary Kaldor, David Held, Andrew Linklater, Richard Falk, and Daniele Archibugi, who argued for, and identified the emergence of, a new cosmopolitan political order based on the extension of political community beyond the nation-state (for an overview, see Archibugi et al. (1998)).
3. The 'pro-choice' movement in the United Kingdom is perhaps the best example of a mobilisation that has emerged to defend the 'liberal' status quo (the Abortion Act 1967) and to counter attempts to overturn the ruling. However, as Amery (2014, 2020) illustrates, pro-/anti-abortion activism has, inter alia, focused on the rights of medical professionals and the regulation of terminations rather than on overturning the law itself.

4   We received responses from all regions/countries of the United Kingdom, although Londoners (239) were clearly overrepresented, and only a few responses were collected from Northern Ireland and Yorkshire (four each). The different regional response rates were reasonably indicative of the cross-national variety in levels of activism. As further discussed in chapter 4, more than two-thirds of respondents were aged 55 and above, and more than two-fifths were retirees. By far most respondents were highly educated (a graduate or postgraduate degree) and white. These figures also seem to reflect the typical anti-Brexit activist demographic reasonably well. In terms of the gender of respondents, the survey was almost perfectly balanced.

CHAPTER THREE

1   Subsequent and more contemporary research on LGBT+ politics in the United Kingdom has tended to place greater emphasis on the impact of civil society mobilisations, pressure from the EU and transnational networks, the changing dynamic of LGBT+ activism, and altered public attitudes (Holzhacker 2012; Ayoub and Kollman 2021). However, Kollman and Waites's assertion about points of access in the UK system for campaigns and issues that run counter to majority opinion remains relevant for understanding the politics of pro-EU/anti-Brexit activism in the wake of the June 2016 referendum.
2   Nigel Farage was a key figure in UKIP from the time of its foundation in 1993, and he was the party's leader for most of the period between 2006 and 2016. Farage left UKIP in December 2018, returning several months later as leader of the newly founded Brexit Party. The latter party's principal aim was to secure a very 'hard' form of Brexit. It was renamed Reform UK in January 2021.

CHAPTER FOUR

1   One respondent answered: 'Oh, my goodness too many to list.' Another said: 'To be honest there are quite a few and I am a bit confused.' Yet another replied: 'This has been part of the remain problem. I cannot even now remember any of their names and whether I "joined" them or not. There have been many and I don't distinguish between them except "sound"/not "sound". I stand with Sodem most days. I have delivered leaflets for People's Vote (when

I could get hold of some) except when the leaflet said Labour was a Remain party.'

2 Non-exhaustive yet useful lists of pro-European organisations and local groups can be found on the websites of Scientists for EU (https://www.scientistsforeu.uk/pro_eu_organisations), the United Kingdom pro-European Network (https://ukpen.eu/ukpen-linked/), and European Movement (https://www.europeanmovement.co.uk/our_branch_network).

References

Abou-Chadi, Tarik, and Werner Krause. 2020. 'The Causal Effect of Radical Right Success on Mainstream Parties' Policy Positions: A Regression Discontinuity Approach'. *British Journal of Political Science* 50(3): 829–47.

Adams, Tim. 2020. 'A Year On, Did Change UK Change Anything?'. *The Observer*, April 19 (https://www.theguardian.com/politics/2020/apr/19/a-year-on-did-change-uk-change-anything).

Albertazzi, Daniele, and Duncan McDonnell. 2015. *Populists in Power*. Abingdon: Routledge.

Alimi, Eitan. 2015. 'Repertoires of Contention'. In *The Oxford Handbook of Social Movements*, edited by Donatella della Porta and Mario Diani. Oxford: Oxford University Press (DOI: 10.1093/oxfordhb/9780199678402.013.42).

Amenta, Edwin, and Francesca Polletta. 2019. 'The Cultural Impacts of Social Movements'. *Annual Review of Sociology* 45(1): 279–99.

Amery, Fran. 2014. 'Abortion Politics in the UK: Feminism, Medicine and the State'. Doctoral dissertation, University of Birmingham.

– 2020. *Beyond Pro-life and Pro-choice: The Changing Politics of Abortion in Britain*. Bristol: Bristol University Press.

Another Europe is Possible. 2021. 'Another Europe is Possible – About'. Web page (https://www.anothereurope.org/about/, accessed February 17, 2021).

Archibugi, Daniele, David Held, and Martin Kohler, eds. 1998. *Re-imagining Political Community: Studies in Cosmopolitan Democracy*. Cambridge: Polity Press.

Aspinwall, Mark. 2002. 'Preferring Europe: Ideology and National Preferences on European Integration'. *European Union Politics* 3(1): 81–111.

Ayoub, Phillip, and Agnès Chetaille. 2020. 'Movement/Countermovement Interaction and Instrumental Framing in a

Multi-level World: Rooting Polish Lesbian and Gay Activism'. *Social Movement Studies* 19(1): 21–37.

Ayoub, Philip, and Kelly Kollman. 2021. '(Same) Sex in the City: Urbanisation and LGBTI Rights Expansion'. *European Journal of Political Research* 60(3): 603–24.

Bacchi, Carol, and Joan Eveline. 2010. *Mainstreaming Politics: Gendering Practices and Feminist Theory*. Adelaide: University of Adelaide Press.

Baker, David, Andrew Gamble, Nick Randall, and David Seawright. 2008. 'Euroscepticism in the British Party System: "A Source of Fascination, Perplexity, and Sometimes Frustration"'. In *Opposing Europe? The Comparative Party Politics of Euroscepticism. Volume 1: Case Studies and Country Surveys*, edited by Aleks Szczerbiak and Paul Taggart, 83–116. Oxford: Oxford University Press.

Bale, Tim. 2003. 'Cinderella and Her Ugly Sisters: The Mainstream and Extreme Right in Europe's Bipolarising Party Systems'. *West European Politics* 26(3): 67–90.

– 2014. 'Putting It Right? The Labour Party's Big Shift on Immigration since 2010'. *Political Quarterly* 85(3): 296–303.

– 2017. *The Conservative Party: From Thatcher to Cameron*. Chichester: John Wiley & Sons.

– 2018. 'Who Leads and Who Follows? The Symbiotic Relationship between UKIP and the Conservatives – And Populism and Euroscepticism'. *Politics* 38(3): 263–77.

Bale, Tim, and Cristóbal Rovira Kaltwasser, eds. 2021. *Riding the Populist Wave: Europe's Mainstream Right in Crisis*. Cambridge: Cambridge University Press.

Balme, Richard, and Didier Chabanet. 2008. *European Governance and Democracy: Power and Protest in the EU*. Lanham, MD: Rowman & Littlefield.

Batrouni, Dimitri. 2020. *The Battle of Ideas in the Labour Party: From Attlee to Corbyn and Brexit*. Cambridge: Policy Press.

BBC. 2018. 'People's Vote March: Hundreds of Thousands Attend London Protest'. *BBC News*, October 10 (https://www.bbc.co.uk/news/uk-45925542).

– 2020. 'MSPs Vote to Reject UK Brexit Legislation'. *BBC News*, January 8 (https://www.bbc.co.uk/news/uk-scotland-scotland-politics-51026014).

Behr, Rüdiger. 2016. 'How Remain Failed: The Inside Story of a Doomed Campaign'. *The Guardian*, July 7 (https://www.theguardian.com/politics/2016/jul/05/how-remain-failed-inside-story-doomed-campaign).

Benford, Robert, and David Snow. 2000. 'Framing Processes and Social Movements: An Overview and Assessment'. *Annual Review of Sociology* 26: 611–39.

Bennett, W. Lance, and Alexandra Segerberg. 2013. *The Logic of Connective Action: Digital Media and the Personalization of Contentious Politics*. Cambridge: Cambridge University Press.

– 2015. 'Communication in Movements'. In *The Oxford Handbook of Social Movements*, edited by Donatella della Porta and Mario Diani. Oxford: Oxford University Press (DOI: 10.1093/oxfordhb/9780199678402.013.39).

Bertuzzi, Niccolo. 2020. 'Normalising the "Alter-Europe" or Going Beyond This Europe? Italian Environmental Movements' Perspectives on Europe, Democracy and the Ecological Crisis'. *European Journal of Cultural and Political Sociology* 7(3): 291–315.

Bickerton, Christopher. 2019. '"Parliamentary", "Popular" and "Pooled": Conflicts of Sovereignty in the United Kingdom's Exit from the European Union'. *Journal of European Integration* 41(7): 887–902.

Blee, Kathleen, and Kimberly Creasap. 2010. 'Conservative and Right-Wing Movements'. *Annual Review of Sociology* 36(1): 269–86.

Blee, Kathleen, and Elizabeth Yates. 2015. 'The Place of Race in Conservative and Far-Right Movements'. *Sociology of Race and Ethnicity* 1(1): 127–36.

Boomgaarden, Hajo, Andreas Schuck, Matthijs Elenbaas, and Claes De Vreese. 2011. 'Mapping EU Attitudes: Conceptual and Empirical Dimensions of Euroscepticism and EU Support'. *European Union Politics* 12(2): 241–66.

Börzel, Tanja, and Thomas Risse. 2018. 'From the Euro to the Schengen Crises: European Integration Theories, Politicization, and Identity Politics'. *Journal of European Public Policy* 25(1): 83–108.

Brack, Nathalie, and Nicholas Startin. 2015. 'Introduction: Euroscepticism, from the Margins to the Mainstream.' *International Political Science Review* 36(3): 239–49.

Brändle, Verena, Charlotte Galpin, and Hans-Jörg Trenz. 2018. 'Marching for Europe? Enacting European Citizenship as Justice during Brexit'. *Citizenship Studies* 22(8): 810–28.

– 2022. 'Brexit as "Politics of Division": Social Media Campaigning after the Referendum'. *Social Movement Studies* 21(1–2): 234–53.

Bruter, Michael, 2003. 'Winning Hearts and Minds for Europe: The Impact of News and Symbols on Civic and Cultural European Identity'. *Comparative Political Studies* 36(10): 1148–79.

– 2004. 'On What Citizens Mean by Feeling "European": Perceptions of News, Symbols and Borderlessness'. *Journal of Ethnic and Migration Studies* 30(1): 21–39.

Bush, Stephen. 2015. 'Labour's Anti-immigrant Mug: The Worst Part Is, It Isn't a Gaffe'. *New Statesmen*, March 28 (https://www.newstatesman.com/politics/2015/03/labours-anti-immigrant-mug-worst-part-it-isnt-gaffe).

Butler, Judith. 2016. 'Rethinking Vulnerability and Resistance'. In *Vulnerability in Resistance*, edited by Judith Butler, Zeynep Gambetti, and Leticia Sabsay, 12–27. New York: Duke University Press.

Caiani, Manuela, and Ondrej Cisar, eds. 2019. *Radical Right Movement Parties in Europe*. London: Routledge.

Caiani, Manuela, and Manès Weisskircher. 2019. 'How Many "Europes"? Left-Wing and Right-Wing Social Movements and Their Visions of Europe'. In *The Handbook of Contemporary European Social Movements*, edited by Cristina Flesher Fominaya and Ramon Feenstra, 30–45. Oxford: Routledge.

– 2022. 'Anti-Nationalist Europeans and Pro-European Nativists: Visions of Europe from the Left to the Far Right'. *Social Movement Studies* 21(1–2): 216–33.

Campbell, Rosie. 2006. *Gender and the Vote in Britain: Beyond the Gender Gap?* Colchester: ECPR Press.

Chabanet, Didier. 2002. 'Les marches européennes contre le chomage, la précarité et les exclusions'. In *L'action collective en Europe*, edited by Richard Balme, Didier Chabanet, and Vincent Wright, 461–94. Paris: Presses de Sciences Po.

Chironi, Daniela. 2020. 'A Fragile Shield for Protecting Civil Rights: The European Union in the Eyes of Italian Feminists'. *European Journal of Cultural and Political Sociology* 7(3): 316–46.

Cichowski, Rachel A., and Alec Stone Sweet. 2003. 'Participation, Representative Democracy and the Courts'. In *Democracy Transformed*, edited by Bruce E. Cain, Russel J. Dalton, and Susan E. Scarrow, 192–220. Oxford: Oxford University Press

Clarke, Harold D., Matthew Goodwin, and Paul Whiteley. 2017. *Brexit: Why Britain Voted to Leave the European Union*. Cambridge: Cambridge University Press.

Clements, Ben. 2017. 'The Referendums of 1975 and 2016 Illustrate the Continuity and Change in British Euroscepticism'. *LSE Brexit Blog*, July 31 (https://blogs.lse.ac.uk/brexit/2017/07/31/the-referendums-of-1975-and-2016-illustrate-the-continuity-and-change-in-british-euroscepticism/).

Cole, Josh. 2020. 'UK Labour and the EU Single Market: "Social Europe" or "Capitalist Club"?'. *Political Quarterly* 91(2): 430–41.

Crewe, Ivor. 1983. 'The Electorate: Partisan Dealignment Ten Years On'. *West European Politics* 6(4): 183–215.

Crines, Andrew Scott, David Jeffery, and Timothy Heppell. 2017. 'The British Labour Party and Leadership Election Mandate(s) of Jeremy Corbyn: Patterns of Opinion and Opposition within the Parliamentary Labour Party'. *Journal of Elections, Public Opinion and Parties* 28: 361–79.

Curtice, John, 2016. 'Brexit: Behind the Referendum'. *Political Insight* 7(2): 4–7.

Cutts, David, and Andrew Russell. 2015. 'From Coalition to Catastrophe: The Electoral Meltdown of the Liberal Democrats'. *Parliamentary Affairs* 68(Supplement 1): 70–87.

De Cleen, Benjamin, Benjamin Moffitt, Panos Panayotu, and Yannis Stavrakakis. 2020. 'The Potentials and Difficulties of Transnational Populism: The Case of the Democracy in Europe Movement 2025 (DiEM25)'. *Political Studies* 68(1): 146–66.

della Porta, Donatella. 1988. 'Recruitment Processes in Clandestine Political Organizations'. *International Social Movement Research* 1: 155–69.

– 2016. *Where Did the Revolution Go? Contentious Politics and the Quality of Democracy*. Cambridge: Cambridge University Press.

– 2020a. 'Europeanisation from Below: Still Time for Another Europe? Introduction to the Special Issue of the European Journal of Cultural and Political Sociology'. *European Journal of Cultural and Political Sociology* 7(3): 225–41.

– 2020b. 'A Europe of Struggles: Blockupy as a Political Moment'. *European Journal of Cultural and Political Sociology* 7(3): 378–404.

– 2020c. 'Protests as Critical Junctures: Some Reflections towards a Momentous Approach to Social Movements'. *Social Movement Studies* 19(5–6): 556–75.

– 2021. 'From Another Europe to Beyond Europe? Visions of Europe in Movements'. *Social Movement Studies* 21(1–2): 180–98.

della Porta, Donatella, and Manuela Caiani. 2007. 'Europeanization from Below? Social Movements and Europe'. *Mobilization: An International Quarterly* 12(1): 1–20.

– 2009. *Social Movements and Europeanization*. Oxford: Oxford University Press.

della Porta, Donatella, and Mario Diani. 1999. *Social Movements: An Introduction*, 1st ed. Oxford: Blackwell.

– 2020. *Social Movements. An Introduction*, 3rd ed. Oxford: Wiley Blackwell.

della Porta, Donatella, and Lorenzo Mosca. 2005. 'Global-Net for Global Movements? A Network of Networks for a Movement of Movements'. *Journal of Public Policy* 25(1): 165–90.

della Porta, Donatella, and Louisa Parks. 2018. 'Social Movements, the European Crisis, and EU Political Opportunities'. *Comparative European Politics* 16(1): 85–102.

Dennis, James. 2020. 'A Party within a Party Posing as a Movement? Momentum as a Movement Faction'. *Journal of Information Technology & Politics* 17(2): 97–113.

de Vries, Catherine. 2007. 'Sleeping Giant: Fact or Fairytale? How European Integration Affects National Elections'. *European Union Politics* 8(3): 363–85.

– 2010. 'EU Issue Voting: Asset or Liability? How European Integration Affects Parties' Electoral Fortunes'. *European Union Politics* 11(1): 89–117.

– 2018a. *Euroscepticism and the Future of European Integration*. Oxford: Oxford University Press.

– 2018b. 'The Cosmopolitan–Parochial Divide: Changing Patterns of Party and Electoral Competition in the Netherlands and Beyond'. *Journal of European Public Policy* 25(11): 1541–65.

de Vries, Catherine, and Erica Edwards. 2009. 'Taking Europe to Its Extremes: Extremist Parties and Public Euroscepticism'. *Party Politics* 15(1): 5–28.

de Wilde, Pieter, Anna Leupold, and Henning Schmidtke. 2016. 'Introduction: The Differentiated Politicization of European Governance'. *West European Politics* 39(1): 3–22.

de Wilde, Pieter, and Michael Zürn. 2012. 'Can the Politicization of European Integration Be Reversed?'. *Journal of Common Market Studies* 50(S1): 137–53.

Diamond, Patrick. 2018. 'Brexit and the Labour Party: Euro-caution vs. Euro-fanaticism? The Labour Party's "Constructive Ambiguity" on Brexit and the European Union'. In *The Routledge Handbook of the Politics of Brexit*, edited by Patrick Diamond, Peter Nedergaard, and Ben Rosamond, 167–78. Oxford: Routledge.

Diani, Mario, and Maria Kousis. 2014. 'The Duality of Claims and Events: The Greek Campaign against the Troika's Memoranda and Austerity, 2010–2012'. *Mobilization: An International Quarterly* 19(4): 387–404.

Diani, Mario, and Ann Mische. 2015. 'Network Approaches and Social Movements'. In *The Oxford Handbook of Social Movements*, edited by Donatella della Porta and Mario Diani. Oxford: Oxford University Press (DOI: 10.1093/oxfordhb/9780199678402.013.9).

Diez Medrano, Juan. 2003. *Framing Europe: Attitudes to European Integration in Germany, Spain, and the United Kingdom*. Princeton, NJ: Princeton University Press.

Dolezal, Martin, and Johan Hellström. 2016. 'The Radical Right as Driving Force in the Electoral Arena?'. In *Politicising Europe: Integration and Mass Politics*, edited by Swen Hutter, Edgar Grande, and Hanspeter Kriesi, 156–80. Cambridge: Cambridge University Press.

Dolezal, Martin, Swen Hutter, and Regina Becker. 2016. 'Protesting European Integration: Politicisation from Below?'. In *Politicising Europe: Integration and Mass Politics*, edited by Swen Hutter, Edgar Grande, and Hanspeter Kriesi, 112–34. Cambridge: Cambridge University Press.

Donati, Pierpaolo. 1992. 'Political Discourse Analysis'. In *Studying Collective Action*, edited by Mario Diani and Ron Eyerman, 136–67. Newbury Park, CA/London: SAGE.

Dorey, Peter. 2017. 'Towards Exit from the EU: The Conservative Party's Increasing Euroscepticism since the 1980s'. *Politics and Governance* 5(2): 27–40.

Dryzek, John S., David Downes, Christian Hunold, David Schlosberg, and Hans-Kristian Hernes. 2003. *Green States and Social Movements: Environmentalism in the United States, United Kingdom, Germany, and Norway*. Oxford: Oxford University Press.

Eder, Klaus. 2003. 'Identity Mobilization and Democracy: An Ambivalent Relationship'. In *Social Movements and Democracy*, edited by Paloma Ibarra, 61–80. Basingstoke: Palgrave Macmillan.

Eisinger, Peter K. 1973. 'The Conditions of Protest Behavior in American Cities'. *American Political Science Review* 67(1): 11–28.

Elgot, Jessica. 2018. 'George Soros Raises Donation to Anti-Brexit Best for Britain Group'. *The Guardian*, February 11 (https://www.theguardian.com/business/2018/feb/11/george-soros-best-for-britain-pro-eu-100000).

Elster, Jon. 1989. *Nuts and Bolts for the Social Sciences*. Cambridge: Cambridge University Press.

Entman, Robert. 1993. 'Framing: Toward Clarification of a Fractured Paradigm'. *Journal of Communication* 43(4): 51–8.

European Commission. 2015. 'Standard Eurobarometer 83/Spring 2015. Public Opinion in the European Union'. Survey results, July 31 (https://ec.europa.eu/commission/presscorner/detail/en/IP_15_5451).

European Movement. 2018. 'Pro-European Grassroots Campaigns Step Up a Gear with New Shared Office Headquarters'. *European*

Movement, March 12 (https://www.europeanmovement.co.uk/shared_headquarters).

Evans, Geoffrey. 2017. 'Brexit Britain: Why We Are All Postindustrial Now'. *American Ethnologist* 44(2): 215–19.

Evans, Geoffrey, and Anand Menon. 2017. *Brexit and British Politics*. Cambridge: Polity Press.

Fella, S., 2006. 'Robin Cook, Tony Blair and New Labour's Competing Visions of Europe'. *Political Quarterly* 77(3): 388–401.

FitzGibbon, John. 2013. 'Citizens Against Europe? Civil Society and Eurosceptic Protest in Ireland, the United Kingdom and Denmark.' *Journal of Common Market Studies* 51(1): 105–21.

Ford, Robert, and Matthew Goodwin. 2014. 'Understanding UKIP: Identity, Social Change and the Left Behind'. *Political Quarterly* 85(3): 277–84.

– 2010. 'Angry White Men: Individual and Contextual Predictors of Support for the British National Party'. *Political Studies* 58(1): 1–25.

Ford, Robert, Matthew Goodwin, and David Cutts. 2012. 'Strategic Eurosceptics and Polite Xenophobes: Support for the United Kingdom Independence Party (UKIP) in the 2009 European Parliament Elections'. *European Journal of Political Research* 51(2): 204–34.

Fuchs, Christian. 2006. 'The Self-organization of Social Movements'. *Systemic Practice and Action Research* 19(1): 101–37.

Galpin, Charlotte, and Hans-Jörg Trenz. 2017. 'The Spiral of Euroscepticism: Media Negativity, Framing and Opposition to the EU'. In *Euroscepticism, Democracy and the Media*, edited by Mauela Caiani and Simona Guerra, 49–72. London: Palgrave Macmillan.

Gamson, William A. 1992. *Talking Politics*. Cambridge: Cambridge University Press.

Gamson, William A., and David Meyer. 1996. 'Framing Political Opportunity'. In *Comparative Perspectives on Social Movements: Political Opportunities, Mobilizing Structures, and Cultural Framings*, edited by Doug McAdam, John McCarthy, and Mayer Zald, 275–90. Cambridge: Cambridge University Press.

Garry, John, and James Tilley. 2015. 'Inequality, State Ownership and the European Union: How Economic Context and Economic Ideology Shape Support for the European Union.' *European Union Politics* 16(1): 39–154.

Gerhards, Jürgen, and Dieter Rucht. 1992. 'Mesomobilization: Organizing and Framing in Two Protest Campaigns in West Germany'. *American Journal of Sociology* 98: 555–95.

Gifford, Chris. 2010. 'The UK and the European Union: Dimensions of Sovereignty and the Problem of Eurosceptic Britishness'. *Parliamentary Affairs* 63(2): 321–38.

Giugni, Marco, and Maria Grasso. 2019. *Street Citizens: Protest Politics and Social Movement Activism in the Age of Globalization.* Cambridge: Cambridge University Press.

Goodhart, David. 2017. *The Road to Somewhere: The Populist Revolt and the Future of Politics.* Oxford: Oxford University Press.

Goodwin, Matthew, Simon Hix, and Mark Pickup. 2020. 'For and Against Brexit: A Survey Experiment of the Impact of Campaign Effects on Public Attitudes toward EU Membership'. *British Journal of Political Science* 50(2): 481–95.

Grande, Edgar, and Swen Hutter. 2016a. 'Introduction: European Integration and the Challenge of Politicisation'. In *Politicising Europe: Integration and Mass Politics*, edited by Swen Hutter, Edgar Grande, and Hanspeter Kriesi, 3–31. Cambridge: Cambridge University Press.

– 2016b. 'Beyond Authority Transfer: Explaining the Politicisation of Europe'. *West European Politics* 39(1): 23–43.

Grande, Edgar, Swen Hutter, Alena Kerscher, and Regina Becker. 2016. 'Framing Europe: Are Cultural-Identitarian Frames Driving Politicisation?'. In *Politicising Europe: Integration and Mass Politics*, edited by Swen Hutter, Edgar Grande, and Hanspeter Kriesi, 181–206. Cambridge: Cambridge University Press.

Grande, Edgar, and Hanspeter Kriesi. 2016. 'Conclusion: The Postfunctionalists Were (Almost) Right'. In *Politicising Europe: Integration and Mass Politics*, edited by Swen Hutter, Edgar Grande, and Hanspeter Kriesi, 279–300. Cambridge: Cambridge University Press.

Grant, Charles. 2008. 'Why Is Britain Eurosceptic?'. Report, Centre for European Reform, December 19 (http://www.leceonline.org/custom/uploads/2017/11/71182634essay_eurosceptic_19dec08.pdf).

Green-Pedersen, Christoffer. 2012. 'A Giant Fast Asleep? Party Incentives and the Politicisation of European Integration'. *Political Studies* 60(1): 115–30.

Griggs, Steven, and David Howarth. 2007. 'Protest Movements, Environmental Activism and Environmentalism in the United Kingdom'. In *The SAGE Handbook of Environment and Society*, edited by Jules Pretty, Andy Ball, Ted Benton, Julia Guivant, David R. Lee, David Oee, Max Pfeffer, and Hugh Ward, 314–24. London: SAGE.

Hayton, Richard. 2021. 'Brexit and Party Change: The Conservatives and Labour at Westminster'. *International Political Science Review*, published online (DOI: 10.1177/01925121211003787).

Heal, Alexandra. 2018. '"Bollocks to Brexit" Bus to Tour Constituencies of May and Corbyn'. *The Guardian*, November 25 (https://www.theguardian.com/politics/2018/nov/25/bollocks-to-brexit-bus-to-tour-constituencies-of-may-and-corbyn).

Helbling, Marc, Dominic Höglinger, and Bruno Wüest. 2010. 'How Political Parties Frame European Integration'. *European Journal of Political Research* 49(4): 495–521.

Helm, Toby, and Henry McDonald. 2016. 'Two-Thirds of Tory MPs Want Britain to Quit European Union'. *The Guardian*, January 9 (https://www.theguardian.com/politics/2016/jan/09/tory-mps-britain-european-union-eu-brexit).

Heppell, Timothy, Andrew Scott Crines, and David Jeffery. 2017. 'The United Kingdom Referendum on European Union Membership: The Voting of Conservative Parliamentarians'. *Journal of Common Market Studies* 55(4): 762–78.

Hess, David, and Kate Pride Brown. 2017. 'Green Tea: Clean-Energy Conservatism as a Countermovement'. *Environmental Sociology* 3(1): 64–75.

Heuser, Beatrice. 2019. *Brexit in History: Sovereignty or a European Union?* London: Hurst & Company.

Hobolt, Sara. 2016. 'The Brexit Vote: A Divided Nation, a Divided Continent'. *Journal of European Public Policy* 23(9): 1259–77.

– 2019. 'European Elections 2019: A More Fragmented Parliament'. *Political Insight* 10(3): 16–19.

Hobolt, Sara, and Catherine de Vries. 2016. 'Public Support for European Integration'. *Annual Review of Political Science* 19: 413–32.

Holzhacker, R., 2012. 'National and Transnational Strategies of LGBT Civil Society Organizations in Different Political Environments: Modes of Interaction in Western and Eastern Europe for Equality'. *Comparative European Politics* 10(1): 23–47.

Hooghe, Liesbet, and Gary Marks. 2004. 'Does Identity or Economic Rationality Drive Public Opinion on European Ontegration?'. *PS: Political Science and Politics* 37(3): 415–20.

– 2009. 'A Postfunctionalist Theory of European Integration: From Permissive Consensus to Constraining Dissensus'. *British Journal of Political Science* 39(1): 1–23.

– 2018. 'Cleavage Theory Meets Europe's Crises: Lipset, Rokkan, and the Transnational Cleavage'. *Journal of European Public Policy* 25(1): 109–35.

Hooghe, Liesbet, Gary Marks, and Carole J. Wilson. 2002. 'Does Left/ Right Structure Party Positions on European Integration?'. *Comparative Political Studies* 35(8): 965–89.

Hutter, Swen. 2012a. 'Restructuring Protest Politics: The Terrain of Cultural Winners'. In *Political Conflict in Western Europe*, edited by Hanspeter Kriesi, Edgar Grande, Martin Dolezal, Marc Helbling, Dominic Höglinger, Swen Hutter, and Bruno Wüest, 151–81. Cambridge: Cambridge University Press.

– 2012b. 'Congruence, Counterweight, or Different Logics? Comparing Electoral and Protest Politics'. In *Political Conflict in Western Europe*, edited by Hanspeter Kriesi, Edgar Grande, Martin Dolezal, Marc Helbling, Dominic Höglinger, Swen Hutter, and Bruno Wüest, 182–203. Cambridge: Cambridge University Press.

Hutter, Swen, and Edgar Grande. 2014. 'Politicizing Europe in the National Electoral Arena: A Comparative Analysis of Five West European Countries, 1970–2010'. *Journal of Common Market Studies* 52(5): 1002–18.

Hutter, Swen, Edgar Grande, and Hanspeter Kriesi, eds. 2016. *Politicising Europe: Integration and Mass Politics.* Cambridge: Cambridge University Press.

Hutter, Swen, and Hanspeter Kriesi. 2019. 'Politicizing Europe in Times of Crisis'. *Journal of European Public Policy* 26(7): 996–1017.

Imig, Doug. 2004. 'Contestation in the Streets: European Protest and the Emerging Euro-Polity'. In *European Integration and Political Conflict* edited by Gray Marks and Marco Steenbergen, 216–34. Cambridge: Cambridge University Press.

Imig, Doug, and Sidney Tarrow. 1999. 'The Europeanization of Movements? A New Approach to Transnational Contention'. In *Social Movements in a Globalizing World*, edited by Donatella della Porta, Hanspeter Kriesi, and Dieter Rucht, 112–33. London: Palgrave Macmillan.

– eds. 2001. *Contentious Europeans: Protest and Politics in an Emerging Polity.* Oxford: Rowman & Littlefield.

Jabko, Nicolas, and Meghan Luhman. 2019. 'Reconfiguring Sovereignty: Crisis, Politicization, and European Integration'. *Journal of European Public Policy* 26(7): 1037–55.

Jasper, James. 2015. 'Introduction. Playing the Game'. In *Players and Arenas: The Interactive Dynamics of Protest*, edited by Jan Willem Duyvendak and James Jasper, 9–32. Amsterdam: Amsterdam University Press.

Katwala, Sunder, and Steve Ballinger. 2016. *How (Not) to Talk about Europe*. London: British Future.

Kitschelt, Herbert. 1986. 'Political Opportunity Structures and Political Protest: Anti-nuclear Movements in Four Democracies'. *British Journal of Political Science* 16(1): 57–85.

– 2006. 'Movement Parties'. In *Handbook of Party Politics*, edited by Richard Katz and William Crotty, 278–90. London: SAGE.

Klandermans, Bert. 1988. 'The Formation and Mobilization of Consensus'. In *International Social Movement Research. Volume 1. From Structure to Action: Comparing Movement Participation Across Cultures*, edited by Bert Klandermans, Hanspeter Kriesi, and Sidney Tarrow, 173–97. Greenwich, CN: JAI Press.

– 2015. 'Motivations to Action'. In *The Oxford Handbook of Social Movements*, edited by Donatella della Porta and Mario Diani. Oxford: Oxford University Press (DOI: 10.1093/oxfordhb/9780199678402.013.30).

Kollman, Kelly, and Matthew Waites. 2009. 'The Global Politics of Lesbian, Gay, Bisexual and Transgender Human Rights: An Introduction'. *Contemporary Politics* 15(1): 1–17.

Koopmans, Ruud. 1996. 'New Social Movements and Changes in Political Participation in Western Europe'. *West European Politics* 19(1): 28–50.

Koopmans, Ruud, and Paul Statham. 1999. 'Political Claims Analysis: Integrating Protest Event and Political Discourse Approaches'. *Mobilization: An International Quarterly* 4(2): 203–21.

Kriesi, Hanspeter. 1995a. *New Social Movements in Western Europe: A Comparative Analysis*. Minneapolis, MN: University of Minnesota Press.

– 1995b. 'The Political Opportunity Structure of New Social Movements: Its Impact on Their Mobilization'. In *The Politics of Social Protest: Comparative Perspectives on States and Social Movements*, edited by J. Craig Jenkins and Bert Klandermans, 167–98. Minneapolis, MN: University of Minnesota Press.

– 2007. 'The Role of European Integration in National Election Campaigns'. *European Union Politics* 8(1): 83–108.

– 2008. 'Political Context and Opportunity'. In *The Blackwell Companion to Social Movements*, edited by David Snow, Sarah Soule, and Hanspeter Kriesi, 67–90. Oxford: Blackwell.

– 2016. 'The Politicization of European Integration'. *Journal of Common Market Studies* 54(S1): 32–47.

Kriesi, Hanspeter, Edgar Grande, Martin Dolezal, Marc Helbling, Dominic Höglinger, Swen Hutter, and Bruno Wüest. 2012. *Political Conflict in Western Europe*. Cambridge: Cambridge University Press.

Kriesi, Hanspeter, Edgar Grande, Romain Lachat, Martin Dolezal, Simon Bornschier, and Timotheos Frey. 2006. 'Globalization and the Transformation of the National Political Space: Six European Countries Compared'. *European Journal of Political Research* 45(6): 921–56.

– 2008. *West European Politics in the Age of Globalization.* Cambridge: Cambridge University Press.

Lindberg, Leon N., and Stuart A. Scheingold. 1970. *Europe's Would-Be Polity: Patterns of Change in the European Community.* Englewood Cliffs, NJ: Prentice-Hall.

Lord, Christopher. 2018. 'The Brexit Vote Has Only Deepened the Political and Social Divisions within British Society'. *LSE Brexit,* February 1 (https://blogs.lse.ac.uk/brexit/2018/02/01/the-brexit-vote-has-only-deepened-the-political-and-social-divisions-within-british-society/).

Lubbers, Marcel, and Peer Scheepers. 2010. 'Divergent Trends of Euroscepticism in Countries and Regions of the European Union'. *European Journal of Political Research* 49(6): 787–817.

Lynch, Philip, and Richard Whitaker. 2013. 'Where There Is Discord, Can They Bring Harmony? Managing Intra-party Dissent on European Integration in the Conservative Party'. *British Journal of Politics and International Relations* 15(3): 317–39.

Lynskey, Dorian. 2018. '"It's Not a Done Deal": Inside the Battle to Stop Brexit'. *The Guardian,* April 28 (https://www.theguardian.com/politics/2018/apr/28/brexit-not-a-done-deal-battle-to-stay-in-eu-second-referendum).

Mance, Henry. 2020. 'How the People's Vote Fell Apart'. *Financial Times,* August 7 (https://www.ft.com/content/e02992f6-cf9e-46b3-8d45-325fb183302f).

Manthorpe, Rowland. 2019. 'Remain Facebook Pages "Professionalised" by £100,000 Campaign'. *Sky News,* September 3 (https://news.sky.com/story/remain-facebook-pages-professionalised-by-100-000-campaign-11800848).

Marks, Gary, and Doug McAdam. 1999. 'On the Relationship of Political Opportunities to the Form of Collective Action: The Case of the European Union'. In *Social Movements in a Globalizing World,* edited by Donatella della Porta, Hanspeter Kriesi, and Dieter Rucht, 97–111. London: Palgrave Macmillan.

Marks, Gary, and Carole Wilson. 2000. 'The Past in the Present: A Cleavage Theory of Party Response to European Integration'. *British Journal of Political Science* 30(3): 433–59.

Marsh, Sarah. 2019. 'In Their Own Words: Why Seven MPs Are Quitting Labour. Who Are the MPs Who Are Leaving the Party to Form a New Independent Group?'. *The Guardian*, February 18 (https://www.theguardian.com/politics/2019/feb/18/in-their-own-words-why-seven-mps-are-quitting-labour-independent-group).

Mason, Rowena. 2018. 'Groups Opposed to Hard Brexit Join Forces under Chuka Umunna'. *The Guardian*, February 1 (https://www.theguardian.com/politics/2018/feb/01/groups-opposed-to-hard-brexit-join-forces-under-chuka-umunna).

Mason, Rowena, Helen Pidd, and Robert Booth. 2014. 'UKIP Results Reveal Divide between London and Rest of England'. *The Guardian*, May 23 (https://www.theguardian.com/politics/2014/may/23/ukip-results-divide-london-rest-england).

McAdam, Doug. 1996. 'Conceptual Origins, Current Problems, Future Directions'. In *Comparative Perspectives on Social Movements: Political Opportunities, Mobilizing Structures, and Cultural Framings*, edited by Doug McAdam, John D. McCarthy, and Mayer N. Zald, 23–40. Cambridge: Cambridge University Press.

McAdam, Doug, John D. McCarthy, and Mayer N. Zald, eds. 1996a. *Comparative Perspectives on Social Movements: Political Opportunities, Mobilizing Structures, and Cultural Framings*. Cambridge: Cambridge University Press.

– 1996b. 'Introduction: Opportunities, Mobilizing Structures, and Framing Processes – Towards a Synthetic, Comparative Perspective on Social Movements'. In *Comparative Perspectives on Social Movements: Political Opportunities, Mobilizing Structures, and Cultural Framings*, edited by Doug McAdam, John D. McCarthy, and Mayer N. Zald, 1–20. Cambridge: Cambridge University Press.

McAdam, Doug, and David A. Snow. 1997. *Social Movements: Readings on Their Emergence, Mobilization, and Dynamics*. Los Angeles, CA: Roxbury.

McAdam, Doug, Sidney Tarrow, and Charles Tilly. 2001. *Dynamics of Contention*. Cambridge: Cambridge University Press.

McCaffrey, Dawn, and Jennifer Keys. 2000. 'Competitive Framing Processes in the Abortion Debate: Polarization–Vilification, Frame Saving, and Frame Debunking'. *Sociological Quarterly* 41(1): 41–61.

McCammon, J. Holly, and Minyoung Moon. 2015. 'Social Movement Coalitions'. In *The Oxford Handbook of Social Movements*, edited by Donatella della Porta and Mario Diani. Oxford: Oxford University Press (DOI: 10.1093/oxfordhb/9780199678402.013.38).

McCarthy, John D. 1996. 'Constraints and Opportunities in Adopting, Adapting, and Inventing. In *Comparative Perspectives on Social Movements: Political Opportunities, Mobilizing Structures, and Cultural Framings*, edited by Doug McAdam, John McCarthy, and Mayer N. Zald, 141–51. Cambridge: Cambridge University Press.

McCarthy, John D., and Mayer N. Zald. 1977. 'Resource Mobilization and Social Movements: A Partial Theory'. *American Journal of Sociology* 82(6): 1212–41.

McDonnell, Duncan, and Annika Werner. 2019. 'Differently Eurosceptic: Radical Right Populist Parties and Their Supporters'. *Journal of European Public Policy* 26(12): 1761–78.

McVeigh, Rory. 1999. 'Structural Incentives for Conservative Mobilization: Power Devaluation and the Rise of the Ku Klux Klan, 1915–1925'. *Social Forces* 77(4): 1461–96.

Meijers, Maurits J. 2017. 'Contagious Euroscepticism: The Impact of Eurosceptic Support on Mainstream Party Positions on European Integration'. *Party Politics* 23(4): 413–23.

Milan, Chiara. 2020. 'Beyond Europe: Alternative Visions of Europe Amongst Young Activists in Self-managed Spaces in Italy'. *European Journal of Cultural and Political Sociology* 7(3): 242–64.

Miller, Vaughne. 2015. 'The 1974–75 UK renegotiation of EEC Membership and Referendum'. House of Commons Library Briefing Paper 7253.

Monforte, Pierre. 2014. *Europeanizing Contention. The Protest against 'Fortress Europe' in France and Germany*, Oxford: Berghahn Books.

Moore, Peter. 2016. 'How Britain Voted at the EU Referendum'. YouGov, June 27 (https://yougov.co.uk/topics/politics/articles-reports/2016/06/27/how-britain-voted).

Mottl, Tahi. 1980. 'The Analysis of Countermovements'. *Social Problems* 27(5): 620–35.

Mudde, Cas. 2019. *The Far Right Today*. Cambridge: Polity Press.

Murphy, Justin, and Daniel Devine. 2020. 'Does Media Coverage Drive Public Support for UKIP or Does Public Support for UKIP Drive Media Coverage?' *British Journal of Political Science* 50(3): 893–910.

Nepstad, Sharon Erickson. 1997. 'The Process of Cognitive Liberation: Cultural Synapses, Links, and Frame Contradictions in the US–Central America Peace Movement'. *Sociological Inquiry* 67(4): 470–87.

New European, The. 2021. 'The New European – About Us.' Web page (https://www.theneweuropean.co.uk/about-us, accessed February 16, 2021).

Oberschall, Anthony. 1973. *Social Conflict and Social Movements.* Englewood Cliffs, NJ: Prentice-Hall.

Office for National Statistics. 2019. 'The Number of EU Citizens Living in London'. Office for National Statistics (https://www.ons.gov.uk/aboutus/transparencyandgovernance/freedomofinformationfoi/thenumberofeucitizenslivinginlondon).

Pattie, Charles, and Ron Johnston. 2001. 'Losing the Voters' Trust: Evaluations of the Political System and Voting at the 1997 British General Election'. *British Journal of Politics and International Relations* 3(2): 191–222.

Pirro, Andrea, Paul Taggart, and Stijn van Kessel. 2018. 'The Populist Politics of Euroscepticism in Times of Crisis: Comparative Conclusions'. *Politics* 38(3): 378–90.

Pirro, Andrea, and Stijn van Kessel. 2017. 'United in Opposition? The Populist Radical Right's EU-Pessimism in Times of Crisis'. *Journal of European Integration* 39(4): 405–20.

– 2018. 'Populist Eurosceptic Trajectories in Italy and the Netherlands During the European Crises'. *Politics* 38(3): 327–43.

Piven, Frances Fox, and Richard Cloward. 1977. *Poor People's Movements: Why They Succeed, How They Fail.* New York: Pantheon Books.

Pogrund, Gabriel, and Patrick Maguire. 2020. *Left Out: The Inside Story of Labour Under Corbyn.* London: Random House.

Portos, Martín. 2020. 'Europe in the Procés: European (Dis-)integration and Catalan Secessionism'. *European Journal of Cultural and Political Sociology* 7(3): 265–90.

Reising, Uwe. 1999. 'United in Opposition?: A Cross-National Time-Series Analysis of European Protest in Three Selected Countries, 1980–1995'. *Journal of Conflict Resolution* 43(3): 317–42.

Rhodes, Abi. 2020. 'Social Movement–Voter Interaction: A Case Study of Electoral Communication by The People's Assembly Against Austerity in the UK'. *Social Movement Studies*, published online (DOI: 10.1080/14742837.2020.1837103).

Rolfe, Brett. 2005. 'Building an Electronic Repertoire of Contention'. *Social Movement Studies* 4(1): 65–74.

Rucht, Dieter. 1996. 'The Impact of National Contexts on Social Movement Structures: A Cross-Movement and Cross-National Comparison'. In *Comparative Perspectives on Social Movements: Political Opportunities, Mobilizing Structures, and Cultural Framings*, edited by Doug McAdam, John McCarthy, and Mayer N. Zald, 185–204. Cambridge: Cambridge University Press.

Rüdig, Wolfgang. 1988. 'Peace and Ecology Movements in Western Europe'. *West European Politics* 11(1): 26–39.

Russell, Meg. 2013. *The Contemporary House of Lords: Westminster Bicameralism Revived*. Oxford: Oxford University Press.

Russell, Meg, and Daniel Gover. 2017. *Legislation at Westminster: Parliamentary Actors and Influence in the Making of British Law*. Oxford: Oxford University Press.

Saunders, Robert. 2018. *Yes to Europe! The 1975 Referendum and Seventies Britain*. Cambridge: Cambridge University Press.

Schmidt, Vivien. 2019. 'Politicization in the EU: Between National Politics and EU Political Dynamics'. *Journal of European Public Policy* 26(7): 1018–36.

Schradie, Jen. 2019. *The Revolution That Wasn't. How Digital Activism Favors Conservatives*, Cambridge, MA: Harvard University Press.

Sherwood, Harriet. 2019. 'Interview. Led By Donkeys Show Their Faces at Last: "No One Knew It Was Us"'. *The Observer*, May 25 (https://www.theguardian.com/politics/2019/may/25/led-by-donkeys-reveal-identities-brexit-billboards-posters).

Smedley, Stuart. 2020. 'Making a Federal Case: Youth Groups, Students and the 1975 European Economic Community Referendum Campaign to Keep Britain in Europe'. *Twentieth Century British History* 31(4): 454–78.

Smith, Naomi. 2021. 'Naomi Smith's Speech: What Is Best for Britain?'. Website post, April 27 (https://www.bestforbritain.org/what_is_best_for_britain).

Smith, Wade P. 2020. 'Social Movement Framing Tasks and Contemporary Racisms: Diagnostic and Prognostic Forms'. *Sociology of Race and Ethnicity*, published online (https://doi.org/10.1177/2332649220922564).

Snow, David, E. Bruke Rochford, Steven Worden, and Robert Benford. 1986. 'Frame Alignment Processes, Micromobilization, and Movement Participation'. *American Sociological Review* 51: 464–81.

Snow, David, Rens Vliegenthart, and Pauline Ketelaars. 2018. 'The Framing Perspective on Social Movements: Its Conceptual Roots and Architecture'. In *The Wiley Blackwell Companion to Social Movements*, edited by David Snow, Sarah Soule, Hanspeter Kriesi, and Holly McCammon, 392–410. Oxford: Wiley Blackwell.

Sobolewska, Maria, and Robert Ford. 2020. *Brexitland: Identity, Diversity and the Reshaping of British Politics*. Cambridge: Cambridge University Press.

Statham, Paul, and Hans-Joerg Trenz. 2015. 'Understanding the Mechanisms of EU Politicization: Lessons from the Eurozone Crisis'. *Comparative European Politics* 13(3): 287–306.

Steenbergen, Marco, Erica Edwards, and Catherine de Vries. 2007. 'Who's Cueing Whom? Mass–Elite Linkages and the Future of European Integration'. *European Union Politics* 8(1): 13–35.

Steenbergen, Marco, and David J. Scott. 2004. 'Contesting Europe? The Salience of European Integration as a Party Issue'. In *European Integration and Political Conflict*, edited by Gary Marks and Marco Steenbergen, 165–92. Cambridge: Cambridge University Press.

Taggart, Paul. 1998. 'A Touchstone of Dissent: Euroscepticism in Contemporary Western European Party Systems'. *European Journal of Political Research* 33(3): 363–88.

Taggart, Paul, and Aleks Szczerbiak. 2013. 'Coming in from the Cold? Euroscepticism, Government Participation and Party Positions on Europe'. *Journal of Common Market Studies* 51(1): 17–37.

Tilly, Charles. 1978. *From Mobilization to Revolution*. Reading, MA: Addison Wesley.

– 1979. 'Social Movements and National Politics." CRSO Working Paper #197.

– 1995. 'To Explain Political Processes'. *American Journal of Sociology* 100(6): 1594–610.

Townsend, Mark. 2019. 'March Organisers Hail "One of the Greatest Protest Marches in British History"'. *The Guardian*, October 19 (https://www.theguardian.com/uk-news/2019/oct/19/peoples-vote-march-hailed-as-one-of-greatest-protest-marches-in-british-history).

Uba, Katrin, and Fredrik Uggla. 2011. 'Protest Actions Against the European Union, 1992–2007'. *West European Politics* 34(2): 384–93.

Usherwood, Simon, and Katherine Wright. 2017. 'Sticks and Stones: Comparing Twitter Campaigning Strategies in the European Union Referendum'. *British Journal of Politics and International Relations* 19(2): 371–88.

van Biezen, Ingrid, Peter Mair, and Thomas Poguntke. 2012. 'Going, Going, ... Gone? The Decline of Party Membership in Contemporary Europe'. *European Journal of Political Research* 51(1): 24–56.

van der Eijk, Cees, and Mark Franklin. 2004. 'Potential for Contestation on European Matters at National Elections in Europe'. In *European Integration and Political Conflict*, edited by Gary Marks and Marco Steenbergen, 33–50. Cambridge: Cambridge University Press.

van der Zwet, Arno, Murray Stewart Leith, Duncan Sim, and Elizabeth Boyle. 2020. 'Brexit, Europe and Othering'. *Contemporary Social Science* 15(5): 517–32.

van Elsas, Erika, Armen Hakhverdian, and Wouter van der Brug. 2016. 'United Against a Common Foe? The Nature and Origins of Euroscepticism among Left-wing and Right-wing Citizens'. *West European Politics* 39(6): 1181–204.

van Elsas, Erika, and Wouter van der Brug. 2015. 'The Changing Relationship Between Left–Right Ideology and Euroscepticism, 1973–2010'. *European Union Politics* 16(2): 194–215.

Vanhala, Lisa. 2012. 'Legal Opportunity Structures and the Paradox of Legal Mobilization by the Environmental Movement in the UK'. *Law & Society Review* 46(3): 523–56.

van Kessel, Stijn. 2015. *Populist Parties in Europe: Agents of Discontent?* Basingstoke: Palgrave MacMillan.

van Kessel, Stijn, Nicola Chelotti, Helen Drake, Juan Roch, and Patricia Rodi. 2020. 'Eager to Leave? Populist Radical Right Parties' Responses to the UK's Brexit Vote'. *British Journal of Politics and International Relations* 22(1): 65–84.

van Kessel, Stijn, and Adam Fagan. 2022a. 'Defending Europe from Below: Pro-European Activism in Germany and the UK and Its Contribution to the Politicisation of Europe'. Paper presented at ECPR General Conference, 22–26 August 2022, Innsbruck, Austria.

– 2022b. 'Mobilising around Europe: A Conceptual Framework and Introduction to the Special Section'. *Social Movement Studies* 21(1–2): 169–79.

Vasilopoulou, Sofia. 2018. *Far Right Parties and Euroscepticism: Patterns of Opposition*. Colchester: ECPR Press.

Volt. 2018. 'The Amsterdam Declaration. Volt's Programme for the European Parliament 2019–2024'. Election manifesto.

Vüllers, Johannes, and Sebastian Hellmeier. 2021. 'Does Counter-mobilization Contain Right-wing Populist Movements? Evidence from Germany'. *European Journal of Political Research*, published online (https://doi.org/10.1111/1475-6765.12439).

Werts, Han, Peer Scheepers, and Marcel Lubbers. 2013. 'Euro-scepticism and Radical Right-wing Voting in Europe, 2002–2008: Social Cleavages, Socio-political Attitudes and Contextual Characteristics Determining Voting for the Radical Right'. *European Union Politics* 14(2): 183–205.

What UK Thinks. n.d. 'EURef2 Poll of Polls'. Web page (https://whatukthinks.org/eu/opinion-polls/euref2-poll-of-polls-2/, accessed July 30, 2021).

Wincott, Daniel. 2020. 'Symposium Introduction: The Paradox of Structure: The UK State, Society and "Brexit"'. *Journal of Common Market Studies* 58(6): 1578–86.

Wintour, Patrick. 2017. 'Former Diplomat to Lead Remainers' Bid to Shift Public Opinion on Brexit'. *The Guardian*, December 17 (https://www.theguardian.com/politics/2017/dec/17/senior-ex-diplomat-to-advise-pro-eu-campaigns-before-brexit-deal-vote).

Wolinetz, Steven, and Andrej Zaslove, eds. 2018. *Absorbing the Blow. Populist Parties and Their Impact on Parties and Party Systems*. Colchester: ECPR Press.

Zald, Mayer 1996. 'Culture, Ideology, and Strategic Framing'. In *Comparative Perspectives on Social Movements: Political Opportunities, Mobilizing Structures, and Cultural Framings*, edited by Doug McAdam, John McCarthy, and Mayer N. Zald, 261–74. Cambridge: Cambridge University Press.

Zald, Mayer, and Roberta Ash. 1966. 'Social Movement Organizations: Growth, Decay and Change'. *Social Forces* 44(3): 327–41.

Zald, Mayer, and John McCarthy. 1987. *Social Movements in an Organizational Society: Collected Essays*. New Brunswick, NJ: Transaction Books.

Zamponi, Lorenzo. 2020. 'Challenging Precarity, Austerity and Delocalisation: Italian Labour Struggles from Euro-criticism to Euro-disenchantment'. *European Journal of Cultural and Political Sociology* 7(3): 347–77.

Zappettini, Franco. 2019. 'From Euroscepticism to Outright Populism: The Evolution of British Tabloids'. LSE Blog, January 4 (https://blogs.lse.ac.uk/brexit/2019/01/04/from-euroscepticism-to-outright-populism-the-evolution-of-british-tabloids/).

Zeitlin, Jonathan, Francesco Nicoli, and Brigid Laffan. 2019. 'Introduction: The European Union Beyond the Polycrisis? Integration and Politicization in an Age of Shifting Cleavages'. *Journal of European Public Policy* 26(7): 963–76.

Zürn, Michael. 2019. 'Politicization Compared: At National, European, and Global Levels'. *Journal of European Public Policy* 26(7): 977–95.

Index

Page references in **bold** indicate a table; page references in *italics* indicate a figure.

action mobilisation, 70
actor expansion, 23
actor polarisation, 23
Alexander, Danny, 62
Amery, Fran, 161n3
Amnesty International, 8
Amsterdam Treaty, 26
Another Europe Is Possible: activities of, 79, 82–3, 143; creation of, 72, *76*; criticism of UK politicians, 115; ideological profile of, 92; pan-Europeanism of, 146; position on Brexit deal, 81; slogans of, 116–17
anti-Brexit activists: activities of, 97–102; demographic characteristics of, 68, 90, 93–7; education levels of, 93–4; ethnic minorities and, 95–6; interaction with Eurosceptics, 127–9, 138; interviews with, 118–19, 153; key challenges for, 122, 152; lack of prognostic perspective, 135–6; messages of, 122, 123, 150; motivations of, 91–2, *93*; perspectives on Brexit, 91, 102, *103*, 108–11, *111*, 119–23; political engagement of, 91, 92–3; profile of, 67–8, 151–2; social status of, 94; strategies of, 102; survey of, 154–60, 162n4; vision of Europe, *109, 110*, 110–11, 130–1, 137–8
anti-Brexit movement: analytical framework, 18, 30, 41, 141; campaign materials of, 13–14; causes of failure of, 141, 143, 150–1; in comparative perspective, 141, 148–9; discursive context of, 48–50, 144; efficacy of, 4, 29, 33–4, 140–1; elite alignments and, 66; emergence of, 140–1, 143, 147; evolution of, 18, 70–90; expansion of actors, 24–5, 150; fragmentation of, 142–3; framing strategies, 11, 35–8, 108, 122, 139, 144–5, 149; historical context of, 141; ideological divisions within, 78–9, 106, 144; legacy of, 68, 146; local activist networks, 11; media outlets of, 79; messages of, 107, 108, 113, 144, 145, 146; mobilisation timeline, *76*; mobilising structures of, 11, 34–5, 67, 69, 70; organizational structure of, 35, 63–4, 82–4; political context of, 42–3, 44, 149–50; political opportunity structure of, 11, 31–4, 50–1, 64; politicisation of Europe

and, 70, 147, 150; protest activities organised by, 7, **7**, 70, 98; resources of, 35; scholarly literature on, 19, 40; shortcomings of, 75, 105–6, 128, 139, 146, 148; study of, 3–4, 9, 12–14, 16, 67; target audience of, 100–2, 150; tension within, 133; websites, 79–80
anti–Poll Tax protests, 8
anti-racist activism, 40

Baldwin, Tom, 88
Balme, Richard, 26
Banks, Arron, 60
Bath for Europe, 77
Becker, Regina, 25, 26
Benford, Robert, 11, 37, 39
Best for Britain, 143; activities of, 80, 82–3, 97, 102–3; creation of, 63, *76*; message of, 114–15, 132; pan-Europeanism of, 146
Blair, Tony, 54, 61
Bolkestein Directive, 27
'Bollocks to Brexit' bus, 98
Börzel, Tanja, 24
Brack, Nathalie, 17
Brändle, Verena, 100
Bray, Steven, 80, 83, 99
Brexit: economic impact of, 47, 115; elite alignments and, 51, 66; 'hard' deal, 4, 146, 162n2; key events, **6**; LGBT+ community and, 117; media coverage of, 45, 49–50; political context of, 26, 44–8, 50–1, 52–7, 60, 151; public attitudes towards, 7, 17, 44, 51, 108–11, *111*, 113–14, 119–23; referendum, 5, 17–18, 50, 71, 121; roots of, 5; 'soft' deal, 102, 103, 106, 142, 143
Brexitometer, 98
Brexit Party. *See* Reform UK
Britain for Europe (BfE): activities of, 97, 142; collaboration with pro-EU groups, 82, 84; creation of, 63, 75, *76*; local grassroots groups and, 77–8, 79, 81

Britain in Europe group, 61
Britain Stronger In Europe: community level activism, 63; creation of, 8; criticism of, 73–4, 105; elite actors of, 62, 63; evolution of, *76*, 141–2; leadership of, 63; local chapters of, 12; messages of, 62–3, 108; as official pro-Remain campaign, 46, 62, 63–4, 66, 72
Brufatto, Tom, 84, 87–8, 89, 133
Business for New Europe, 62, 72

Caiani, Manuela, 26
Cameron, David: Bloomberg speech, 62; call for Brexit referendum, 50–1, 58, 141; political leadership of, **6**, 62; pro-Remain position of, 53, 63, 65
Campaign for Nuclear Disarmament (CND), 8
Campbell, Alistair, 83, 88
Carswell, Douglas, 59
Chabanet, Didier, 26
Change UK, 57, 65
Churchill, Winston, 5, 42
Clarke, Ken, 62, 63
Clegg, Nick, 56, 82
configuration of actors, 32, 33, 43, 57
consensus mobilisation, 37, 70
conservative 'counter-movements', 38–9
Conservative Party: EEC membership referendum and, 52, 53; European integration and, 19, 45, 141; internal division, 53; position on Brexit, 46, 51, 52, 53–4, 60, 65, 144
Conservatives In group, 72
Corbyn, Jeremy: anti-Brexit movement and, 72, 78; call for second referendum, 65; political leadership of, 55, 57, 144
critical Europeanism, 27, 28, 148

De Gaulle, Charles, 5
della Porta, Donatella, 26, 28, 35, 152
Democracy in Europe Movement 2025 (DiEM25), 28, 148, 152

Index

Democratic Unionist Party (DUP), 51
de Wilde, Pieter, 24
diagnostic framing, 37–8, 39–40, 108, 119, 122, 129, 150
Diani, Mario, 28
discursive opportunity structures, 33–4, 37, 43–4, 48, 61, 144
Dixon, Hugo, 79, 88
Dolezal, Martin, 25, 26

EEC membership referendum of 1975: comparison to anti-Brexit movement, 14, 66, 141; ideological cleavage and, 52; mobilisation of citizens in, 8; Plaid Cymru position in, 51; political context of, 5, 44–5, 49, 52, 53, 54–5, 142; results of, 48; in timeline of anti-Brexit mobilisation, 76; 'Yes' campaign, 61–2
elite alignments, *31*, 43, 45–6, 51, 60–1, 66
elite allies, *31*, 32, 43, 46, 57, 61, 64, 142, 146
Elster, Jon, 33
Environmentalists for Europe, 72
environmental movements, 27, 92, 112–13, 117, 125
Ethnic Minorities for a People's Vote group, 96
EU Flag Mafia, 81
Europe: call for radical democratisation of, 28, 148
European integration: domestic politics of, 18–19, 24; historical and cultural conditions of, 112; left–right realignment and, 52–3; mainstream parties and, 19, 20; opposition to, 19; public attitudes towards, 9, 16–17, 23, 24–5, 44, 45, 47, 48–9, 73; saliency of, 147; scholarship on, 4, 9–11, 19, 25–6, 40; social movements and, 27–8; supporters of, 4, 9–10
European Movement (EM): affiliation with BfE, 84; community-level activism and, 12, 13; creation of, 63, 71, *76*; as dormant organisation, 104–5; influence of, 61; membership of, 103; as national umbrella for local groups, 77–8, 142; referendum of 1975 and, 142; as social network, 75, 77; UK chapter of, 8, 29, 71
European Parliament: 2019 elections, 24, 25, 28, 57, 58, 114, 148, 149
European Social Forum, 27
European Union (EU): criticism of, 27, 28, 130–1; environmental policy of, 117; evolution of, 52–3; globalisation and, 21–2; media coverage of, 5, 119–20, 139, 144; public attitudes towards, 16, 17, 21, 45, 108–11, *109*, 121, 123, 124, 127–8, 130
'Europe from below', 25, 27, 41
Euroscepticism: political parties and, 19–21, 40, 141; politicisation of Europe and, 26; rise of, 4, 8, 17, 20, 45; scholarship on, 9–10, 19; in UK media, 105, 119–20

Facebook, 100
Farage, Nigel, 59–60, 65, 114, 162n2
far-right movements, 26
'#FBPE' (Follow Back, Pro-EU) community, 99
FitzGibbon, John, 26
Ford, Robert, 45, 51, 55, 58, 151
For our Future's Sake (FFS): activities of, 101; campaign messages of, 113; creation of, 64, *76*, 81; office location, 82; young people and, 95
framing: alignment, 36–7; categories, 112–13, *114*, 117; concept of, 10, 30, *31*, 35–8, 41, 107; constructivist perspective of, 35–6; core task of, 37; empowerment and, 37; internal and external dimension of, 37–8; resonance, 36–7. *See also* diagnostic framing; motivational framing; prognostic framing

Galsworthy, Mike, 74, 87, 88, 89–90
Gamson, William A., 38
globalisation, 21–2, 27, 40, *110*
Global Justice Movement, 27
Gove, Michael, 60, 65
Grande, Edgar, 23, 112, 150
Grassroots for Europe, *76,* 86, 103, 106, 135
grassroots mobilisation, 17–18, 25, 72, 73, 74, 77, 78, 146, 161n1
grassroots organisations: activities of, 97–102; development of, 141–2; emergence of, 3, 6–7, 8, 46, 64, 77, 105, 161n1; failure of, 150–1; mutual support of, 79; tensions between, 87, 100; use of social media, 99–100
Great Recession of 2007–9, 28, 41, 53, 55
Greece: anti-EU sentiment in, 28
Greenpeace, 8

Healthier IN the EU, 82
Heath, Edward, 42
Helbling, Marc, 112
Hopkinson, Nick, 71, 74
House of Lords: influence over the Commons, 47
Hutter, Swen, 23, 25, 26, 150

Identarians (far-right movement), 26
immigration: public discussion of, 22, 110, 127, 129, 138
Independent Group for Change, **6**
InFacts website, 79, 82
institutionalised political system, 32, 43
interest groups: anti-Brexit movement and, 69, 72; lobbying efforts, 29; main resources of, 47, **69**; mode of operation of, **69**; plurality of, 46; structural features of, **69**
Iraq war, 8

Johnson, Boris: Brexit deal of, 7, 114, 146; political leadership of, **6,** 54, 87–8, 143; pro-Leave position of, 60, 65, 144

Kay, Madeleina, 81, 95
Kennedy, Charles, 56
Kitschelt, Herbert, 31, 43
Klandermans, Bert, 37, 70
Kollman, Kelly, 47, 162n1
Koopmans, Ruud, 31, 33, 43, 55
Kousis, Maria, 28
Kriesi, Hanspeter, 21, 23, 32, 33, 43

Labour In for Britain, 72
Labour Party: EEC membership referendum and, 52, 54–5; European integration and, 45, 51, 55, 141, 144; evolution of, 53, 54; immigration policy of, 58; internal divisions of, 19, 54, 55, 57, 82; political agenda of, 58; position on Brexit, 46, 51, 52, 55–6, 65; UKIP and, 58; voter base, 54–5
Lawyers In for Britain, 72
Leave campaign: appeal to local context, 117–18; criticism of, 108; division within, 60; framing categories, 115–16; immigration issue, 138; key messages of, 116, 117; political parties and, 65; slogan of, 138
Leave.EU campaign, 60, 115
Led by Donkeys, 81, 98
left-liberal movements, 9, 11, 38, 39, 125–6
Let Us Be Heard, **7**
Leupold, Anna, 24
LGBT+ movement, 27, 38, 47, 162n1
liberal-cosmopolitan movements, 9, 22, 38, 39, 149, 161n2
Liberal Democrats, 51, 56, 61, 142
Lisbon Treaty, 27
Liverpool for Europe, 78, 117
London4Europe, 78, 81
Lucas, Caroline, 82

Maastricht Treaty, 16, 26–27
Macron, Emmanuel, 24
Malloch-Brown, Mark, 82
Mandelson, Peter, 62, 63, 83, 88

Index

March for Change: activities of, **7**, 102–3; creation of, *76*, 88; messages of, 113; view of EU integration, 116
March for Europe, **7**
May, Theresa, **6**, 80, 87–8, 98, 132, 136
McAdam, Doug, 18, 30, 32, 43, 67, 107, 141
McCarty, John, 18, 30, 34, 35, 37, 67, 141
McGrory, James, 88
McVeigh, Rory, 39
Medrano, Diez, 112
Meyer, David, 38
Miliband, Ed, 58
mobilising agents: motivations of, 69–70; typology of, **69**
mobilising structures: concept of, 30, *31*, 34–5, 41, 67; irrational, 36; operationalisation of, 68; purpose of, 68–9
Momentum movement, 50, 72
Mothers' Unions, 62
motivational framing, 37

National Health Service (NHS), 60, 112, 115–16
National Union of Students (NUS), 81
'New Labour', 54
North East for Europe, 116
Northern Ireland: attitudes to Brexit, 117, 121
Northern Ireland protocol, 4, 146
Northern Irish Democratic Unionist Party, 80

Ofcom, 58–9
Oluwole, Femi, 96
online activism ('slacktivism'), 100
Open Britain: activities of, 79, 82, 97, 143; conflicts within, 88; corporate structure of, 88; creation of, 63, 74; position on Brexit, 130, 142
Open Society Foundation (OSF), 97
Osborne, George, 63
Our Future Our Choice (OFOC): activities of, 101–2; 'Battle Bus' of, 98; creation of, 64, *76*, 80; office location, 82; young people and, 95

PEGIDA (Patriotic Europeans Against the Islamicisation of the Occident), 26
People's Assembly Against Austerity, 50
People's March for Europe, **7**
People's Vote (PV) campaign: call for second referendum, 85; collaboration within, 143; collapse of, *76*, 106, 143; criticism of, 85, 86–7, 89–90, 135; ethnic minorities and, 96; growth of, 84; influence of, 146; internal politics of, 88–9; lack of prognostic frames, 136–7; launch of, 64, 68, 71, *76*, 81, 82, 105, 131, 143; local activists and, 133; main goal of, 103–4, 138; messaging of, 84, 132–4; popular support for, 84–5; reputation of, 134–5; strategy of, 89–90, 131–2, 134; tensions within, 82–4, 85, 87, 89, 132; young people and, 103–4
People's Vote March, **7**
People's Vote March for the Future, **7**
Pirro, Andrea, 112
Plaid Cymru (Welsh nationalist political party), 51
political mobilisation, 24
political opportunities, 30, *31*, 32–3, 41, 43
political opportunity structure (POS): anti-Brexit movement and, 14; concept of, 11, 29–30, 32; configuration of political actors and, 32, 33; filtering mechanisms, 33; four dimensions of, 32; shortcoming of, 36; studies of, 33, 35
political parties: evolution of, 66; ideology of, 22; main resources of, **69**; mode of operation of, **69**; social movement access to, 31–2; structural features of, **69**

political system, *31*; anti-Brexit movement and, 43–4; institutionalised, 32, 43; openness and closure of, 37, 43, 64; relational power within, 43, 57; social movements and, 47; strategies within, 33; supranational, 52
politicisation: dimensions of, 23
politicisation of Europe: actors of, 23; anti-Brexit movement and, 70, 147, 150; mass protest mobilisation and, 25; rise of, 23–4; scholarship on, 9–10, 14, 22–4, 26, 40; stimulants of, 24
'pro-choice' movement, 161n3
pro-European movement: *vs.* conservative movements, 39; dilemmas of, 39–40; efficacy of, 4; emergence of, 61; framing strategies of, 11–12, 39–40, 149; future of, 5, 102–4, 151; influence of, 61; lack of infrastructure of, 104–5, 106; messages of, 108; mobilisation of, 16
prognostic framing, 37, 38, 39–40, 108, 119, 129, 149, 150
protest politics, 33, 41, 69, 70
Pulse of Europe (PoE), 10, 41; formation of, 18, 24–5; messaging of, 148, 149; organisational structure of, 25; support for European integration, 148–9
punctuated politicisation, 23

racism, 40
Rees-Mogg, Jacob, 123, 125
referendum on the Brexit withdrawal agreement. *See* second referendum
Reform UK, 162n2
Remain campaign: analysis of, 61; economic arguments of, 115, 126; elite allies and, 61; emergence of, 57, 60–1, 62; environment argument of, 113–14; failure of, 74; framing categories, 113–15, 129; groups and representatives of, 8, 13, 72; immigration theme, 127, 129, 138; lack of infrastructure, 75; local activists and, 74, 129, 130; open borders argument, 125, 126; socio-economic arguments, 115, 118, 123–5, 139; supporters of, 51, 63, 65, 72
repertoires of contention, 70
resonance: concept of, 36–7
resource mobilisation theory (RMT), 11, 30, 34, 35
'Revoke Article 50 and to remain in the EU' petition, 100
right-wing parties and organisations, 9, 21, 24, 39, 52, 79
Risse, Thomas, 24
Rucht, Dieter, 67, 68
Rudd, Roland, 62, 72, 88

Sainsbury, David, 62
salience: as dimension of politicisation, 23, 150
salience of Europe, 9, 16, 19, 73
Schmidtke, Henning, 24
Scientists for Europe, *76*, 79, 82, 143
Scientists for Labour, 72
Scotland: attitudes to Brexit, 117, 121; grassroots mobilisation in, 73
Scottish National Party (SNP), 47–8, 142
second referendum: activists' views of, 81, 85, 101–2, *103*, 136, 145; call for, 65, 81–2, 106, 113, 137, 139, 143
Single Member Plurality system, 58
Smith, Naomi, 86, 96, 132
Snow, David, 11, 37, 39
snow-balling technique, 12–13
Sobolewska, Maria, 45, 51, 55, 58, 151
social media: grassroot activism and, 79, 99–100
social movement organisation (SMO): at grassroot level, 72–3; influence of, 47; issue of European integration, 147; main resources of, **69**; mobilisation opportunities, 25–6, 34–5, 67; mode of operation of, **69**; structural features of, **69**

Index

social movements: access to electoral systems, 31–2; agency of, 35, 67; agendas of, 30, 38; analytical framework, 29–30, *31*, 31–5, 41; context structure of; 67; counter-movement and, 38–9; definition of, 30, 38; dynamic and interactive nature of, 33–4; efficacy of, 29, 30, *31*, 43–4; emergence of, *31*; framing processes of, 11, 35–8; goals of, 43; institutional setting of, 31–2, 38, 43; mobilising structures of, 34–5; networks of, 69; political opportunity structure of, 29–30, 43, 50; scholarship on, 14, 25–6, 29–30, 32, 38–9, 42–3, 147; visions of Europe, 152

societal activism: emergence of, 10, 29

Soros, George, 97

Soubry, Anna, 57, 82

'Standing on motorway bridges with pro Remain banner', 99

Stand of Defiance European Movement (SODEM): activities of, 99; creation of, 64, *76,* 80; People's Vote campaign and, 83, 132; slogan of, 80; view of EU membership, 81

Startin, Nicholas, 17, 20

Statham, Paul, 33, 43

'Stop Brexit' hat, 99

Stronger In. *See* Britain Stronger In Europe

Swinson, Jo, 82

Taggart, Paul, 20

Thatcher, Margaret, 53

The New European (TNE) (newspaper), 79

Tilly, Charles, 70

Treaty for the European Constitution, 27

Trump, Donald, 25, 96

UK Independence Party (UKIP): creation of, 49, 57, 65, 162n2; electoral success of, 58–9; Euroscepticism of, 45, 58, 59; influence of, 49, 51, 59, 66, 141; key figures of, 162n2; media attention to, 59, 60; political agenda of, 58, 59; popularity of, 53, 56, 57–8, 141

UK politicians: criticism of, 98, 111, 113, 114

Umunna, Chuka, 57, 82

United Kingdom: European integration and, 5, 17, 48–9; Euroscepticism in, 19–20, 21, 105, 119–20; general elections, 80; grassroots activism in, 7–8; political cleavages in, 151; political system, 44, 45, 46–7, 48; pro-European organisations, 71–72; prorogation of Parliament, 5; street protests, 29

Unite for Europe, **7**

Van Kessel, Stijn, 112

Varoufakis, Yanis, 28, 148

Veterans for Europe, 81

Volt Europa, 148, 152

Vote Leave campaign, 60

Waites, Matthew, 47, 162n1

Wales for Europe, 90, 115

Weisskircher, Manès, 26

Welsh Labour Party, 47–8

Wilson, Harold, 5, 48, 54

Wilson, Richard, 86, 135

'Yes' campaign, 8

young people: organisations of, 95; political apathy of, 94–5; view of issue of EU membership, 145–6

Zald, Mayer, 18, 30, 34, 37, 67, 141